The
EVERYTHING®
Food Allergy Cookbook

Dear Reader,

As an adult, my mother developed food allergies to shellfish and artichokes. She learned this the way anyone learns of an allergy—by becoming sick after eating the food. She has been lucky so far; the reactions haven't been life threatening, but they are becoming more severe.

My face gets flushed and I feel warm when I eat foods that contain a large amount of FD&C Yellow No. 5, a food dye. This is a sensitivity to an additive, not an allergy. But it makes me wonder if I'm going to develop food allergies. An allergy to shellfish would be difficult for me to adjust to, since shrimp is one of my favorite foods.

While it's true that most food allergies start early, you can develop allergies at any time in your life. It's important for all of us to learn the signs of an allergy and what to do if they appear.

Thankfully, the government has been a bit more proactive in this area, and labeling requirements are becoming more stringent. Manufacturers are responding to people with allergies, creating dedicated factories and developing many new products. Many schools are becoming peanut free.

All of these are responsible, prudent reactions to these potentially life-threatening situations. But if you or someone in your family has a food allergy, it's still ultimately up to you to be vigilant. Reading labels and asking questions of food preparers will become second nature. The good news is, if you take control of the situation, you can eat better and more varied food than you ever dreamed. Let's get started!

Linda Larsen

Welcome to the EVERYTHING® Series!

These handy, accessible books give you all you need to tackle a difficult project, gain a new hobby, comprehend a fascinating topic, prepare for an exam, or even brush up on something you learned back in school but have since forgotten.

You can choose to read an *Everything*® book from cover to cover or just pick out the information you want from our four useful boxes: e-questions, e-facts, e-alerts, e-ssentials. We give you everything you need to know on the subject, but throw in a lot of fun stuff along the way, too.

We now have more than 400 *Everything*® books in print, spanning such wide-ranging categories as weddings, pregnancy, cooking, music instruction, foreign language, crafts, pets, New Age, and so much more. When you're done reading them all, you can finally say you know *Everything*®!

QUESTION?
Answers to
common questions

FACTS
Important snippets
of information

ALERTS!
Urgent
warnings

Quick
handy tips

PUBLISHER Karen Cooper

DIRECTOR OF ACQUISITIONS AND INNOVATION Paula Munier

MANAGING EDITOR, EVERYTHING SERIES Lisa Laing

COPY CHIEF Casey Ebert

ACQUISITIONS EDITOR Brielle Matson

DEVELOPMENT EDITOR Brett Palana-Shanahan

EDITORIAL ASSISTANT Hillary Thompson

Visit the entire Everything® series at *www.everything.com*

THE
EVERYTHING®
FOOD ALLERGY
COOKBOOK

Prepare easy-to-make
meals—without nuts, milk,
wheat, eggs, fish, or soy

Linda Larsen,
B.S. in Food Science and Nutrition

Aadamsmedia
Avon, Massachusetts

The nutritional information provided with all of the recipes
in this book was calculated using NutriBase Clinical Version 7.0.

An Everything® Series Book.
Everything® and everything.com® are registered trademarks of F+W Publications, Inc.

Published by Adams Media, an F+W Publications Company
57 Littlefield Street, Avon, MA 02322. U.S.A.
www.adamsmedia.com

ISBN 10: 1-59869-560-6
ISBN 13: 978-1-59869-560-1
Printed in the United States of America.

J I H G F E D C B A

Library of Congress Cataloging-in-Publication Data
available from the publisher.

This publication is designed to provide accurate and authoritative information with regard to the subject matter covered. It is sold with the understanding that the publisher is not engaged in rendering legal, accounting, or other professional advice. If legal advice or other expert assistance is required, the services of a competent professional person should be sought.
 —From a *Declaration of Principles* jointly adopted by a Committee of the American Bar Association and a Committee of Publishers and Associations

Many of the designations used by manufacturers and sellers to distinguish their products are claimed as trademarks. Where those designations appear in this book and Adams Media was aware of a trademark claim, the designations have been printed with initial capital letters.

The Everything® Food Allergy Cookbook is intended as a reference volume only, not as a medical manual. In light of the complex, individual, and specific nature of health problems, this book is not intended to replace professional medical advice. The ideas, procedures, and suggestions in this book are intended to supplement, not replace, the advice of a trained medical professional. Consult your physician before adopting the suggestions in this book, as well as about any condition that may require diagnosis or medical attention. The author and publisher disclaim any liability arising directly or indirectly from the use of this book.

Although these recipes have been thoroughly edited for accuracy, there are many sources of hidden allergens and the final responsibility for making these recipes and eating them rests with the consumer. Carefully reading labels is the only way to guarantee that processed foods are free from the allergens in question.

This book is available at quantity discounts for bulk purchases.
For information, please call 1-800-289-0963.

Dedication

To my sisters, Laura and Lisa, for being my best friends. We had a great time growing up together, and we still do.

Acknowledgments

To my dear husband, Doug, as always. And to my agent, Barb Doyen, and Kerry Smith and Brielle Matson, my editors. And to my family, especially my parents, Duane and Marlene Johnson, for their love and support.

Contents

Introduction

There have been many news stories lately about severe food allergies and anaphylactic reactions that have ended in death. If you have a food allergy, you know about it because you have a reaction to food. But what's the difference between a true food allergy, food intolerance, and sensitivity to food? What are the medical tests you need, and how can you take care of yourself?

Food allergies are the fastest-growing form of allergies in the world. In the United States, while asthma rates have stabilized, allergic reactions to food are skyrocketing. In the United Kingdom, anaphylaxis cases have tripled in the last five years. Symptoms can range from a flushed face and upset stomach to full-blown anaphylactic shock and death.

These allergies are difficult to deal with because of our intimate relationship to food. What we eat literally becomes part of our bodies. What causes food allergies? How can you get an accurate diagnosis and keep yourself healthy? And is there hope for treatment and cures in the future?

Only about 2 percent of the American adult population and 8 percent of children have a true food allergy. Many people think they have food allergies when they actually don't. The only way to know if you are truly allergic to a food is to be tested by a doctor, using one or more accurate, proven tests.

More people are intolerant of foods or sensitive to ingredients in them. The differences do not necessarily include difference in severity, but whether the reaction to the food takes place in the immune system or is confined to the digestive tract. Food intolerances and sensitivities, however, usually do not include anaphylactic reactions.

On the surface, it may seem easy to just avoid the foods you are allergic to, but the food industry is a large and complex organization: Many foods are manufactured with dozens of ingredients, and the food you are allergic to can hide behind many names. Cross-contamination, whether in the final stages of cooking or food production or while the food is growing, is also a huge problem, especially for those with life-threatening food allergies.

At the time of this writing, researchers at the North Carolina Agricultural and Technical State University have produced allergen-free peanuts. Tests show 100 percent inactivation of the allergens in assays and serum tests. We'll see how this works in the real world. Will it be possible to completely replace peanuts with this new strain? Or will this breakthrough just confuse the matter?

Meanwhile, if you shop carefully, read labels, and have found good substitutes for the food or foods you are allergic to, you can transform most recipes to fit your needs. For instance, if you are allergic to milk, and a recipe calls for butter but everything else is fine, substitute solid shortening or vegetable oil or a dairy-free vegan margarine.

With help from this book, your doctor, friends and family, and compliant food manufacturers, you can eat a healthy, well-balanced, delicious diet with a little bit of work, knowledge, and care. As you look through the recipes, focus on those that are safe for you to eat. The recipes were developed to be as safe as possible for the most allergens possible, but you don't have to use every allergy-free ingredient listed.

For example, if a recipe is free from soy, wheat, fish, nuts, eggs, and milk, but you're only allergic to wheat and fish, you can use real cheese, soy sauce, pistachios, and real eggs if substitutes for them are used in a recipe.

This book uses icons to alert you as to which allergy each recipe is safe for. For example, if a recipe contains no milk, you will see the No Milk icon. The icons you will see in this book are:

No Milk   No Wheat   No Eggs   No Soy   No Fish   No Nuts

Chapter 1
Introduction to Food Allergies

*F*ood allergies are an immune-system reaction to protein molecules found on food. This reaction is actually a mistake your body makes. Your immune system is set up to defend your body against viruses, toxins, and bacteria, foreign invaders that have no place in the body. When cells in your body think of food as a foreign invader, they attack, leading to all of the reactions known as symptoms of an allergy. For a true food allergy, reaction time is usually within minutes to two hours.

What Is a Food Allergy?

You cannot be allergic to a substance your body hasn't been exposed to. So the first time you eat a food your body decides to attack, you won't have a reaction. This is called sensitizing.

Allergens and Antigens

When the protein, also called an antigen, of the allergenic food meets some of the cells in your body, the cells produce an antibody specifically created to bind to the antigen in the food. These antibodies, also known as Immunoglobulin E (IgE), attach themselves to large cells called mast cells and basophils, forming a complex that is now ready to defend your body.

The next time you come in contact with that food antigen, it fits into the antibody like a key into a lock, releasing chemicals from the mast cells that provoke your body into a response. Those chemicals include histamines, which cause swelling of tissue, itching, hives, breathing problems, and irregular heartbeat. No one knows why this overreaction occurs. Scientists have various theories they are currently studying, but there is no one answer. Food-allergy symptoms include:

- Itching
- Hives
- Eczema
- Swelling of the lips, tongue, and mouth
- Breathing difficulties
- Coughing
- Stuffy nose and congestion
- Gastrointestinal (GI) problems (vomiting, diarrhea)
- Irregular heartbeat
- Anaphylaxis

TH1 and TH2 Cells

Your immune system has two main branches of white blood cells that respond to real and perceived attacks on the body. One is called TH1, which is responsible for corralling and neutralizing bacteria and viruses. The other is called TH2 and will respond to substances like protein molecules in food.

QUESTIONS

I never had allergies as a child; why am I allergic now?
You can develop allergies to any substance at any time of your life. Scientists aren't sure why these allergies develop, just that they can. Any time you experience any of the symptoms in the allergy-symptom list, get to a doctor or emergency room for medications that may help prevent a life-threatening reaction.

These two branches are joined by regulatory cells, which track, monitor, and regulate the TH1 and TH2 cells. It may be that if your immune system isn't stimulated by bacteria and viruses at an early age, the regulatory or helper cells don't learn how to control the TH1 and TH2 cells, and they will overreact. Autoimmune diseases like celiac disease and Multiple Sclerosis can result from overactive TH1 cells. And food allergies result from overactive TH2 cells.

The Diagnosis

There are several ways to diagnose a food allergy, including medical tests, food challenges, elimination diets, and self-screening. Mild allergies can be difficult to diagnose, but if your reaction has been severe the suspect food can usually be quickly identified.

Start with Yourself

A self-screening test can be helpful, and is usually the first step toward an accurate diagnosis. Start keeping a food diary, and carefully observe and record your symptoms: when they occurred; which foods you have eaten and how much you consumed; time from eating the food to when symptoms appeared; and the severity of symptoms.

Visit the Doctor

Most people visit their regular doctor when they are just not feeling well. You may have had digestive problems, skin irritation, breathing problems, depression, or tiredness and weakness. Your doctor will do a general workup on you, and if you are in general good health, the sleuthing begins.

When you begin the journey to diagnosis, find an allergy specialist. General practitioners and internists do not have the experience in diagnostic tools and treatments that specialists do. General practitioners can do preliminary work and exclude some diseases, but when interpreting test results, a specialist is more qualified. The following organizations can help you find a qualified specialist:

- American Academy of Allergy, Asthma and Immunology
- American Board of Medical Specialists
- American College of Allergy, Asthma and Immunology
- American Board of Allergy and Immunology
- National Institute of Allergy and Infectious Diseases

Get Tested

There are two basic types of medical tests used to diagnose allergies: skin tests and RAST (radioallergosorbent test), which is a blood test that looks for the presence of IgEs specific to different foods. Your IgE number must be above a certain threshold for diagnosis of a food allergy.

The skin-prick test, while less accurate than the RAST, is also less expensive and faster. A solution containing the suspect proteins is scratched onto the skin, along with a control of salt water. The size of the reaction determines the allergy, with a negative reaction being the most accurate diagnosis. With a statistically significant positive skin test, the RAST test is the next step.

For the RAST (also called CAP-RAST and ImmunoCap test), blood is drawn and is tested against the different antigens from the suspect food. If IgEs are found with numbers above a certain threshold, a diagnosis of a food allergy is made. The higher the score, the more accurate the diagnosis. Doctors have set thresholds (in KUA/L, or kilounits of antibody per liter) above which there is a 95 percent chance that you do have an allergy to that food.

95 Percent Diagnostic Certainty CAP-RAST Test (0 to 100)

Allergen	KUA/L Number
Peanuts	14
Wheat	80
Eggs	7
Milk	15
Fish	20
Shellfish	20
Soy	65
Tree nuts	15

Other Tests

The elimination diet is a less scientific, but simple, way of determining food allergies when medical tests are inconclusive or contradictory. With this diet, which should be planned with the help of a nutritionist to make sure the diet is wholesome and meets all your needs, you are started on some hypoallergenic foods, including rice, bananas, vegetables, millet, and lamb.

Once you start feeling better, other foods are added slowly, at the rate of one every few days to a week. This is called the challenge phase of the diagnosis. If symptoms appear, the suspect food can be identified. Use of a food diary is critical during this test. If allergy reactions have been life threatening, this test should only be conducted in a physician's office where there are appropriate remedies.

You may see ads or pamphlets for other types of allergy tests that are not accepted by the medical community. Don't waste your time and money on hair testing, NAET, energy pathway diagnosis, kinesiology, cytotoxic food testing, the IgG ELISA test, Vega, or electrodermal testing. These tests have not been peer reviewed using double-blind studies and are unproven.

The rotation diet is another possible diagnostic tool. In some people with less severe allergies, the rotation diet may be used to prevent future allergies. It can also uncover allergies to other foods, including corn, tomatoes, strawberries, and yeast. In the rotation system, a very strict diet of only a certain number of biologically related foods is eaten every day for four or five days.

The premise is that "masking antibodies" your body produces for a food will diminish in that time frame, because your immune system "rests" when not exposed to those allergens. This diet should not be followed long term because it limits entire food groups necessary for good health. Some doctors think this diet does not work. It is very limiting and can be quite challenging to maintain. While the diet may be a diagnostic tool, claims that it can cure food allergies should be viewed with skepticism. Only you and your doctor can decide if a rotation diet is a good tool for you.

Now What?

Once you have a firm diagnosis, it's time to start learning which foods you must avoid and how to prepare for any potential reactions. Your doctor may prescribe an emergency kit including oral antihistamines along with an Epi-Pen, which is a small syringe filled with epinephrine. It's important that you review the instructions with this kit, and even stage a mock emergency so you understand how to use the kit and can implement the medication as quickly as possible. If your child is allergic, you must inform all of the key people in his life about the allergy, so they can eliminate these foods and watch for symptoms of a reaction.

You may have heard of food challenges or oral challenge, where you are fed increasing amounts of the suspect food to see when a reaction occurs. Never attempt this outside of a doctor's office. A doctor and lifesaving equipment must be on hand. While this test can lead to an accurate diagnosis, it also carries a high risk. And for an accurate result, you have to be off antihistamines.

Not only should you educate yourself and your family about your allergy, but you have to educate the community you live in. Wear a medical-alert bracelet, let those close to you (teachers, friends) know about the allergy, and keep an emergency kit on hand to live well with allergies.

Ask your doctor for a list of words and terms that cover your food allergy and bring it with you when you shop and when you eat in restaurants. Become familiar with these terms so you know what to look for when reading food labels.

Why Are Cases Increasing?

Food-allergy rates around the world are skyrocketing. Twenty years ago, there may have been one or two children in an entire school population with a severe allergy; today there are at least ten times as many. What is causing this increase?

Genetics

Scientists believe that many, if not most, food allergies have a genetic basis. That is, if food allergies run in your family, your chances of developing one are increased. If both parents have food allergies, there is a 60 percent chance that at least one of their children will have an allergy. But even if there is no history of food allergies in the family, 5–15 percent of children will develop one.

Too Clean, or Too Dirty

You may have heard warnings about overuse of antibiotics and antibacterial cleansers. Not only do these practices force bacteria and viruses to mutate, but the evolved germs can become resistant to current drugs and medicines. And there's another angle: Children who grow up in a very clean environment don't develop as many antibodies to germs, so their immune system may be underused or "bored," and will strike out against other substances, like food. This is called the Hygiene Hypothesis.

Should I ditch the soap?
Proponents of the Hygiene Hypothesis don't want you to stop washing your hands or cleaning the kitchen. But using plain soap and water instead of antibacterial solutions and soaps may lead to a healthier family. Children who play in the dirt, have pets, and contract normal childhood diseases can be healthier than those who are overly protected.

Studies have shown that allergies are less common in children who attend daycare and early preschool; who grow up in rural areas, especially farms; who have pets; and who have older brothers and sisters who bring germs and illnesses home from school.

Conversely, inner-city children, children of smokers, and children who live in very polluted areas have more allergies and food sensitivities. Rates of asthma are particularly high in the most polluted areas. So, environmental toxins and pollution may also play a role in allergy development.

Moderation May Be Key

The lesson may be to simply avoid the extremes. Don't become obsessed with cleanliness. Let your children play in the dirt and with animals, and don't shy away from anyone who sneezes.

Finally, don't smoke! Smoking is a proven cause of maladies that range from asthma, SIDS, allergies, bronchitis, and cancer. Secondhand smoke is particularly dangerous for children.

Eight Allergenic Foods

There are eight foods that comprise 90 percent of all food allergies. They are peanuts, tree nuts, wheat, milk, eggs, soy, shellfish, and fish. A person may be allergic to just one of these foods, or may have multiple allergies to two or more of these substances.

Peanuts

An allergy to peanuts is the most publicized and widely known, because there have been news reports about spectacular anaphylactic reactions to unbelievably minute quantities of the peanut protein. There are a few reasons why peanut allergies can be so severe.

The protein responsible for the allergy has a unique shape that is very easy for your immune system to recognize. All proteins have bends and folds in their structure, but the peanut proteins are folded so the allergenic molecules are right on the surface.

QUESTIONS

Is it Aflatoxin?

Recently, a company made a claim that their product, which contains peanuts, is safe for those allergic to peanuts because the peanuts did not have Aflatoxin, a mold that can grow on the nut. This is a misleading and dangerous claim, because peanut allergies have nothing to do with mold. It's the protein in peanuts that causes the reaction.

There are also three specific protein molecules in peanuts that provoke an allergic reaction, called Ara h 1, 2, and 3, so your immune system has three times the targets and three times the potential response, as opposed to all other allergic reactions.

The antibody in your blood that is created when you have a peanut allergy is called PN-IgE.

Milk

There are two main types of milk allergies: slow onset and rapid onset. Rapid onset can occur within minutes of consuming the milk protein. Symptoms include itching, hives, difficulty breathing, and anaphylaxis. It is less common than slow onset, which is manifested in vomiting, fussiness in babies, and failure to thrive. The slow-onset allergy can be more difficult to diagnose, as the RAST test isn't very accurate for this type.

Most milk allergies are reactions to both the casein and whey portions of the milk protein. The casein protein is heat stable, that is, cooking will not destroy its configuration. Heated milk products are therefore still allergenic. Whey is not heat stable, so if your allergy is to the protein in whey only, you may be able to consume heated milk products.

When you're looking for foods that are milk or cheese substitutes, it can help to look for the word "vegan." Vegan means that no animal products whatsoever were used in the making of that food. The word "pareve" can also be a good clue. This is a kosher term meaning no dairy or meat, although it does not mean the product is 100 percent dairy-free.

The good news about milk allergies is that most children outgrow it after avoiding milk and milk products for one to two years. However, if a young child is allergic to milk, the odds are fairly good that she will develop allergies to other foods as well.

Fish and Shellfish

There is usually no cross-reactivity to shellfish (shrimp, crab, and lobster) and finfish (grouper, haddock, walleye), but there are people who are allergic to both. If you have a severe allergy to one or the other, it's best to simply avoid both.

This is an allergy that can, and does, occur at any time of life, not in childhood. And it's a tricky allergy to manage because of cross-contamination. Cross-contamination in this subgroup can occur when the oil used to fry shrimp is then used to fry French fries. Or a spoon that contained fish-based Worcestershire sauce could contaminate a salad.

Some people with a fish allergy can actually consume certain species of fish. The canning process that tuna and salmon undergo may remove the allergenic proteins. Also, some people allergic to shellfish (shrimp) aren't always allergic to mollusks (clams, oysters). An elimination diet or food challenge, *only* in your doctor's presence, will help determine the extent of your allergy.

Fish proteins can even become airborne during the cooking process, and can cause reactions. Make sure the fish you do eat is very fresh: Fish that has begun to spoil will have a buildup of histamine in the flesh, which can cause a reaction even in people who are not allergic. And here's a common confusion: Iodine is not the cause of fish allergies, as many people believe; the reaction is to the protein in fish.

Eggs

It's the proteins in egg whites that cause most of the allergic reactions in those allergic to eggs. In fact, uncooked or poorly cooked egg whites can cause the most severe reactions. But some people are also allergic to the proteins in egg yolks. This is another one of the very serious reactions that can be life threatening. In fact, some people who are allergic to eggs can get a reaction from skin contact with egg products or even fumes from cooking eggs.

One of the best ways to avoid eggs is to read labels. With the new labeling requirements now in effect, look for terms like "made in a facility that also processes eggs." But, as with all processed foods, mistakes can happen. It's a good idea to become familiar with the names eggs can hide behind in processed foods, and scan the ingredient list even if the label reassures you the product doesn't contain egg. Again, the word "vegan" is probably your best clue, since these foods are made with no animal products whatsoever.

People generally outgrow egg allergies. Most allergies begin in young children, who outgrow the reaction by age five. Food challenges are usually used to diagnose egg allergies.

Some vaccines, including the flu vaccine and the shot for measles/mumps/rubella, are developed and made using egg proteins. Your doctor can actually test the vaccine to see if it contains egg proteins before it is administered to you or your child.

Wheat

An allergy to wheat is sometimes a reaction to the gluten, or protein, found in wheat and some other grains, and other times a reaction to the grain itself. A pure reaction to wheat is different from celiac disease, also known as celiac sprue. Some researchers think that gluten allergies may go far beyond celiac disease, and if there are IgE antibodies to gluten in the blood, avoiding gluten may improve symptoms.

Other grains to avoid if you are allergic to wheat include barley, rye, triticale, and sometimes oats. Cross-contamination can be a problem with wheat allergies, so make sure the grains you consume are pure, from the field to the packing plant.

Starting in 2008, the Food and Drug Administration is tightening guidelines for food labeling. New standards are going to apply to products labeled "gluten free," which will help those allergic to gluten more readily identify safe foods. Guidelines labeling other allergenic foods were put into effect January 2006. However, there is a caveat with this rule. The claim "gluten free" will only apply to products containing wheat. Oats, barley, rye, and triticale, which can be sources of gluten through cross-contamination, are not included in this claim, so you still *must* read labels carefully.

Gluten can hide in lots of foods that seem innocuous. Thoroughly study labels on all the processed foods you buy and learn about these hidden sources. The only way to be safe is to study labels on all foods more complicated than lettuce. Gluten can be found in some unlikely places including:

- Sour cream, ice cream, and cheese
- Nondairy creamers
- Meat patties and sausages
- Soy meat substitutes
- Malt flavoring and caramel coloring
- Rice mixes and seasoning mixes
- Some medications
- Canned soups and bouillon cubes
- Salad dressing, mustard, flavored vinegars, and mayonnaise
- Canned baked beans and vegetables with sauces
- Nonstick baking sprays with flour
- Cocoa mixes and chocolate drinks

Wheat allergies can be difficult to diagnose, because the skin tests and blood tests are usually inconclusive. An elimination diet, under the supervision of a doctor or nutritionist, may be your best bet.

Soy

Soy is a legume, as are peanuts. If you are allergic to peanuts, you may have a cross-reactivity to soy or other legumes, including chick peas, lima beans, and Great Northern Beans. But an allergy to one does not guarantee an allergy to another.

It's rare for adults to develop an allergy to soy. Soy allergies usually develop at around three months, and many children do outgrow it. The allergy usually begins as a reaction to soy-based formulas; breastfeeding is one of the best ways to prevent allergies to soy and milk.

ALERT!

Soy can hide behind certain terms in food that aren't included in labeling laws. "Vegetable protein" and "natural flavors" are blanket terms manufacturers are allowed to use that can contain soy. Monoglycerides and diglycerides may be derived from soy, so avoid foods that include those terms on the label.

Some of the symptoms more unique to soy allergies include skin reactions like eczema and acne, along with canker sores and hives. These reactions are more uncomfortable than life threatening, although an anaphylactic reaction is still possible. For mild reactions, taking an antihistamine will help reduce symptoms.

There are five different types of taste buds on your tongue: sweet, salty, sour, bitter, and umami. Umami is less commonly known and understood. In 2000, researchers isolated the receptor for umami, and officially added it to the types of taste buds. It is a "meaty" taste triggered by the presence of glutamate amino acids, found in soy sauce, mushrooms, and monosodium glutamate. If you are allergic to soy, you must omit soy sauce from your diet, or use a substitute you can make at home (see Chapter 4: Substitutions and Mixes).

If you are allergic to soy, you have to carefully read labels of medications, too. Some of the fast-melt medicines are soy based.

Tree Nuts

As with peanut allergies, tree-nut allergies can be very severe and usually last your entire life. If you have an allergy to peanuts, there is about a 40–50 percent chance that you will develop an allergy to tree nuts as well. Nuts can hide in processed and prepared foods, and cross-contamination is a great risk, even if the food has been properly labeled. Avoid all nut butters and pastes as well. Tree nuts include:

- Walnuts
- Pecans
- Pistachios
- Chestnuts
- Hazelnuts
- Almonds
- Macadamia nuts
- Cashews
- Beechnuts
- Brazil nuts

Nut oils may or may not be safe for you to eat. The processing that extracts oil from nuts usually removes the allergenic proteins. But if you have a severe allergy, it's best to simply avoid all nut oils. Natural extracts like almond extract should also be avoided. Also be aware that nut products and oils can be found in some lotions and shampoos; skin contact can trigger a severe reaction with these allergies.

Coconut, water chestnuts, and nutmeg are not part of the tree-nut family. Unless you are specifically allergic to these foods, they don't cross-react with the tree-nut families.

Cross-Contamination

One of the most insidious problems for those with food allergies and celiac disease is cross-contamination. From buying a food from a plant that uses peanuts to eating oatmeal grown in a field next to a wheat field, cross-contamination is a serious health risk. But you can take steps to minimize this risk.

Dedicated Mill

When you buy soy, potato, millet, or any other type of gluten-free flours, look for the words "dedicated mill" on the label. This means that the mill only produces that particular kind of flour, so there is less chance of cross-contamination with gluten. If your allergies are severe, you may even want to find a company that purchases raw produce from farms that do not rotate their crops.

The same is true for peanut and nut allergies. If a nut-free candy is made in the same plant as one that has nuts, cross-contamination becomes a real issue. Look for products from companies that guarantee nut-free manufacturing environments. And be on the lookout for recalls, too; mistakes do happen.

Clean Kitchens

If you have a severe allergy, the foods you eat must come from clean kitchens. This doesn't mean bacteria free, but it means free of cross-contamination. In restaurants, oil that was used to fry fish can then contaminate the potatoes that are fried next.

With peanut allergies, more than any other allergy, reaction to an incredibly tiny amount of the protein can be spectacular and very serious. Cross-contamination can be caused by using the same spatula to transfer peanut cookies and sugar cookies to a cooling rack. Concentrations as low as 1 in 10,000 can trigger the immune response.

Celiac Disease Is Different

Celiac disease (also called celiac sprue) isn't an immune reaction to gluten, the protein in wheat and other grains, it's a genetic autoimmune disease caused by gluten. The presence of this protein triggers the immune response and your body attacks the villi, or cells, lining the small intestine, causing inflammation. This can lead to malnutrition as well as other painful symptoms like vomiting, abdominal pain, and diarrhea. People who have this disease must avoid grains that have gluten, including wheat, barley, rye, and sometimes oats. There is no cure.

Gliadin Is the Culprit

Gluten is made up of two main proteins, called glutenin and gliadin. If you have celiac disease, your body reacts to the gliadin protein by creating antibodies against an enzyme called tissue transglutaminase, or tTG. This causes the villi on the intestine lining to flatten. The reaction may even destroy the villi, and also causes inflammation.

Some health practitioners believe that "leaky gut" leads to food allergies and celiac disease. This theory is unproven and is not scientifically defined. There may be some conditions that result from your intestine inappropriately allowing substances through the intestinal wall, but food allergies are not believed to be caused by this malady.

The best way to diagnose celiac disease is with a biopsy of the small intestine, which shows the damage to the villi and mucosa caused by the immune system overreaction. Or you can have a series of four blood tests, including testing for IgA, IgG, antigliadin antibodies, and antiendomysial antibodies. All of the tests should be run for the most accurate diagnosis, since the body's reaction to other diseases can create tTG antibodies, for instance.

Other Grains

If you have celiac disease, the kinds of grains you can safely consume vary widely from person to person. Unfortunately, cross-contamination among grains is very common. This contamination can range from grains growing in adjacent fields to mills processing more than one type of grain.

Hidden Sources

Once again, it's hidden sources of gluten that can cause problems. Processed grains that a celiac patient could normally eat, like oats, can, if grown next to a field of wheat, contain gluten proteins. Gluten can also be found in foods like soy sauce and rice cereal.

The Plan

Once you have been diagnosed and understand how to manage your allergy, you should develop a plan. Clean out your pantry, removing all suspect foods. Collect recipes that omit your allergens. Get used to reading labels. Keep your allergy kit with you at all times; and aggressively ask questions of those serving you food.

How to Read Labels

In January 2006, the FDA changed standards on food labels to make it easier to find suspect foods in the products you buy. The product must clearly state if it contains any of the eight groups of foods most responsible for allergic reactions. The language is simple: If a product contains casein, a milk protein, the label has to show the words "contains milk," or if it has some seitan, the label must read "contains gluten."

A few words of warning: the word "free" isn't regulated by the FDA. A product that says "milk free" may still contain milk protein. And the phrase "may contain" can be a blanket legal loophole for manufacturers, indicating that cross-contamination is possible.

So read labels, every single time. Products can change formulas, so even if a food is safe for you to eat one month, it may not be the next month. The best foods are the ones with labels that do not have the words "contains X."

Cooking Techniques and Tips

If you have a severe food allergy, it can be a good idea to stock your kitchen with homemade foods. That means you make your own stocks, sauces, seasoning mixes, and baking mixes. This is really the only way to manage a severe allergy, because you control exactly what goes into the food you eat. This may seem bothersome, but compare the time spent in the kitchen to the time you won't have to spend worrying about a reaction and getting medical help for symptoms.

Genetic engineering may be a future solution to food allergies. Scientists have been able to produce hypoallergenic strains of food-allergy molecules that can be used in treatments. The treatments could also have few, if any, side effects. These treatments may be some years in the future, but the research is promising.

Eating Out

Talk to the chef! Not the server, or the maitre d', but the chef. Quiz her extensively about the foods you want to eat, and reiterate the severity of your allergy. Think about making up a card stating which food or foods you are allergic to, and having the chef sign it to prove he has read it. This will heighten sensitivity to your condition and may help you avoid a reaction.

There are some types of restaurants that are more dangerous than others. For those with a peanut or soy allergy, avoiding Chinese, Japanese, and other Asian restaurants is a good idea. Even if food you order from these restaurants doesn't contain peanuts or soy, the risk for cross-contamination is great. Avoid restaurants with buffet service. Cross-contamination risk is very high when people serve themselves. Also avoid restaurants with attached bakeries, for the same reason.

There are some restaurants that are intrinsically safer than others. Look for places that cook their food from scratch. Ask for recommendations from others who have food allergies. And if you've had luck with a large chain restaurant, other branches may be safe. But still be aware that chefs change their recipes. Always talk to the chef before you order from any restaurant, even one you've safely dined at before.

Hope for the Future

Currently, the only treatment for food allergies is to avoid the suspect food, in all its incarnations. Having an emergency kit on your person at all times is essential. But researchers are working on possible treatments and cures that offer hope.

Researchers are working on a vaccine using genetically engineered proteins similar to those that cause the allergy, but that have been changed to reduce their effect.

ALERT!

Scientists hope that food allergies may be eradicated in about ten years. They are currently working on many treatments that appear promising. So there is hope for the future. In the meantime, read labels, be prepared, and try to relax and enjoy life, knowing that you can take care of yourself.

Researchers have also found that mice bred to have a peanut allergy were missing a crucial molecule called Interlukin-12. This study has also shown that with peanut allergies, some of the immune cells last longer, which can provoke the immune system into a reaction. Interlukin-12 may be the missing factor that helps subdue this reaction.

Outgrowing Allergies

Many people can outgrow their food allergies, with the exception of allergies to peanuts and tree nuts. Scientists think that avoiding that food for years may "reset" your body's immune system. Or, it may be that the immune system in the digestive tract matures and no longer reacts to that protein or proteins.

Children with allergies to soy, egg, milk, and wheat can outgrow their allergies; about 85 percent are no longer allergic at the age of five. Peanut allergies are usually lifelong, but 20 percent of children do outgrow it.

Preventing Allergies

No one is sure why people develop food allergies in the first place. Some studies suggest that if food allergies run in a family, pregnant women should avoid those foods while they are pregnant and nursing. Other studies have found that there is no effect. The exception to this is peanuts. If there is a strong peanut allergy in your family, avoid peanuts while pregnant and nursing.

To help prevent food allergies, breastfeed your child until he is six months old, and avoid feeding him solid foods until that age. Add cow's milk to his diet after he is one year old, and introduce eggs only after the age of two. Add seafood and nuts to his diet when he is three years old, and be sure to add foods gradually as he grows. Introducing one new food at a time, waiting for a couple of weeks in between each introduction, will help you identify the food if he is allergic to it.

About These Recipes

For the purposes of this book, the eight allergenic foods have been condensed to six. Because so many people who are allergic to peanuts are also allergic to tree nuts, peanuts and tree nuts have been combined into one category. And those allergic to shellfish are often allergic to fish, so those two categories have been combined.

Be flexible when choosing these recipes, and don't be afraid to substitute. A recipe that uses flour can work for those allergic to wheat if you substitute one of the flour mixes found in Chapter 4. Recipes for egg substitutes can also be found in Chapter 4.

Conversely, if you aren't allergic to eggs, use real eggs in these recipes (1 egg per 3–4 tablespoons of the substitute), add chopped nuts if you don't have nut allergies, or use butter, milk, and cheese if you don't have an allergy to dairy.

Also, if you are allergic to anything else, from tomatoes to strawberries to onions, just leave them out of recipes. Most recipes are quite tolerant and will work with substitutions and or omissions. You will find that your diet isn't as limited as you thought!

Chapter 2
Breakfast

Creamy Millet Porridge

Yes, this is the same millet you feed the birds. But buy your millet at a grocery store or food co-op, not in the pet store! If you have a peanut allergy with a cross-reaction to soy, do not make this recipe.

Calories: 324.60
Fat: 2.77 grams
Saturated Fat: 0.44 grams
Carbohydrates: 69.88 grams
Sodium: 201.98 mg

1½ cups millet
½ cup dried chopped apricots
¼ cup honey
2 cups apricot nectar
3 cups water
½ teaspoon salt
½ cup silken tofu

1. In large saucepan, combine millet, apricots, and honey and stir to mix. Add nectar, water, and salt. Bring to a boil over medium-high heat, then reduce heat to low. Cover saucepan and cook 20–30 minutes, until millet is tender.

2. Uncover saucepan and stir. Stir in tofu and serve immediately.

Scrambled Eggs

Scrambled eggs are usually made with eggs beaten with milk or cream. Using water actually makes them lighter and fluffier!

Serves 4

Calories: 206.67
Fat: 16.69 grams
Saturated Fat: 4.03 grams
Carbohydrates: 0.77 grams
Sodium: 430.82 mg

2 tablespoons olive oil
8 eggs
2 tablespoons water
½ teaspoon salt
Dash white pepper

1. Heat medium skillet over medium heat. Add olive oil. Meanwhile, combine remaining ingredients in a medium bowl and beat until frothy.

2. Add egg mixture to pan and cook, running a heatproof spatula along the bottom occasionally, until eggs form soft curds that are just set. Serve immediately.

milk wheat fish nuts

Bacon Eggs Benedict

You can make the sauce, rice cakes, and bacon ahead of time. When you want to eat, cook the Scrambled Eggs, assemble the dish, and broil until hot.

Serves 6

Calories: 417.53
Fat: 25.03 grams
Saturated Fat: 6.25 grams
Carbohydrates: 25.31 grams
Sodium: 902.62 mg

¾ cup short-grain rice
1 egg
½ teaspoon dried basil
    leaves
¼ teaspoon salt
1 tablespoon olive oil
4 slices gluten-free bacon
1 recipe Scrambled Eggs
    (page 22)
1 cup rice or soy milk
2 tablespoons cornstarch
    or superfine rice flour
¼ teaspoon salt
½ cup shredded, dairy-free
    soy cheese

1. In medium saucepan, cook rice according to package directions for sticky rice. Cool completely. When cold, beat in egg, basil leaves, and ¼ teaspoon salt. Form mixture into 6 cakes.

2. Heat olive oil in a medium saucepan. Pan-fry cakes on both sides for 4–6 minutes per side, until golden brown. Remove from pan.

3. Cook bacon until crisp, crumble, and set aside. Prepare Scrambled Eggs.

4. In a microwave-safe measuring cup, combine rice or soy milk with cornstarch or rice flour and ¼ teaspoon salt. Microwave on high 1–2 minutes, stirring once with wire whisk during cooking time, until thick. Stir in cheese until melted.

5. Preheat broiler. Place rice cakes on a broiler pan. Top with crumbled bacon, some of the Scrambled Eggs, and the cheese sauce. Broil 6" from heat source until food is hot and the top starts to brown and bubble. Serve immediately.

Soy Cheese

Many brands of soy cheese contain whey or casein, both dairy products, to improve mouthfeel and texture. If you are allergic to milk, you must read labels carefully to make sure no cow's milk products appear on the ingredient list. Some brands truly are dairy free, including The Vegan Gourmet.

Calories: 312.64
Fat: 6.71 grams
Saturated Fat: 0.99 grams
Carbohydrates: 60.30 grams
Sodium: 23.16 mg

4 cups gluten-free rolled oats
3 cups flaked rice cereal
2 cups gluten-free corn flakes
½ cup sesame seeds
1 cup honey
⅓ cup vegetable oil
¼ cup orange juice
1 cup brown sugar
2 teaspoons cinnamon
1 teaspoon ground ginger
½ teaspoon ground cardamom
2 teaspoons gluten-free vanilla extract
2 cups golden raisins
1 cup dried blueberries
1 cup dried cranberries

milk   wheat   eggs   soy   fish   nuts

Spicy and Sweet Granola

You can add or subtract spices as you'd like in this excellent breakfast-cereal recipe. The oats can be omitted if you can't find those guaranteed gluten-free; just use more corn and rice cereal.

1. Preheat oven to 300°F. In large roasting pan, combine oats, flaked rice cereal, corn flakes, and sesame seeds and mix well.

2. In small saucepan, combine honey, vegetable oil, orange juice, brown sugar, cinnamon, ginger, and cardamom and mix well. Heat until warm, then remove from heat and stir in vanilla. Drizzle over cereal in roasting pan and toss to coat.

3. Bake 40–50 minutes, stirring twice, until cereals are glazed and toasted. Stir in dried fruits, then cool completely. When cool, break into pieces and store at room temperature in airtight container.

Gluten-Free Oats

Cross-contamination can be a big problem with most brands of commercial oatmeal. Even if the mill is dedicated only to oats, if the grains are planted in a field near wheat it can become polluted. There are some companies working on this. Gluten Free Oats and Chateau Cream Hill Estates both claim their oats are gluten free.

milk   wheat   eggs   fish   nuts

Blueberry Pancakes

If you can't find superfine rice flour, try processing some regular rice flour in a food processor until the particles are fine.

1. Place rice flour, potato flour, tapioca flour, baking powder, baking soda, salt, and cinnamon in a sieve. Sieve into a large bowl; stir in sugar.

2. In small bowl, combine applesauce, oil, soy milk, and orange juice and mix well. Add all at once to dry ingredients and mix just until combined; there will still be some lumps. Gently stir in blueberries and let batter stand for 10 minutes.

3. Heat nonstick skillet over medium heat. Pour batter onto skillet in ¼-cup amounts. Cook until edges appear dry and bubbles form and just start to break on the surface. Gently turn pancakes and cook on second side until done.

Gluten-Free Baking Products

There are quite a few varieties of wheat-free and gluten-free baking mixes on the market. Buy them in small quantities to try before you stock up. Again, read labels carefully, and look for reviews of these products on gluten-free Web sites like *www.celiac.com*.

Yields 12 pancakes; Serves 6

Calories: 329.14
Fat: 6.18 grams
Saturated Fat: 0.55 grams
Carbohydrates: 64.22 grams
Sodium: 130.74 mg

1¼ cups superfine rice flour
⅓ cup potato-starch flour
3 tablespoons tapioca flour
1 teaspoon gluten-free baking powder
1 teaspoon baking soda
¼ teaspoon salt
½ teaspoon cinnamon
⅓ cup sugar
¼ cup applesauce
2 tablespoons vegetable oil
1¼ cups soy milk
¼ cup orange juice
1½ cups blueberries

Crisp Brown-Sugar Waffles

The brown sugar caramelizes when the waffles cook, adding an extra layer of flavor to these delicious waffles.

Serves 4

Calories: 365.81
Fat: 8.97 grams
Saturated Fat: 0.86 grams
Carbohydrates: 63.62 grams
Sodium: 179.31 mg

1 cup superfine rice flour
½ cup millet flour
3 tablespoons brown sugar
1½ teaspoons gluten-free baking powder
½ teaspoon baking soda
½ teaspoon xanthan gum
¼ teaspoon salt
¼ cup Egg Substitute for Baking (page 66)
½ cup apple juice
2 tablespoons vegetable oil

1. Combine rice flour, millet flour, sugar, baking powder, baking soda, xanthan gum, and salt in large bowl; mix with wire whisk until blended.

2. In small bowl, combine Egg Substitute, apple juice, and oil; mix well. Stir into flour mixture and mix well; let stand for 10 minutes.

3. Preheat waffle iron and brush with solid shortening. Pour batter by scant ⅓-cup measures onto heated iron, close, and cook until steaming stops. Serve waffles immediately.

milk wheat soy fish nuts

Scroddled Eggs

Scroddled eggs are just barely mixed, so the white and yellow portions are still visible in the finished product.

Serves 4

Calories: 180.44
Fat: 13.89 grams
Saturated Fat: 3.68 grams
Carbohydrates: 0.79 grams
Sodium: 431.78 mg

8 eggs
1 tablespoon olive or vegetable oil
½ teaspoon salt
⅛ teaspoon pepper

1. Place eggs in medium bowl. Beat with a fork just until yolks are broken and mixture is slightly frothy. Do not beat until the yolks and whites are combined.

2. Heat medium nonstick skillet over medium heat. Add oil and swirl around pan. Pour in eggs and sprinkle with salt and pepper. Cook, shaking pan occasionally and running a heatproof spatula around the edges of the eggs, until set.

3. Carefully turn eggs with a large spatula and cook until second side is set. Eggs should be visibly white and yellow. Cut into quarters to serve.

Scroddled Eggs

Back in the Great Depression, customers at diners would ask for "scroddled" eggs because they couldn't be made with powdered egg. The white and yellow color of the partially beaten eggs can't be imitated by anything other than fresh eggs, unlike traditional scrambled eggs or omelets.

milk eggs fish nuts

Multigrain Pancakes

Serves 6

Calories: 226.55
Fat: 1.17 grams
Saturated Fat: 0.18 grams
Carbohydrates: 49.95 grams
Sodium: 241.11 mg

1 cup whole-wheat flour
½ cup all-purpose flour
¼ cup rye flour
¼ cup cornmeal
1 teaspoon baking powder
¼ cup brown sugar
½ teaspoon salt
1 teaspoon cinnamon
2 teaspoons vanilla
1 ripe banana
½ cup soy or rice milk
½ cup orange juice
½ cup apple juice

You can omit the soy or rice milk in this recipe and increase the orange and apple juices, if you'd like.

1. In large bowl, combine flours, cornmeal, baking powder, brown sugar, salt, and cinnamon and mix well with wire whisk.

2. In blender or food processor, combine vanilla, banana, and soy or rice milk; blend until smooth. Add orange and apple juices; blend until smooth again.

3. Add all at once to dry ingredients; mix with wire whisk until blended. Let batter stand for 15 minutes.

4. Heat large nonstick skillet over medium heat. Brush oil over surface. Pour batter onto skillet ¼ cup at a time. Cook until edges appear dry and bubbles form and just start to break on the surface. Gently turn pancakes and cook on second side until done.

milk *eggs* *soy* *fish* *nuts*

Fruity Waffles

**Yields 12 waffles;
Serves 6**

Bananas, orange juice, and blueberries combine to make an excellent, crisp waffle perfect for a luxurious breakfast.

Calories: 239.83
Fat: 4.69 grams
Saturated Fat: 0.43 grams
Carbohydrates: 46.65 grams
Sodium: 182.33 mg

1. In large bowl, combine flours, sugar, baking powder, baking soda, cinnamon, and salt and mix well with wire whisk.

2. In blender or food processor, combine bananas and rice milk; blend or process until smooth. Add orange juice and vegetable oil and blend or process until smooth.

3. Add all at once to dry ingredients and mix until just combined. Fold in blueberries.

4. Preheat the waffle iron according to directions and make waffles; brush waffle iron with a bit of vegetable oil before making first waffle.

*1 cup all-purpose flour
½ cup whole-wheat flour
½ cup superfine rice flour
¼ cup sugar
1½ teaspoons baking
   powder
1½ teaspoons baking soda
1 teaspoon cinnamon
¼ teaspoon salt
2 ripe bananas
1 cup rice milk
½ cup orange juice
2 tablespoons vegetable oil
1½ cups blueberries*

Making Waffles

Follow the directions that come with your waffle iron to make the best waffles. Generally, you preheat the iron, grease it a bit, add the batter, close the iron, and cook until the steaming stops. The first waffle almost always sticks; after that, you should be able to turn out perfect waffles.

Calories: 409.01
Fat: 30.35 grams
Saturated Fat: 6.86 grams
Carbohydrates: 7.90 grams
Sodium: 887.74 mg

2 tablespoons vegetable oil
½ cup chopped onion
1 cup chopped gluten-free ham
1 (8-ounce) can pineapple tidbits
9 eggs
½ teaspoon salt
⅛ teaspoon pepper
1 cup shredded dairy-free soy cheese

milk   wheat   fish   nuts

Ham Omelet

The pineapple liquid adds a bit of sweetness to the eggs, which complements the salty ham beautifully.

1. In large saucepan, heat vegetable oil over medium heat. Add onion and ham; cook and stir 4–5 minutes, or until onion is crisp-tender. Remove ham and onions from skillet and set aside.

2. Drain pineapple, reserving liquid. In medium bowl, combine 2 tablespoons reserved pineapple liquid, eggs, salt, and pepper; beat until frothy.

3. Add to hot saucepan; cook over medium heat, lifting egg mixture occasionally to let uncooked egg flow underneath. When top is set but still moist, add ham, onion, and drained pineapple.

4. Cover and cook 2 minutes, then top with cheese. Fold omelet in half and slide onto serving plate. Serve immediately.

milk wheat eggs soy fish

Puffed-Rice Granola

*If someone in your family has a nut allergy,
you can simply omit the nuts in this recipe and increase
the puffed rice, oatmeal, and sesame seeds.*

Yields 12 cups; Serves 24

Calories: 294.13
Fat: 13.73 grams
Saturated Fat: 2.46 grams
Carbohydrates: 38.74 grams
Sodium: 63.29 mg

3 cups puffed rice
3 cups gluten-free, quick-cooking oatmeal
2 cups gluten-free buckwheat flakes
1 cup coconut
½ cup sesame seeds
⅓ cup flaxseed, ground
2 cups assorted chopped nuts, if desired
½ cup honey
⅓ cup brown sugar
¼ cup vegetable oil
¼ cup pineapple juice
2 teaspoons gluten-free vanilla
½ teaspoon salt
2 teaspoons cinnamon
2 cups dried cherries

1. Preheat oven to 300°F. In large roasting pan, combine puffed rice, oatmeal, buckwheat flakes, coconut, sesame seeds, flaxseed, and nuts; toss to mix.

2. In small saucepan, combine honey, brown sugar, oil, pineapple juice, vanilla, salt, and cinnamon; bring to a simmer over low heat. Stir until combined, then drizzle over ingredients in roasting pan and stir to coat.

3. Bake 35–40 minutes, stirring twice, until ingredients are glazed and mixture is light golden brown. Remove from oven and stir in dried cherries. Cool completely, then break into pieces and store in air-tight container at room temperature.

Cereals for Granola

The cereals you choose to make your own granola will determine its final texture. Puffed cereals will make a lighter granola that is more crisp than crunchy or chewy, and may be easier for some to eat. Flakes and rolled oats tend to stick together and become crunchy clusters.

Calories: 278.85
Fat: 21.34 grams
Saturated Fat: 4.88 grams
Carbohydrates: 4.63 grams
Sodium: 381.96 mg

2 tablespoons olive oil
½ cup chopped onion
1 cup sliced mushrooms
½ cup chopped red bell
  pepper
¼ teaspoon salt
⅛ teaspoon pepper
½ teaspoon dried thyme
  leaves
8 eggs
2 tablespoons water
½ cup grated, dairy-free
  soy cheese

Serves 6

Calories: 327.05
Fat: 3.66 grams
Saturated Fat: 0.64 grams
Carbohydrates: 67.22
grams
Sodium: 201.27 mg

2 cups water
2 cups applesauce
1½ teaspoons cinnamon
¼ cup brown sugar
2 tablespoons honey
½ teaspoon salt
2 cups gluten-free, quick-
  cooking oatmeal
½ cup dried currants

Egg and Veggie Scramble

Use your favorite vegetables in this easy breakfast recipe.

1. In large skillet, heat olive oil over medium heat. Add onion, mushrooms, and red bell pepper; cook and stir 4–5 minutes, or until vegetables are tender. Sprinkle with salt, pepper, and thyme leaves.

2. Meanwhile, in medium bowl combine eggs and water and beat until frothy. Add to skillet when vegetables are tender. Cook, stirring occasionally, until eggs are just set but still moist.

3. Sprinkle with cheese, remove from heat, and cover. Let stand 3–4 minutes, or until cheese melts. Serve immediately.

Creamy Oatmeal

Applesauce adds creamy texture and nutrition to this simple oatmeal recipe. Serve it hot with some warmed maple syrup or honey.

1. In large saucepan, combine water, applesauce, cinnamon, brown sugar, honey, and salt and bring to a boil.

2. Stir in oatmeal and cook 2–4 minutes, or until mixture thickens. Stir in currants, cover, and remove from heat. Let stand 5 minutes. Stir and serve immediately.

Cornmeal-Cranberry Pancakes

Apple juice adds a nice bit of sweetness to these tender pancakes. Serve them with cranberry sauce or warmed honey for a fabulous breakfast.

Serves 6

Calories: 286.39
Fat: 7.68 grams
Saturated Fat: 2.91 grams
Carbohydrates: 50.54 grams
Sodium: 317.07 mg

¾ cup cornmeal
½ teaspoon salt
2 tablespoons honey
2 tablespoons butter
½ cup water
1 cup apple juice
1 egg
½ cup flour
¼ cup whole-wheat flour
1 teaspoon baking powder
½ teaspoon baking soda
1 cup dried cranberries
1 tablespoon vegetable oil

1. In large bowl, combine cornmeal, salt, honey, and butter. In microwave-safe glass measuring cup, combine water and apple juice. Microwave on high 1–2 minutes, or until mixture boils. Add to cornmeal mixture, stir, and let stand for 5 minutes.

2. Beat in egg until mixed. Then add flours, baking powder, and baking soda and stir just until combined. Add cranberries.

3. Heat large skillet over medium heat. Brush the surface with oil. Pour batter onto skillet using ¼ cup measure. Cook until edges appear dry and bubbles form and just start to break on the surface, about 4 minutes. Gently turn pancakes and cook on second side until done. Serve immediately.

Making Pancakes

For the best pancakes, the griddle should be hot enough that a drop of water skips and steams as soon as it's dropped onto the surface. Cook pancakes until the sides look dry and bubbles form on the surface and begin to break. Use a large spatula to easily turn the pancakes. The second side will never brown as much as the first, so don't worry about it!

Yields 2 cups; Serves 16

Calories: 68.05
Fat: 2.71 grams
Saturated Fat: 1.68 grams
Carbohydrates: 9.98 grams
Sodium: 81.50 mg

2 mangoes, peeled and
    chopped
2 tablespoons lime juice
¼ cup honey
1 cup vegan tofu cream
    cheese
¼ teaspoon salt
⅛ teaspoon cardamom

Mango Spread

This spread is excellent as a sandwich spread, to top hot-cooked cereal, or as a pancake and waffle spread.

Combine all ingredients in blender or food processor; blend or process until smooth. Place in medium bowl, cover, and refrigerate 1–2 hours before using. Store in refrigerator up to 3 days.

Serves 2

Calories: 286.06
Fat: 6.59 grams
Saturated Fat: 0.65 grams
Carbohydrates: 53.32 grams
Sodium: 87.64 mg

½ cup soy milk
1¼ cups frozen blueberries
¼ cup honey
½ cup silken tofu
2 tablespoons ground
    flaxseed

Blueberry Smoothie

You can vary the fruit you use in this smoothie; frozen raspberries or strawberries would be delicious.

Combine all ingredients in blender or food processor. Blend or process until mixture is smooth. Serve immediately.

milk wheat eggs soy fish nuts

Eggless French Toast

Serve this French Toast hot from the griddle with some whipped honey and fresh raspberries.

1. In blender or food processor, combine all ingredients except bread and oil; blend or process until smooth. Pour into shallow bowl.

2. Soak bread in mixture 2–3 minutes. Heat vegetable oil in a large skillet over medium heat. Cook bread in skillet, turning once, until golden brown on both sides and slightly puffy, about 4–6 minutes. Serve immediately.

Serves 4

Calories: 148.33
Fat: 5.16 grams
Saturated Fat: 0.49 grams
Carbohydrates: 24.04 grams
Sodium: 130.37 mg

1 ripe banana, mashed
1 tablespoon lemon juice
⅓ cup vanilla rice milk
½ teaspoon cinnamon
1 tablespoon sugar
Dash salt
1 teaspoon gluten-free vanilla
4 slices day-old, gluten-free, egg-free bread
1 tablespoon vegetable oil

Calories: 371.64
Fat: 15.09 grams
Saturated Fat: 3.20 grams
Carbohydrates: 35.27 grams
Sodium: 367.58 mg

6 russet potatoes, peeled
    and sliced
1 tablespoon vegetable oil
1 onion, chopped
8 hard-cooked eggs, sliced
4 Chicken and Apple
    Patties (page 39),
    cooked and crumbled
1¼ cups grated, dairy-free
    soy cheese

milk   wheat   fish   nuts

Egg and Potato Casseroles

Individual breakfast casseroles are great for families when people eat at different times. Just leave them in the fridge with a note about how to bake them.

1. Bring a large pot of water to a boil. Cook sliced potatoes until tender but still firm, about 10–12 minutes. Drain well and let cool.

2. Grease eight (10-ounce) custard cups with oil. In small skillet, heat vegetable oil over medium heat. Add onion; cook and stir until tender, about 5 minutes.

3. Layer potatoes, eggs, onion, and Chicken and Apple Patties in prepared custard cups. Top with cheese. Cover and refrigerate for 2 days, or bake immediately.

4. To bake, preheat oven to 350°F. Bake casseroles 15–20 minutes, until hot. Add 5–10 minutes baking time for refrigerated casseroles.

Hard-Cooked Eggs

To make hard-cooked eggs, place eggs in cold water to cover. Place pan over high heat and bring to a boil; boil hard for 1 minute. Cover pan, remove from heat, and let stand for 15 minutes for large eggs. Run under cold running water until eggs feel cold to the touch. Tap eggs on side of pan under water, then peel. Store in refrigerator for 3 days.

milk   wheat   eggs   fish   nuts

Banana-Raspberry Smoothie

Frozen strawberries are also delicious in this simple and creamy smoothie. Serve with cinnamon muffins for a great breakfast.

Combine all ingredients in blender or food processor. Blend or process until mixture is smooth. Serve immediately.

Serves 4

Calories: 278.30
Fat: 2.82 grams
Saturated Fat: 0.41 grams
Carbohydrates: 61.92 grams
Sodium: 58.40 mg

2 cups frozen raspberries
2 bananas, sliced
1 cup rice milk
1 cup frozen, dairy-free tofutti
½ teaspoon cinnamon
⅛ teaspoon cardamom

milk   wheat   eggs   fish   nuts

Egg-Free Scrambled "Eggs"

Turmeric is an inexpensive spice that adds a golden color to these "eggs." It is also a good source of antioxidants.

1. Heat olive oil in large skillet over medium heat. Add mushrooms, onion, and garlic; cook and stir until tender, about 6 minutes. Sprinkle with salt and pepper.

2. Add crumbled tofu to skillet. In small bowl, combine water and turmeric; mix well. Sprinkle evenly over tofu. Cook and stir until heated and most of the moisture has been absorbed.

3. Sprinkle with cheese, cover, remove from heat, and let stand 2–3 minutes to melt cheese. Serve immediately.

Serves 4

Calories: 266.54
Fat: 20.82 grams
Saturated Fat: 3.31 grams
Carbohydrates: 5.80 grams
Sodium: 489.75 mg

2 tablespoons olive oil
1 cup sliced mushrooms
½ cup chopped onion
2 cloves garlic, minced
½ teaspoon salt
⅛ teaspoon pepper
1 (8-ounce) block medium-firm tofu, crumbled
1 tablespoon water
½ teaspoon turmeric
1 cup shredded, nondairy vegan soy cheese

Calories: 270.69
Fat: 7.06 grams
Saturated Fat: 3.46 grams
Carbohydrates: 44.14 grams
Sodium: 173.31 mg

1 cup steel-cut, gluten-free oats
1¾ cups water
¼ cup frozen orange juice concentrate, thawed
1 cup mixed dried fruit
¼ teaspoon salt
2 tablespoons sugar
1 (13-ounce) can evaporated milk

Fruity Slow-Cooker Oatmeal

Waking up to hot oatmeal in the slow cooker is very luxurious. Drizzle this with some maple syrup and top with fresh fruit.

1. Place oats in a dry, heavy saucepan over medium-low heat. Toast oats 5–7 minutes, stirring frequently, until oats are deeper golden brown and fragrant. Cool completely.

2. In 2-quart slow cooker, combine oats, water, orange juice concentrate, dried fruit, and salt; mix well. Cover and cook on low 7–9 hours.

3. In the morning, stir in the sugar and evaporated milk; cook for another 30 minutes until hot. Stir well and serve immediately.

Steel-Cut Oats

Steel-cut oats are really essential when cooking oatmeal in the slow cooker. They have a firmer texture and stand up to the long cooking time. They are made from the whole-oat grain, also known as groats, cut into pieces. All types of oatmeal have the same nutritional qualities, although instant oatmeal may have less fiber.

milk *wheat* *eggs* *soy* *fish* *nuts*

Chicken and Apple Patties

Rather than feed your kids sausages full of nitrates, try this easy recipe that is flavorful and good for you, too.

1. In large saucepan, heat olive oil over medium heat. Add onion and garlic; cook and stir until tender, about 5 minutes. Remove from heat and add apple, brown sugar, and lemon juice. Let cool for 20 minutes.

2. Place in large bowl and add chicken, salt, pepper, and thyme leaves; work with your hands until combined.

3. Form mixture into 16 patties. You can freeze the patties at this point, or cook them in more olive oil, turning once, until thoroughly cooked, about 3–4 minutes per side. To cook frozen patties, let thaw in refrigerator overnight, then proceed as directed.

milk *wheat* *eggs* *soy* *fish* *nuts*

Cinnamon French Toast

Purchased gluten-free bread can be dense and rather stiff; perfect for making the best French Toast.

1. In food processor or blender, combine orange juice, rice milk, and banana and blend until smooth. Pour into a shallow bowl and stir in sugar, cinnamon, cardamom, vanilla, and salt; mix well.

2. Soak bread in mixture for 2–3 minutes. Heat vegetable oil in a large skillet over medium heat. Cook bread in skillet, turning once, until golden brown on both sides and slightly puffy, about 4–6 minutes. Serve immediately.

Serves 8

Calories: 163.41
Fat: 4.51 grams
Saturated Fat: 0.76 grams
Carbohydrates: 10.39 grams
Sodium: 347.50 mg

2 tablespoons olive oil
1 onion, finely chopped
3 cloves garlic, minced
1 cup finely chopped, peeled apple
1 tablespoon brown sugar
2 tablespoons lemon juice
1½ pounds gluten-free ground chicken
1 teaspoon salt
¼ teaspoon white pepper
1 teaspoon dried thyme leaves

Serves 4–6

Calories: 132.17
Fat: 3.89 grams
Saturated Fat: 0.47 grams
Carbohydrates: 22.75 grams
Sodium: 222.32 mg

¼ cup orange juice
¼ cup rice milk
1 ripe banana
2 tablespoons sugar
½ teaspoon cinnamon
⅛ teaspoon cardamom
1 teaspoon gluten-free vanilla
¼ teaspoon salt
6 slices day-old gluten-free, dairy-free bread
1 tablespoon vegetable oil

Serves 12

Calories: 417.83
Fat: 12.40 grams
Saturated Fat: 1.95 grams
Carbohydrates: 71.99 grams
Sodium: 117.64 mg

¼ cup dairy-free vegan
   margarine
2 tablespoons vegetable oil
¼ cup applesauce
½ cup sugar
½ cup brown sugar
2 eggs
1 teaspoon gluten-free
   vanilla
1 cup superfine rice flour
½ cup white sorghum flour
½ cup millet flour
1 teaspoon xanthan gum
1 teaspoon gluten-free
   baking powder
1 teaspoon cinnamon
1 (21-ounce) can gluten-free
   cherry pie filling
¼ cup dairy-free vegan
   margarine
½ cup brown sugar
½ teaspoon cinnamon
1 cup gluten-free oatmeal

Cherry Coffee Cake

*This coffee cake is for a special occasion.
Make it for Christmas morning breakfast or brunch.*

1. Preheat oven to 350°F. Spray a 9" × 13" pan with nonstick gluten-free cooking spray and set aside.

2. In large bowl, combine ½ cup margarine, oil, applesauce, sugar, and ½ cup brown sugar; beat until smooth. Add eggs and vanilla and beat again until smooth.

3. In medium bowl, combine rice flour, sorghum flour, millet flour, xanthan gum, baking powder, and 1 teaspoon cinnamon; mix well. Add to egg mixture and beat just until combined. Spread evenly in prepared pan and top with cherry-pie filling.

4. In small bowl, combine ¼ cup margarine, ½ cup brown sugar, ½ teaspoon cinnamon, and oatmeal; mix until crumbly. Sprinkle over pie filling.

5. Bake 45–55 minutes, or until it is deep golden brown and starts to pull away from sides of pan. Let cool for 30 minutes, then serve.

Gluten-Free Oatmeal?

Many celiacs and others who avoid gluten have had reactions to oatmeal, because it is processed in the same plants used to mill wheat. You can find gluten-free oatmeal from a plant that has a dedicated mill, with oats grown in dedicated fields—one that only produces oats, like Bob's Red Mill and Cream Hill Estates. McCann's uses dedicated mills, but doesn't have a guaranteed supply chain from the farms.

milk wheat soy fish nuts

Wild Blueberry-Raspberry Pancakes

You can find sweet, light sorghum flour in health food stores, or order it online. It's sweeter and lighter than amaranth flour.

1. In medium bowl, combine juice, oil, and egg yolk; mix well. Add sorghum flour, tapioca flour, cornstarch, xanthan gum, baking soda, and salt; mix just until combined.

2. In small bowl, beat egg whites with sugar until stiff peaks form. Fold into batter.

3. Heat a nonstick skillet over medium heat. Pour batter by ¼-cup measure onto skillet. Cook until edges appear dry and bubbles form and just start to break on the surface, about 4 minutes. Sprinkle each pancake with a few spoonfuls of blueberries and raspberries and gently turn pancakes. Cook on second side until done. Serve immediately.

Wild Blueberries

Many dried blueberries are made with wild blueberries, which are tangier than cultivated blueberries. They have much more Vitamin A and antioxidants than the cultivated variety. You can find them in the health food aisle or baking aisle of the grocery store. Stir them into everything from pancake batter to snack mixes to sugar cookies.

Serves 6

Calories: 339.21
Fat: 6.09 grams
Saturated Fat: 0.63 grams
Carbohydrates: 67.57 grams
Sodium: 225.09 mg

½ cup pineapple juice
2 tablespoons vegetable oil
1 egg yolk
½ cup sweet, light
    sorghum flour
½ cup tapioca flour
6 tablespoons cornstarch
½ teaspoon xanthan gum
1 teaspoon baking soda
½ teaspoon salt
3 egg whites
2 tablespoons sugar
¾ cup dried wild
    blueberries
1 cup raspberries

Chapter 3
Breads

Calories: 365.16
Fat: 7.04 grams
Saturated Fat: 2.52 grams
Carbohydrates: 73.49 grams
Sodium: 342.62 mg

2 cups Gluten-Free, Soy-Free Baking Mix (page 67)
¼ cup brown sugar
¼ cup sugar
¼ cup Egg Substitute for Baking (page 66)
1 tablespoon vegetable oil
½ cup buttermilk
½ cup sour cream
1 cup raisins
2 teaspoons caraway seeds

wheat eggs soy fish nuts

Irish Soda Bread

This bread is one of the best gluten-free choices around, and it's quick to make. You don't have to wait to have corned beef and cabbage to make it!

1. Preheat oven to 350°F. Spray a 9" round cake pan with nonstick gluten-free cooking spray and set aside.

2. In large bowl, combine Baking Mix, brown sugar, and sugar; mix well with wire whisk. In small bowl, combine Egg Substitute, oil, buttermilk and sour cream; beat well.

3. Add buttermilk mixture to dry ingredients and stir just until moistened. Add raisins and caraway seeds. Spoon batter into the prepared pan.

4. Bake 55–65 minutes, or until bread is deep golden brown and toothpick inserted in center comes out clean. Remove from pan and cool on wire rack 30 minutes before serving.

milk wheat eggs soy fish nuts

Cornmeal Cranberry Muffins

Warm muffins, fresh from the oven, are a delicious choice for a hearty breakfast or an easy snack.

Yields 12 muffins

Calories: 153.64
Fat: 5.29 grams
Saturated Fat: 0.39 grams
Carbohydrates: 25.17 grams
Sodium: 58.61 mg

1. Preheat oven to 400°F. Spray 12 muffin cups with nonstick gluten-free cooking spray and set aside. In large bowl, combine flours, cornmeal, baking powder, baking soda, xanthan gum, cardamom, and salt; mix well.

2. In small bowl, combine Egg Substitute, oil, brown sugar, rice milk, sparkling water, and vanilla; mix well. Add to dry ingredients and stir just until combined. Fold in cranberries.

3. Divide batter evenly among prepared muffin cups. Bake 18–23 minutes, or until muffins are golden brown and firm. Immediately remove from muffin cups and let cool on wire rack.

¾ cup superfine rice flour
¼ cup potato-starch flour
¼ cup millet flour
½ cup cornmeal
2 teaspoons gluten-free
    baking powder
1 teaspoon baking soda
1 teaspoon xanthan gum
⅛ teaspoon cardamom
¼ teaspoon salt
¼ cup Egg Substitute for
    Baking (page 66)
¼ cup vegetable oil
⅓ cup brown sugar
⅓ cup rice milk
¾ cup sparkling water
1 teaspoon gluten-free
    vanilla
1 cup chopped cranberries

Sparkling Water

Sparkling water is plain water that is carbonated. It has no added ingredients and can be found in any grocery store. In gluten-free breads, it adds a bit of lightness and helps aerate the bread without weakening the structure, as the acids in other sparkling drinks can. Use plain, not flavored, water in baking recipes.

Calories: 396.75
Fat: 17.31 grams
Saturated Fat: 9.68 grams
Carbohydrates: 57.04 grams
Sodium: 313.70 mg

1 cup butter, softened
1 cup brown sugar
1 cup sour cream
2 teaspoons gluten-free vanilla
2 eggs
2 egg whites
2 tablespoons lemon juice
2½ cups Gluten-Free, Soy-Free Baking Mix (page 67)
1 teaspoon cinnamon
1½ cups Spicy and Sweet Granola (page 24)
½ cup dried chopped cherries

Crunchy Coffee Cake

Raisins, chocolate chips, dried cranberries, or chopped nuts (if you're not allergic) could be used in place of the dried cherries if you'd like.

1. Preheat oven to 350°F. Spray a 9" × 13" baking pan with nonstick gluten-free cooking spray and set aside. In large bowl, combine butter and sugar and beat until light and fluffy.

2. Add sour cream, vanilla, eggs, egg whites, and lemon juice; beat until blended. Add Baking Mix and cinnamon; mix just until blended.

3. Spread half of batter into prepared baking pan. Top with half of the granola, remaining batter, then remaining granola. Top with dried cherries.

4. Bake 35–40 minutes, or until cake is golden brown and springs back when lightly touched in center. Let cool completely on wire rack.

milk wheat soy fish nuts

Apple Spice Bread

Applesauce and fresh apple combine in this delicious recipe to make a quick bread perfect for a snack or after-school treat.

Yields 1 loaf; Serves 8

Calories: 314.62
Fat: 5.01 grams
Saturated Fat: 0.69 grams
Carbohydrates: 65.74 grams
Sodium: 102.16 mg

1. Preheat oven to 350°F. Spray a 9" × 5" loaf pan with nonstick gluten-free cooking spray and set aside. In large bowl, combine flours, xanthan gum, salt, cinnamon, nutmeg, allspice, cardamom, baking powder, and baking soda; mix well.

2. In medium bowl, combine brown sugar, eggs, vegetable oil, vanilla, applesauce, apple, and currants; mix well. Stir into dry ingredients just until mixed. Pour into prepared pan.

3. Bake 55–65 minutes, or until deep golden brown and toothpick inserted in center comes out clean. Let cool in pan for 5 minutes; remove to wire rack to cool completely.

1 cup superfine rice flour
½ cup millet flour
¼ cup sweet, white sorghum flour
1 teaspoon xanthan gum
¼ teaspoon salt
1 teaspoon cinnamon
¼ teaspoon nutmeg
⅛ teaspoon allspice
⅛ teaspoon cardamom
1 teaspoon gluten-free baking powder
½ teaspoon baking soda
1 cup brown sugar
2 eggs
2 tablespoons vegetable oil
1 teaspoon gluten-free vanilla
½ cup applesauce
1 cup apple, peeled and grated
½ cup dried currants

Brown Sugar

Brown sugar can dry out quite quickly if kept in its original packaging. To make it last longer, buy a brown-sugar disc, a small pottery disc that is soaked in water. Pack the brown sugar into an airtight container and top with the disc; the brown sugar will not dry out. Make sure the cover is fastened securely and store in a cool, dark place.

Banana-Chocolate Muffins

Bananas are a good substitute for eggs in these tender muffins.

Yields 12 muffins

Calories: 248.94
Fat: 10.95 grams
Saturated Fat: 6.73 grams
Carbohydrates: 39.22 grams
Sodium: 150.14 mg

2 cups Gluten-Free Muffin Mix (page 86)
1 ripe banana, mashed
¼ cup coconut oil, melted
1 tablespoon vegetable oil
10 tablespoons Rice Milk (page 84)
1 teaspoon gluten-free vanilla
1 cup gluten-free semisweet chocolate chips
2 tablespoons sugar
½ teaspoon cinnamon

1. Preheat oven to 400°F. Spray 12 muffin cups with nonstick gluten-free cooking spray and set aside. Place Muffin Mix in a large bowl.

2. In medium bowl, combine banana, coconut oil, vegetable oil, Rice Milk, and vanilla; mix well. Add to Muffin mix and stir just until combined. Stir in chocolate chips.

3. Spoon batter into prepared muffin cups. In small bowl, combine sugar and cinnamon; mix well and sprinkle over muffins. Bake 14–19 minutes, or until muffins are firm and gently rounded. Remove from muffin cups and cool on wire rack.

Seasoned Breadsticks

You'll need a breadstick pan for this easy recipe. They can be found at baking supply stores and online.

Yields 12

Calories: 195.14
Fat: 3.97 grams
Saturated Fat: 0.35 grams
Carbohydrates: 36.81 grams
Sodium: 205.22 mg

2 tablespoons cornmeal
1 recipe French Bread (page 51)
1 teaspoon dried basil leaves
1 teaspoon garlic powder
1 teaspoon celery salt
1 teaspoon dried thyme leaves
2 teaspoons grated lemon zest

1. Spray 12 breadstick molds with nonstick gluten-free cooking spray; sprinkle with cornmeal. Prepare French Bread dough through Step 2. Spoon dough into prepared molds; let rise for about 20 minutes.

2. Preheat oven to 375°F. In small bowl, combine basil, garlic powder, celery salt, thyme, and lemon zest. Sprinkle evenly over breadsticks.

3. Place a pan with 1" of water on rack below bread to create steam. Bake 12–21 minutes, or until deep golden brown. Remove to wire rack; cool for 10 minutes. Serve warm.

wheat   eggs   soy   fish   nuts

Sourdough French Bread

You can play with the flour combinations and proportions in this bread recipe, depending on which ones you need to avoid. Red Star Yeast is gluten-free.

1. In medium bowl, combine flours, cornstarch, dry milk powder, salt, xanthan gum, and baking powder. Remove 1 cup of mixture; combine in large bowl with yeast, sugar, yogurt, gelatin, and ½ cup water. Mix well; let stand for 15 minutes.

2. Add remaining water and apple cider vinegar to yeast mixture; stir well. Add remaining flour mixture to make a very soft dough; beat for 2 minutes.

3. Grease two French-bread baking tins with unsalted butter; sprinkle with cornmeal. Spoon dough into tins; cover and let rise for about 30 minutes, until dough doubles in bulk. While dough is rising, preheat oven to 400°F. Place a pan with 1" of water on rack below bread.

4. Bake 35–45 minutes, or until loaves are deep golden brown and sound hollow when tapped with your fingers. Remove from pan and place on wire rack to cool.

Why Not Quick Rise Yeast?

Because this bread, along with the other gluten-free breads in this chapter, does not have gluten, the xanthan gum needs time to build a structure so the bread keeps its shape. Quick rice or cake yeast will not work as well, because the structure of gluten-free dough is weaker than regular bread containing gluten, and the bread may collapse.

**Yields 2 loaves;
20 servings**

Calories: 170.91
Fat: 0.66 grams
Saturated Fat: 0.35 grams
Carbohydrates: 33.77 grams
Sodium: 165.11 mg

1¼ cups millet flour
1 cup tapioca flour
1 cup white sorghum flour
1 cup potato-starch flour
¼ cup cornstarch
2 tablespoons dry milk powder
1 teaspoon salt
2 teaspoons xanthan gum
1 teaspoon gluten-free baking powder
2 (0.25-ounce) envelopes gluten-free dry yeast
2 tablespoons sugar
1 cup plain yogurt
1 teaspoon unflavored gelatin
1¼ cups warm water, divided
1 tablespoon apple cider vinegar
Unsalted butter
2 tablespoons cornmeal

Calories: 213.38
Fat: 5.64 grams
Saturated Fat: 1.29 grams
Carbohydrates: 34.95 grams
Sodium: 132.98 mg

Solid shortening or unsalted
*   butter*
1½ cups millet flour
½ cup white sorghum flour
½ cup potato-starch flour
¼ cup tapioca flour
½ cup cornstarch
1½ teaspoons xanthan gum
3 tablespoons sugar
½ teaspoon salt
1 tablespoon instant-blend,
*   gluten-free dry yeast*
3 tablespoons olive oil
1 tablespoon honey
1 tablespoon gluten-free
*   apple cider vinegar*
1 cup buttermilk
1 teaspoon unflavored
*   gelatin*
½ cup very warm water
¾ cup sparkling water
2 eggs
2 egg yolks

Light-White Batter Bread

Batter breads are perfect for gluten-free breads because there is no kneading, so you don't have to worry about consistency. Wait 2–3 hours to slice this bread after it comes out of the oven.

1. Grease 9" × 5" loaf pan with shortening or butter; line bottom and long sides with single sheet of parchment paper; set aside.

2. In medium bowl, combine flours, cornstarch, xanthan gum, sugar, salt, and yeast; mix well; set aside.

3. In large mixer bowl, combine oil, honey, and vinegar; mix well. In medium saucepan, combine buttermilk, gelatin, water, and sparkling water; heat until very warm. Add to oil mixture with eggs and egg yolks; stir to combine. Gradually add flour mixture, beating constantly on medium speed.

4. When batter is smooth, pour into prepared pan. Let batter rise 30–40 minutes, or until almost doubled in size.

5. Preheat oven to 400°F. Bake 35–45 minutes, or until deep golden brown and set. You may need to cover the loaf with foil if it becomes too brown. Remove from pan; let cool completely on wire rack.

milk   wheat   eggs   fish   nuts

French Bread

This bread is fabulous toasted and rubbed with garlic, then drizzled with olive oil and served with spaghetti or grilled chicken.

1. In medium bowl, combine rice flour, brown-rice flour, millet flour, tapioca flour, milk substitute, xanthan gum, and salt; mix well. In large bowl, combine water with honey; stir to mix. Add yeast; stir; let stand 15 minutes.

2. Add lemon juice and oil to yeast mixture; add flour mixture and stir to combine; beat for 2 minutes. Dough should be sticky and quite soft.

3. Grease a French-bread tin with solid shortening and sprinkle with cornmeal or millet flour. Spoon dough into prepared tin. Let rise about 20 minutes.

4. Preheat oven to 375°F. Place a pan with 1" of water on rack below bread to create steam. Bake 50–55 minutes, or until deep golden brown. Remove to wire rack to cool completely.

French-Bread Tins

You can find French-bread tins in most baking supply stores or online. When you're making gluten-free French bread, it's important to find tins that are not perforated. Because the dough for this bread is a stiff batter, it will flow into the small holes and "glue" the bread to the pan. If you can't find them, line a perforated tin with heavy-duty foil.

Yields 1 loaf; 12 Servings

Calories: 189.88
Fat: 3.95 grams
Saturated Fat: 0.34 grams
Carbohydrates: 35.69 grams
Sodium: 108.28 mg

1½ cups superfine rice flour
½ cup superfine brown-rice flour
½ cup millet flour
½ cup tapioca flour
3 tablespoons powdered, nondairy vegan milk substitute
2 teaspoons xanthan gum
½ teaspoon salt
1¾ cups water
2 tablespoons honey
2½ teaspoons gluten-free dry yeast
1 tablespoon lemon juice
3 tablespoons vegetable oil
Solid shortening
2 tablespoons cornmeal or millet flour

Calories: 342.61
Fat: 8.55 grams
Saturated Fat: 0.69 grams
Carbohydrates: 64.65 grams
Sodium: 288.07 mg

⅓ cup vegetable oil
1½ cups mashed banana (about 3 bananas)
½ cup sugar
¼ cup brown sugar
1 tablespoon soy yogurt
2 eggs
2¼ cups Gluten-Free, Soy-Free Baking Mix (page 67)
1 teaspoon cinnamon
2 tablespoons sugar
½ teaspoon cinnamon

Banana Bread

This is just pure banana bread, with a wonderful flavor and smooth texture. But you could add ½ cup nuts, chocolate chips, or raisins if you'd like.

1. Preheat oven to 350°F. Spray a 9" × 5" loaf pan with nonstick gluten-free cooking spray and set aside.

2. In large bowl, combine oil, banana, sugar, brown sugar, and soy yogurt; beat until smooth. Stir in eggs one at a time; beat well after each addition.

3. Stir in the Baking Mix and 1 teaspoon cinnamon just until combined. Spoon batter into prepared loaf pan. In small bowl, combine 2 tablespoons sugar and ½ teaspoon cinnamon; sprinkle over batter.

4. Bake 50–60 minutes, or until deep golden brown and firm. Remove from pan and cool completely on wire rack. Store tightly covered at room temperature.

milk wheat eggs soy fish nuts

Fruity-Pear Citrus Bread

Pears add moisture and flavor to this simple quick bread. You can omit the glaze if you'd like.

1. Preheat oven to 375°F. Spray a 9" × 5" loaf pan with nonstick gluten-free cooking spray and set aside.

2. In large bowl, combine flours, xanthan gum, sugar, baking powder, baking soda, and salt; mix well.

3. In small bowl, combine vanilla, pears, orange zest, orange juice, and vegetable oil; mix well. Add to dry ingredients and stir just until combined. Pour into prepared pan.

4. Bake 35–40 minutes, or until bread is golden brown and firm. While bread is baking, combine lemon juice and powdered sugar in small bowl. Drizzle ½ of mixture over bread when it comes out of the oven.

5. Let bread cool 10 minutes in pan; remove to wire rack. Drizzle with remaining ½ of lemon mixture; cool completely.

Storing Quick Breads

Most quick breads, that is, breads made with baking powder or soda instead of yeast, improve in texture and flavor if allowed to stand overnight at room temperature. Cool the bread completely, then either wrap in plastic wrap or place the bread in a plastic food-storage bag and seal. Quick breads can also be frozen for longer storage.

Yields 1 loaf; Serves 12

Calories: 215.11
Fat: 4.88 grams
Saturated Fat: 0.37 grams
Carbohydrates: 41.85 grams
Sodium: 50.79 mg

1½ cups superfine rice flour
¼ cup millet flour
¼ cup potato-starch flour
1 teaspoon xanthan gum
½ cup sugar
2 teaspoons gluten-free baking powder
1 teaspoon baking soda
¼ teaspoon salt
1 teaspoon gluten-free vanilla
½ cup pureed pears
1 teaspoon grated orange zest
½ cup orange juice
¼ cup vegetable oil
3 tablespoons lemon juice
1 cup powdered sugar

2 cups Gluten-Free Muffin Mix (page 86)
⅓ cup rice milk
¼ cup apple juice
⅓ cup vegetable oil
¼ cup Egg Substitute II (page 76)
1 cup fresh or frozen blueberries
¼ cup brown sugar
½ cup quick-cooking, gluten-free oatmeal
1 tablespoon minced candied ginger
½ teaspoon cinnamon
3 tablespoons vegetable oil

milk wheat eggs fish nuts

Blueberry Coffee Cake

Raspberries or blackberries would work well in place of the blueberries in this quick and easy coffee cake.

1. Preheat oven to 375°F. Spray a 9" square pan with nonstick gluten-free cooking spray and set aside.

2. Place Muffin Mix in large bowl. In small bowl, combine rice milk, apple juice, oil, Egg Substitute; mix well. Add to Muffin Mix and stir just until combined; fold in fresh or frozen blueberries. Place in prepared pan.

3. In small bowl, combine brown sugar, oatmeal, ginger, and cinnamon; mix well. Add vegetable oil; work with hands until crumbly. Sprinkle over batter in pan.

4. Bake 25–30 minutes, or until coffee cake is golden brown and pulls away from sides of pan. Let cool 30 minutes; cut into squares to serve.

milk wheat eggs soy fish nuts

Focaccia Bread

You can use this bread as the basis for homemade pizza or top it with fresh vegetables and cut in small squares for an appetizer.

1. In large bowl, combine flours, xanthan gum, yeast, salt, and sugar; mix well.

2. Add vinegar, water, and 3 tablespoons olive oil; beat with mixer for 2 minutes.

3. Line a 10" springform pan with parchment paper; sprinkle bottom with cornmeal. Spoon dough onto paper; drizzle with 1 tablespoon olive oil and sprinkle with coarse salt and thyme.

4. Let rise for 30 minutes. Preheat oven to 400°F. Bake 18–25 minutes, or until golden brown. Let cool 5 minutes; remove from pan and peel off parchment paper; cool on wire rack.

Soft Doughs

Generally, the softer and stickier the dough is for a yeast bread, the coarser the bread texture will be. For focaccia, you want a very coarse bread with lots of big yeast holes and a chewy texture. You can't knead this bread, so beat with an electric mixer for 2 minutes, or beat vigorously by hand for 300 strokes.

Yields 1 loaf; Serves 8

Calories: 175.81
Fat: 3.86 grams
Saturated Fat: 0.58 grams
Carbohydrates: 31.42 grams
Sodium: 228.98 mg

1-½ cups superfine rice flour
½ cup millet flour
⅓ cup tapioca flour
1 teaspoon xanthan gum
1 (0.25-ounce) package instant-blend gluten-free dry yeast
¼ teaspoon salt
2 teaspoons sugar
½ teaspoon gluten-free apple cider vinegar
1⅓ cups warm water
4 tablespoons olive oil
2 tablespoons cornmeal
½ teaspoon coarse salt
1 teaspoon dried thyme leaves

milk   wheat   eggs   soy   fish   nuts

Focaccia Rolls

Serves 6

Calories: 207.75
Fat: 5.01 grams
Saturated Fat: 0.73 grams
Carbohydrates: 37.90 grams
Sodium: 291.98 mg

1 recipe Focaccia
    (page 55)
2 tablespoons cornmeal
½ teaspoon coarse salt

You'll need six 4-inch ring molds for this recipe to make the perfect bun shape. These are fun to make and serve.

1. Prepare Focaccia through step 2. Then set aside dough. Spray six 4-inch ring molds with nonstick gluten-free cooking spray and place on a parchment paper–lined baking sheet.

2. Preheat oven to 375° F. Sprinkle cornmeal on the sides of the molds and on the parchment paper. Spoon dough into the molds; sprinkle with coarse salt. Let rise for 20–30 minutes, and then bake for 9–10 minutes or until set.

3. Carefully remove molds, and bake rolls for 5–8 minutes longer until light golden brown and set. Let cool on wire racks, then cut in half and use for sandwiches.

Freezing Rolls

Most rolls and other baked goods will freeze very well. Let the rolls cool completely on a wire rack. If you try to freeze them while warm, water will condense on the surface and they'll be soggy. Place into freezer bags or hard-sided freezer containers. Label, seal, and freeze up to 6 months. To thaw, let stand on the counter for 1–2 hours.

milk wheat eggs soy fish nuts

Gluten-Free Biscuits

The coconut oil doesn't flavor the biscuits—
it just helps make them flaky and tender.
These are the biscuits to serve with fried chicken!

1. In food processor, combine vegetable shortening and coconut oil; process until blended. Place in freezer.

2. In large bowl, combine Flour Mix, sugar, baking powder, baking soda, cream of tartar, and salt; mix well. In small bowl, combine Egg Substitute, ⅓ cup rice milk, and cider vinegar; mix well.

3. Cut chilled shortening mixture into small pieces and add to flour mixture. Cut in with a pastry blender until particles are fine. Add Egg mixture; stir just until combined, adding more rice milk if necessary to make dough hold together.

4. Wrap dough in plastic wrap; chill for at least 2 hours. Preheat oven to 425°F. Roll-out dough on surface dusted with superfine rice flour, to ½" thickness. Cut into 12 biscuits, using a sharp knife or biscuit cutter.

5. Place biscuits on ungreased cookie sheets. Brush with 1 tablespoon rice milk; bake 12–18 minutes, until biscuits are deep golden brown. Serve hot.

Coconut Oil

Because the coconut palm is a tropical plant, the coconut oil produced from it is solid at room temperature. In fact, the oil is very firm and can be difficult to work with. Blend it with other fats in the food processor so it will blend evenly with the dry ingredients. You can find coconut oil at health food stores and co-ops.

Yields 12 biscuits

Calories: 227.20
Fat: 9.60 grams
Saturated Fat: 3.84 grams
Carbohydrates: 32.34 grams
Sodium: 70.46 mg

⅓ cup solid vegetable shortening
2 tablespoons coconut oil
2 cups Flour Mix II (page 69)
1 tablespoon sugar
2 teaspoons gluten-free baking powder
¼ teaspoon baking soda
¼ teaspoon cream of tartar
¼ teaspoon salt
¼ cup Egg Substitute for Baking (page 66)
⅓–½ cup rice milk
1 tablespoon apple cider vinegar
1 tablespoon rice milk

Cherry Muffins

Muffins are easy and quick to make. If you don't have nut aller-gies, add ½ cup chopped nuts to this simple recipe.

Yields 12 muffins

Calories: 320.24
Fat: 8.26 grams
Saturated Fat: 2.70 grams
Carbohydrates: 59.84 grams
Sodium: 306.87 mg

2 cups Gluten-Free Muffin Mix (page 86)
½ cup cherry juice
¼ cup rice milk
2 tablespoons coconut oil
3 tablespoons vegetable oil
1 egg or ¼ cup Egg Substitute for Baking (page 66)
½ cup dried chopped cherries
2 tablespoons brown sugar

1. Preheat oven to 400°F. Spray 12 muffin cups with nonstick gluten-free cooking spray and set aside.

2. In medium bowl, place Muffin Mix. In small saucepan, combine cherry juice, rice milk, coconut oil, and vegetable oil; heat over low heat until coconut oil melts. Remove from heat.

3. Add cherry juice mixture and egg or Egg Substitute to Muffin Mix; mix just until combined. Fold in cherries.

4. Drop batter into prepared muffin cups. Sprinkle each with a bit of brown sugar. Bake 12–17 minutes, or until muffins are firm and golden brown. Remove from muffin cups; let cool on wire rack.

milk wheat eggs soy fish nuts

Honey Rolls

These soft rolls are flavored with honey, inside and out. You can serve them for breakfast or as a dinner roll.

1. Grease two 9" round cake pans with solid shortening and set aside. In a large saucepan, combine oil, rice milk, honey, and shortening; heat over medium-low heat until mixture is very warm and shortening melts. Remove from heat; let cool for 15 minutes.

2. In large bowl, combine flours, cornstarch, and xanthan gum; mix well. Remove ½ of mixture and set aside.

3. To flour mixture remaining in bowl add yeast, salt, baking soda, and sugar; mix well. Add lukewarm rice milk mixture from Step 1 and Egg Substitute; beat for 2 minutes.

4. Add remaining flour mixture; beat well until combined. Using a large spoon, drop dough into the pan, making 10 rolls per pan. Drizzle remaining 3 tablespoons honey over rolls.

5. Preheat oven to 350°F; let rolls rise in warm place 15 minutes. Bake 15–25 minutes, or until deep golden brown. Remove from pans immediately; cool on wire rack.

Reheating Gluten-Free Rolls

Starch is the main structural component for gluten-free breads and rolls. When starch cools it becomes hard, which is why gluten-free breads become hard when they cool. Reheating these breads, either in the microwave or oven, will make them softer and more palatable. Reheat each roll for about 10 seconds on high power.

Yields 20 rolls

Calories: 158.58
Fat: 5.35 grams
Saturated Fat: 0.72 grams
Carbohydrates: 26.36 grams
Sodium: 71.94 mg

⅓ cup vegetable oil
¾ cup rice milk
¼ cup honey
2 tablespoons solid
    shortening
1 cup superfine rice flour
½ cup potato-starch flour
¾ cup millet flour
1 cup cornstarch
1½ teaspoons xanthan gum
1 (0.25-ounce) package
    instant-blend gluten-
    free dry yeast
½ teaspoon salt
½ teaspoon baking soda
¼ cup sugar
¼ cup Egg Substitute for
    Baking (page 66)
3 tablespoons honey

Calories: 290.76
Fat: 6.36 grams
Saturated Fat: 0.87 grams
Carbohydrates: 55.97
grams
Sodium: 253.96 mg

*2¼ cups Gluten-Free,
Soy-Free Baking Mix
(page 67)*
½ cup sugar
½ cup cranberry juice
¼ cup apple juice
½ cup apple jelly
2 eggs
¼ cup vegetable oil
*1½ cups frozen cranberries,
cut in half*
2 tablespoons sugar
½ teaspoon cinnamon

milk   wheat   soy   fish   nuts

Cranberry Quick Bread

*This delicious bread is perfect for the holidays,
when cranberries are in season. If you aren't allergic to nuts,
add ½ cup chopped pecans or walnuts.*

1. Preheat oven to 350°F. Spray a 9" × 5" loaf pan with nonstick gluten-free cooking spray and set aside.

2. In large bowl, combine Baking Mix and ½ cup sugar; mix well with wire whisk. In small saucepan, combine juices and apple jelly; heat over low heat until jelly melts.

3. Add jelly mixture, eggs, and oil to dry ingredients; stir just until combined. Fold in cranberries; spoon into prepared pan.

4. In small bowl, combine sugar and cinnamon; mix well. Sprinkle over batter. Bake bread 45–50 minutes, until deep golden brown and set. Turn out onto wire rack to cool.

milk wheat soy fish nuts

Corn Bread

*Corn bread must be served with chili or other hot, thick stews.
A little maple syrup drizzled on each piece is a nice touch.*

1. Preheat oven to 400°F. Spray a 9" square baking pan with nonstick gluten-free cooking spray and set aside.

2. In medium bowl, combine corn meal, flours, xanthan gum, baking powder, salt, and sugar; mix well with wire whisk.

3. In small bowl, combine remaining ingredients; mix well with wire whisk. Add to dry ingredients and stir just until combined. Pour into prepared pan. Bake 25–30 minutes, or until bread is golden brown. Serve very warm.

milk wheat eggs soy fish nuts

Mini Pizza Crusts

Make these pizza crusts, partially bake them, then freeze. Then, whenever your kids want pizza, let them pull these crusts out of the freezer, assemble, and bake!

1. Make Pizza Crusts through Step 3. Preheat oven to 400°F. Using 3 cookie sheets, grease four 6" circles on each with the shortening. Sprinkle with cornmeal.

2. Place dough on each circle, dividing evenly; press dough into an even layer, using plastic wrap to protect your hands. Bake 7–12 minutes, or until set and very light golden brown. Cool completely; use in recipes or freeze.

3. You can use these straight from the freezer. Just top with toppings and bake as recipe directs, adding a few more minutes to the baking time.

Serves 9

Calories: 190.12
Fat: 7.31 grams
Saturated Fat: 0.66 grams
Carbohydrates: 28.36 grams
Sodium: 141.77 mg

¾ cup cornmeal
½ cup corn flour
½ cup superfine rice flour
1 teaspoon xanthan gum
1½ teaspoons gluten-free
    baking powder
½ teaspoon salt
¼ cup sugar
½ cup water
¼ cup rice milk
½ cup apple juice
1 egg
¼ cup vegetable oil

Yields 12 crusts

Calories: 283.49
Fat: 5.49 grams
Saturated Fat: 0.93 grams
Carbohydrates: 54.38 grams
Sodium: 202.66 mg

1 recipe Pizza Crust (page
    63)
1 tablespoon solid
    shortening
2 tablespoons cornmeal

Light Dinner Rolls

Yields 12 rolls

Calories: 180.68
Fat: 3.62 grams
Saturated Fat: 0.49 grams
Carbohydrates: 34.02 grams
Sodium: 114.06 mg

1 (0.25-ounce) package instant-blend gluten-free dry yeast
¼ cup rice milk
1 cup warm water
2 eggs
⅓ cup banana, mashed
2 tablespoons vegetable oil
¼ cup sugar
½ teaspoon salt
1 cup superfine rice flour
½ cup cornstarch
⅓ cup potato-starch flour
⅔ cup millet flour
½ cup tapioca flour
1¼ teaspoons xanthan gum

These light dinner rolls taste best the day they are made. Serve them warm with some whipped honey or strawberry jam.

1. Spray 12 muffin cups with nonstick gluten-free cooking spray and set aside. In large bowl, combine yeast and rice milk; let stand 5 minutes. Add warm water, eggs, banana, oil, sugar, and salt; mix well.

2. In medium bowl, combine all remaining ingredients; mix well with wire whisk. Add to yeast mixture, beating well; beat for 4 minutes.

3. Spoon batter into prepared muffin cups. Let rise in warm place for 20 minutes. Preheat oven to 375ºF while rolls are rising. Bake 15–20 minutes, until rolls are deep golden brown. Remove from muffin cups immediately; let cool on wire rack. Serve warm.

milk · wheat · eggs · soy · fish · nuts

Pizza Crust

Yields 2 crusts; Serves 16

Calories: 205.35
Fat: 3.32 grams
Saturated Fat: 0.46 grams
Carbohydrates: 40.78 grams
Sodium: 151.99 mg

You can vary the flours in this crust, as long as you use the cornmeal and flaxseed to give that texture and crunch.

1. In medium bowl, combine flours, ground flaxseed, 3 tablespoons cornmeal, xanthan gum, salt, garlic powder, and sugar; mix well with wire whisk to blend. Place half of this mixture in a large bowl.

2. In small saucepan, combine rice milk, water, and olive oil; heat until very warm. Add to dry ingredients in large bowl; beat with electric mixer for 2 minutes.

3. Let dough stand while you combine yeast with ⅓ cup warm water and let sit until bubbly. Add to dough; beat for 2 minutes longer. Add remaining flour mixture to form stiff dough.

4. Preheat oven to 425°F. Grease two 12" pizza pans with solid shortening; sprinkle with cornmeal. Divide dough in half; place on prepared pans. Using plastic wrap to cover your fingers, press out dough to fill pans.

5. Bake 10–15 minutes, or until the crusts are set, but not browned. Cool completely on wire rack; use as directed in recipe, or top as desired and bake at 400°F 20–25 minutes longer until crust is browned and crisp.

1½ cups superfine rice flour
1¼ cups brown rice flour
1 cup tapioca flour
1 cup millet flour
3 tablespoons flaxseed, ground
3 tablespoons cornmeal
2 teaspoons xanthan gum
1 teaspoon salt
⅛ teaspoon garlic powder
2 tablespoons sugar
½ cup rice milk
1 cup water
2 tablespoons olive oil
2 (0.25 ounce) packages quick-rise gluten-free yeast
⅓ cup warm water
3 tablespoons cornmeal

Freezing Pizza Crusts

Make several of these crusts and freeze them, then you can make homemade pizza in minutes. Prebake the pizzas and cool them completely, then wrap in waxed paper and place in large freezer bags. Label, seal, and freeze the crusts for up to 6 months. To use, bake the frozen crust for another 5 minutes at 400°F, then top and finish baking.

milk wheat soy fish nuts

Bagels

It's difficult to find good bagels that aren't gluten-free, let alone ones a celiac patient can eat. These are best eaten the day they are made; toast and spread with cream cheese!

Yields 8 bagels

Calories: 288.89
Fat: 5.77 grams
Saturated Fat: 1.00 grams
Carbohydrates: 52.03 grams
Sodium: 328.79 mg

2½ cups Flour Mix III (page 70)
½ cup cornstarch
1 (0.25-ounce) package instant blend quick-rise gluten-free yeast
3 tablespoons dry vegan rice milk powder
1 tablespoon flaxseed, ground
1 teaspoon salt
1 tablespoon sugar
2 tablespoons Lyle's Golden Syrup
2 tablespoons extra-virgin olive oil
2 egg whites
1½ cups warm water
2 tablespoons cornmeal
1 tablespoon baking soda

1. In large bowl, combine Flour Mix, cornstarch, yeast, milk powder, flaxseed, salt, and sugar and mix well. In small bowl, combine Syrup, olive oil, eggs, and warm water and beat with wire whisk until blended.

2. Add wet ingredients to dry ingredients and beat with electric stand mixer for 3–5 minutes or until a dough forms. You may need to add more water or Flour Mix to form a workable dough.

3. Divide dough into 8 pieces. Form each piece into a ball; flatten slightly. Poke a hole through the center and work the hole until it's at least 1½"wide. Place on Silpat liner, cover, and let rest for 20 minutes.

4. Preheat oven to 400° F. Line a cookie sheet with parchment paper and set aside. Bring a large pot of water to a boil and add baking soda. Add bagels, four at a time, wait until they rise to the surface, count to one minute, then turn gently. Cook for one minute on the second side, then remove to Silpat sheets.

5. When bagels have boiled, sprinkle bottoms with cornmeal and place on parchment paper–lined cookie sheet. Bake for 20–30 minutes or until deep golden brown. Remove to wire rack to cool; serve warm.

Silpats

Silpat sheets are reusable flexible silicone sheets used to line cookie sheets; food, even sticky doughs, will not stick to them. In essence, Silpats can turn any pan into a nonstick pan. Silpats are made from food-grade silicon reinforced with glass weave and can withstand temperatures between -40°F and 480°F.

Chapter 4
Substitutions and Mixes

Egg Substitute for Baking

This mixture will substitute for one egg in most baking and cooking recipes. The flaxseed acts as a thickener and stabilizer for the batter or dough.

In spice grinder, grind flaxseed until very fine. In very small saucepan, combine with 3 tablespoons water; bring to a boil. Reduce heat to low; simmer until mixture is syrupy, about 3–4 minutes. Remove from heat and let cool completely. Store, covered, in the refrigerator up to 1 week.

There's a Limit to Egg Substitutes
Most egg substitutes will work well in baking and cooking recipes, but only up to a point. If a recipe calls for more than three eggs, the substitute will most probably not work well.

Evaporated Rice or Soy Milk

Evaporated milk is just that—milk with some of the water removed. Just start with twice as much milk as you need.

1. Combine all ingredients except vanilla in medium-heavy saucepan; stir well to blend. Bring to a simmer over low heat; simmer, watching carefully, until mixture is reduced by half.

2. Remove from heat; stir in vanilla. Cover and chill. Store in refrigerator up to 4 days. You can freeze this for longer storage, but it may "break." Thaw in refrigerator; beat well, adding some rice-milk or soy-milk powder to make the mixture blend again.

milk wheat eggs soy fish nuts

Gluten-Free, Soy-Free Baking Mix

Use this baking mix in recipes in place of flour, salt, and baking powder or baking soda. If you're allergic to corn, use more potato-starch flour or millet flour instead. For a simple flour substitute, omit the baking powder, baking soda, cream of tartar, and salt and use cup for cup.

Combine all ingredients; mix very well with wire whisk to blend. Store at room temperature in airtight container. Use as directed in recipes.

Potato Flour Versus Potato Starch

Potato starch is also known as potato-starch flour. This is a very finely milled product used in baking. Potato flour can be very grainy, and it is dense, with a marked potato taste. Do not confuse the two, and be sure to read labels when you're in the health food store.

Yields 6 cups; Nutrition information per cup

Calories: 789.70
Fat: 5.07 grams
Saturated Fat: 0.88 grams
Carbohydrates: 172.57 grams
Sodium: 1266.73 mg

2 cups superfine rice flour
1½ cups white sorghum flour
1 cup millet flour
1 cup potato-starch flour
½ cup coconut flour
½ cup tapioca flour
2½ teaspoons xanthan gum
3 teaspoons gluten-free baking powder
2 teaspoons baking soda
3 teaspoons cream of tartar
1½ teaspoons salt

Yields 1½ cups; Serving
size 2 tablespoons

Calories: 207.62
Fat: 23.03 grams
Saturated Fat: 1.43 grams
Carbohydrates: 0.81 grams
Sodium: 116.67 mg

½ cup gluten-free Dijon
    mustard
1¼ cups vegetable oil
⅛ teaspoon pepper
½ teaspoon paprika, if
    desired

Eggless Mayonnaise

By whipping oil into mustard, you can create a mayonnaise that doesn't contain eggs; quite a feat!

1. Place mustard in blender or food processor. Very slowly, add oil, a drop at a time, processing continually. As the mixture thickens, add the oil more quickly. Keep adding oil until the mixture is light in color, smooth, and thick. You may not need all of the oil.

2. Add pepper and paprika and blend until smooth. Store covered in refrigerator up to 2 weeks.

About Mustard
Mustard is usually made with ground mustard seed, vinegar, and water. Read labels carefully; sometimes wheat flour or gluten is used as a thickener. Some organic brands, including Orphee Organic, are gluten free. You can make your own mustard with many recipes online. Most homemade mustards must stand for a couple of weeks in the refrigerator so the flavors can mellow and blend.

milk wheat eggs fish nuts

Flour Mix I

You can use this substitute, cup for cup, for plain all-purpose flour in any baking recipe.

Combine all ingredients; whisk thoroughly to combine. Store in airtight container at room temperature.

Yields 2 cups; Nutrition information per cup

Calories: 514.06
Fat: 5.37 grams
Saturated Fat: 0.89 grams
Carbohydrates: 101.47 grams
Sodium: 19.24 mg

1 cup superfine rice flour
⅓ cup potato-starch flour
⅓ cup garbanzo-bean flour
⅓ cup debittered soy flour
¾ teaspoon xanthan gum

milk wheat eggs soy fish nuts

Flour Mix II

If you're allergic to rice or soy, this is a good flour blend. Be sure to use potato-starch flour, not regular potato flour.

Combine all ingredients in medium bowl and mix well with wire whisk. Store covered at room temperature up to 2 weeks.

Yields 4 cups; Nutrition information per cup

Calories: 821.11
Fat: 6.83 grams
Saturated Fat: 1.11 grams
Carbohydrates: 159.43 grams
Sodium: 47.82 mg

1¼ cups millet flour
1 cup white sorghum flour
1 cup potato-starch flour
¾ cup coconut flour
1½ teaspoons xanthan gum

Flour Mix III

This flour is a bit lighter than the other blends, because cornstarch is finer than flour. It's a good choice for cookies and muffins.

Yields 4 cups; Nutrition information per cup

Calories: 564.18
Fat: 5.10 grams
Saturated Fat: 1.19 grams
Carbohydrates: 116.07 grams
Sodium: 13.10 mg

1½ cups superfine rice flour
1 cup masa (corn flour)
½ cup cornstarch
1 cup teff flour
1½ teaspoons xanthan gum

Combine all ingredients in medium bowl and mix well with wire whisk. Store covered at room temperature up to 2 weeks.

Soy-Yogurt Cheese

You can flavor this delicious soft cheese with everything from honey to crushed red pepper flakes and olive oil. Roll the finished product into balls to serve with an antipasto platter.

Yields 2 cups; Serving size ¼ cup

Calories: 123.14
Fat: 2.36 grams
Saturated Fat: 0.34 grams
Carbohydrates: 20.91 grams
Sodium: 47.78 mg

4 cups natural soy yogurt

1. Place the yogurt in a strainer lined with a couple of coffee filters or some dampened cheesecloth. Place the strainer in a large bowl, cover with a cloth, and refrigerate for 24 hours. The whey that drains off the yogurt can be used in soups and yeast-bread recipes.

2. The yogurt cheese will keep tightly covered in refrigerator 3–4 days.

milk wheat eggs fish nuts

Nut Substitute

Rolled oats become nutty tasting when toasted, and roasted soy-beans add crunch in this simple nut-substitute recipe.

1. Make the "Nuts," but do not add honey, curry powder, or salt. Roast at the lower temperature plain. Let cool completely.

2. Turn oven to 400°F. Place the rolled oats on a cookie sheet; bake 6–9 minutes, shaking pan occasionally, until oats are golden brown. Let cool completely.

3. Coarsely chop "Nuts" if desired; combine with rolled oats in a glass container. Cover tightly and store in refrigerator up to 1 week. Use as a substitute, cup for cup, for nuts in recipes.

milk wheat fish nuts

Gluten-Free Brownie Mix

To use this simple mix, combine 4 cups of the mix, 3 eggs, and ¼ cup soy yogurt. Mix and bake in a 13" × 9" pan at 350°F 30–35 minutes.

1. Combine all ingredients except solid shortening and coconut oil in large bowl and mix well with wire whisk.

2. Using two knives or a pastry blender, cut in the solid shortening and coconut oil until fine particles form. Store in airtight container in refrigerator up to 1 month.

Yields 3 cups; 6 servings

Calories: 243.06
Fat: 7.65 grams
Saturated Fat: 1.16 grams
Carbohydrates: 31.70 grams
Sodium: 347.82 mg

½ recipe Roasted Sweet and Spicy "Nuts" (page 119)
1 cup gluten-free rolled oats

Yields 4 (13" × 9") brownie batches

Calories: 3126.76
Fat: 114.44 grams
Saturated Fat: 50.10 grams
Carbohydrates: 536.18 grams
Sodium: 2206.32 mg

2 cups superfine rice flour
1 cup millet flour
1 cup potato-starch flour
1½ teaspoons xanthan gum
4 teaspoons gluten-free baking powder
4 cups sugar
3 cups brown sugar
2 cups cocoa powder
3 teaspoons salt
1½ cups solid shortening
½ cup coconut oil

wheat eggs soy fish nuts

Ghee

Yields 1 cup; Serving size 1 tablespoon

Calories: 114.36
Fat: 12.94 grams
Saturated Fat: 8.19 grams
Carbohydrates: 0.01 grams
Sodium: 1.75 mg

2 sticks (¼ pound) unsalted butter
2 tablespoons unsalted butter

The trick to making this as dairy free as possible is to be sure all of the foam and solids are removed from the butterfat. It will still not be 100 percent free of milk proteins.

1. Place all of the butter in a heavy, small saucepan over medium heat. Let butter melt, then bring to a boil.

2. Reduce heat a bit, then cook butter without stirring. A foam will form on the surface; this should disappear in a few minutes.

3. Continue cooking butter until a second foam appears on the surface. The liquid will turn a golden color, and may smell like popcorn.

4. Carefully pour the liquid through cheesecloth into a heatproof container, leaving the solids in the bottom of the pan. You can strain the ghee several times to remove more protein. Store in airtight container in a cool, dark place up to 3 weeks.

Ghee Is Dairy Free?

If you have a severe dairy allergy to milk proteins, don't try ghee as a butter substitute. It's difficult, if not impossible, to remove all of the protein from the fat. Ghee is almost lactose free, so if lactose intolerance is the problem, ghee might work for you. Commercially produced ghee, especially organic brands, may be more pure than homemade.

milk   wheat   eggs   fish   nuts

Not Peanut Butter

*You could use all sunflower seeds or all sesame
seeds or all soybeans in this simple recipe that's
a perfect substitute for peanut butter.*

1. Pick over soybeans, discarding any that are shriveled, and any extraneous material. Rinse in cold water, drain, and place in a large bowl. Cover with water and let soak 12 hours.

2. Preheat oven to 325°F. Drain soybeans; pat dry with paper towels. Place in single layer on a large cookie sheet. Roast 55–65 minutes, turning beans with a spatula every 10 minutes, until crisp and light golden brown. Remove from cookie sheet and let stand on paper towels 10 minutes.

3. Reduce oven temperature to 275°F. Roast the soybeans another 30–40 minutes, stirring every 8 minutes, until crisp. Add sunflower seeds and sesame seeds for last 20 minutes of roasting time. Cool completely.

4. Combine soybeans, sunflower seeds, sesame seeds, salt, and soybean oil in food processor; process until finely ground. With processor running, very slowly add the water, a tablespoon at a time, until desired consistency is reached.

5. Scrape mixture into a small jar or other small container, seal, and store in refrigerator up to 2 weeks.

**Yields ¾ cup; Serving
size 2 tablespoons**

Calories: 111.84
Fat: 9.29 grams
Saturated Fat: 1.12 grams
Carbohydrates: 3.85
grams
Sodium: 74.44 mg

*¾ cup dried soybeans
½ cup hulled sunflower
   seeds
⅓ cup sesame seeds
½ teaspoon salt
¼ cup soybean or
   safflower oil
½ cup cold water*

Calories: 7.00
Fat: 0.0 grams
Saturated Fat: 0.0 grams
Carbohydrates: 1.67 grams
Sodium: 405.89 mg

6 tablespoons cream of
    tartar
3 tablespoons baking soda
1 teaspoon cornstarch or
    potato-starch flour

milk   wheat   eggs   soy   fish   nuts

Baking-Powder Substitute

The cornstarch helps prevent lumps in this homemade substitute.
Store it tightly covered in a cool, dry place.

Combine all ingredients in a sifter. Sift into a small bowl; stir with wire whisk until blended. Decant into a small glass jar with screw-top lid. Store in a cool, dry place up to 2 months.

Homemade Baking Powder

When you use this homemade powder, you must be sure to get the batter or dough into the oven as soon as possible. It's not a double-acting powder like many of the commercial ones, so it only releases CO_2 when combined with liquid, not when the batter is heated. Gluten-free breads are more fragile structures, so they can't hold on to the leavening. Also, try to add this at the last minute, before the batter goes into the oven.

milk wheat eggs soy fish nuts

Apple Butter

*Apple butter is a good substitute for
half of the oil in some simple baked recipes,
and it's also delicious as a spread on toasted bread.*

1. Core apples and cut into pieces. In a 3-quart slow cooker, combine all ingredients; mix well. Cover and cook on low 10–12 hours, stirring occasionally, until apple butter is thick and deep golden brown. Remove lid after 8 hours for a thicker apple butter.

2. As the apple butter cooks, you'll need to stir more often to prevent burning. Be sure to thoroughly scrape sides and bottom of slow cooker each time you stir. If desired, use an immersion blender to make apple butter smoother.

3. Spoon apple butter into 1 cup jars or freezer containers. Refrigerate up to 2 weeks or freeze up to 2 months.

**Yields 4 cups;
Serving size ¼ cup**

Calories: 197.18
Fat: 0.12 grams
Saturated Fat: 0.02 grams
Carbohydrates: 51.11 grams
Sodium: 44.57 mg

*8 large tart apples, peeled
1½ cups brown sugar
1½ cups sugar
¼ cup gluten-free apple
   cider vinegar
2 teaspoons cinnamon
½ teaspoon ground ginger
¼ teaspoon salt*

Egg Substitute II

Because the coconut oil is so thick, you'll need a food processor or strong blender for this recipe.

Enough to substitute for 6 eggs; Two and a half tablespoons substitute for 1 egg

Calories: 121.55
Fat: 8.64 grams
Saturated Fat: 6.42 grams
Carbohydrates: 3.09 grams
Sodium: 113.40 mg

5 tablespoons powdered vegan egg replacer
9 tablespoons water
3 tablespoons coconut oil

1. Combine egg replacer, half of the water, and the coconut oil in food processor or blender; process or blend until well mixed and frothy.

2. With motor running, gradually add remaining water; process until well blended. Store in refrigerator up to four days.

Other Egg Replacers

Other egg replacers for using in baking include ripe mashed bananas (about 2–3 tablespoons of mashed banana per egg); ¼ cup dairy-free vegan mayonnaise; or a combination of soy powder and water, cornstarch and water, or gelatin and water in a 1:2 ratio. Eggs add moisture, contribute protein, and add to the structure of baked products.

milk   wheat   eggs   fish   nuts

Basil Pesto

Most pesto is made with Parmesan cheese and pine nuts, but a vegan alternative works just as well. And nuts aren't necessary!

1. In food processor, combine basil, spinach, garlic, lemon juice, salt, and pepper; process until ground.

2. With motor running, add enough olive oil until desired consistency is reached. By hand, stir in cheese and water, if needed. Store tightly covered in refrigerator up to 3 days. Freeze for longer storage.

Yields 1½ cups pesto; Serving size 2 tablespoons

Calories: 132.00
Fat: 11.92 grams
Saturated Fat: 1.94 grams
Carbohydrates: 0.94 grams
Sodium: 119.20 mg

1½ cups packed fresh basil leaves
1 cup packed baby spinach leaves
3 cloves garlic, chopped
2 tablespoons lemon juice
½ teaspoon salt
⅛ teaspoon pepper
½–⅔ cup extra-virgin olive oil
¼ cup grated soy vegan Parmesan cheese
2 tablespoons water, if necessary

Chili Powder

Make your own chili powder to be sure it's free from allergens. This is also a good way to experiment in the kitchen.

Yields ½ cup; Nutrition information per teaspoon

Calories: 8.19
Fat: 0.30 grams
Saturated Fat: 0.04 grams
Carbohydrates: 1.45 grams
Sodium: 98.65 mg

1 tablespoon sweet paprika
1 tablespoon smoked paprika
2 tablespoons ground cumin
2 tablespoons garlic powder
1 teaspoon black pepper
1 tablespoon ground oregano
1 teaspoon cayenne pepper
1 teaspoon ground red chilies
1 teaspoon salt

Combine all ingredients in small bowl and mix carefully. Decant into a small glass jar with screw lid. Cover tightly and store in dark, cool place up to 2 months.

Uses for Chili Powder

Chili powder is typically used to add flavor to chili, which is a thick soup made from beans, tomatoes, and beef. It is also good sprinkled over grilled cheese sandwiches, as a seasoning for Guacamole, and rubbed into meats as a dry marinade before grilling. You can experiment with other spices, including cinnamon, white pepper, and onion powder.

milk   wheat   eggs   soy   fish   nuts

Curry Powder

Curry powder is a spice blend used in Middle Eastern and Indian cooking. You can vary this any way you'd like, by adding more hot spices like ground chilies or sweet spices like cinnamon.

Combine all ingredients in small glass jar with screw-top lid. Cover and shake to blend. Store covered in cool, dark place up to 4 months.

Yields 6 tablespoons; Serving size ½ teaspoon

Calories: 4.83
Fat: 0.23 grams
Saturated Fat: 0.02 grams
Carbohydrates: 0.73 grams
Sodium: 1.06 mg

2½ teaspoons cinnamon
2 teaspoons ground coriander
2 tablespoons ground cumin
1 tablespoon ground
   turmeric
1 teaspoon mustard powder
2 teaspoons ground ginger
½ teaspoon cayenne pepper
1 teaspoon ground
   cardamom

milk   wheat   eggs   soy   fish   nuts

Eggless Cooked Salad Dressing

This mayonnaise can also be used as a sandwich spread.

1. In small saucepan, combine rice flour, water, and lemon juice; let stand 5 minutes. Then cook over low heat, stirring constantly with a wire whisk, until thick.

2. Remove from heat; beat in mustard. Transfer mixture to a blender or food processor. Very slowly, with the motor running, add oil; mix until desired consistency. Blend in paprika, cover, and chill 1–2 hours before using. Store in refrigerator up to 2 weeks.

Yields 1¼ cups; Serving size 2 tablespoons

Calories: 123.54
Fat: 13.02 grams
Saturated Fat: 1.27 grams
Carbohydrates: 1.94 grams
Sodium: 58.36 mg

2 tablespoons superfine
   rice flour
1 tablespoon water
2 tablespoons lemon juice
¼ cup gluten-free Dijon
   mustard
⅔ to ¾ cup vegetable oil
¼ teaspoon paprika

Taco Seasoning Mix

Yields 8 tablespoons;
Nutrition informa-
tion per tablespoon

Calories: 27.09
Fat: 0.41 grams
Saturated Fat: 0.05 grams
Carbohydrates: 5.74 grams
Sodium: 403.79 mg

3 tablespoons Chili Powder
   (page 78)
2 tablespoons minced dried
   onion
1 tablespoon minced dried
   garlic
2 tablespoons potato-starch
   or superfine rice flour
1 teaspoon onion powder
1 teaspoon salt
1 teaspoon paprika
½ teaspoon dried oregano
   leaves
½ teaspoon dried marjoram
   leaves
½ teaspoon crushed, dried
   red-pepper flakes

Many Mexican and Tex-Mex recipes call for Taco Seasoning Mix. But commercial varieties often have wheat flour, MSG, and other additives. This pure mix is spicy and delicious, and it will thicken sauces.

Combine all ingredients in a small bowl and blend well with wire whisk. Place in small glass jar with screw-top lid and seal. Store in a cool, dry place out of sunlight. Two tablespoons is equivalent to 1 package commercial seasoning mix.

Taco Seasoning Mix

Taco seasoning mix is usually added to tomato sauce when making filling for tacos, tostadas, or enchiladas. One commercial packet is equal to about 2 tablespoons of homemade mix. You can also add it to browned ground beef along with ½ cup of water to make an easy burrito or taco filling.

milk wheat eggs soy fish nuts

Tomato Sauce

Many commercial varieties of tomato sauce have milk protein and or gluten to help add body and thicken the sauce. This simple, classic sauce is perfect.

1. In large skillet, heat olive oil over medium heat. Add onion and garlic; cook and stir until tender, about 5 minutes. Add ginger root; cook for 1 minute longer. Sprinkle with salt and pepper.

2. Add tomato paste, stir, and increase heat. Let tomato paste brown a bit on the bottom (this adds depth of flavor to the sauce), being careful not to let it burn. When there are some brown spots, add tomato juice and wine.

3. Bring back to a simmer, then add chopped tomatoes. Reduce heat to low and simmer 20–25 minutes, or until sauce has thickened, stirring frequently. Cool; store in refrigerator up to 4 days or freeze up to 3 months.

**Yields 3 cups;
Serving size ½ cup**

Calories: 140.01
Fat: 4.94 grams
Saturated Fat: 0.72 grams
Carbohydrates: 16.37 grams
Sodium: 438.73 mg

*2 tablespoons extra-virgin olive oil
1 large onion, chopped
4 cloves garlic, chopped
1 tablespoon minced ginger root
¼ teaspoon salt
⅛ teaspoon white pepper
1 (6-ounce) can gluten-free tomato paste
1 cup tomato juice
1 cup dry red wine
4 large tomatoes, chopped*

milk wheat eggs soy fish nuts

Soy Sauce Substitute

Soy sauce contains glutamate, to which umami taste buds in the tongue respond to create a meaty flavor in your mouth. Marmite also contains this substance without any soy, which is why it's used in this recipe.

Yields 6 tablespoons; Serving size 1 teaspoon

Calories: 6.10
Fat: 0.01 grams
Saturated Fat: 0.0 grams
Carbohydrates: 1.26 grams
Sodium: 36.49 mg

2 small dried mushrooms
½ cup boiling water
1 tablespoon gluten-free, soy-free Marmite
1 tablespoon molasses
2 teaspoons gluten-free balsamic vinegar
⅛ teaspoon pepper
⅛ teaspoon garlic powder

1. Place the dried mushrooms in a small bowl and pour boiling water over. Let steep for 15 minutes; strain liquid into a small saucepan. Chop mushrooms and add to the strained liquid.

2. Add Marmite, molasses, vinegar, pepper, and garlic powder; stir with a wire whisk until combined. Bring to a boil over medium-high heat. Reduce heat to low and simmer 6–8 minutes until slightly reduced, stirring frequently.

3. Strain mixture again, pressing on solids to extract liquid. Cover and store in refrigerator for up to 4 days. Can be frozen for longer storage; freeze in 1 tablespoon quantities.

Marmite

Marmite is a gluten-free, soy-free, vegetarian yeast extract that, when used in small quantities and combined with a few other ingredients, can be substituted for soy sauce for those with an allergy to soy. Like soy, it contains amino acid molecules that trigger the "meaty" taste buds (umami) on your tongue. It's commonly used in Britain and Europe, and can be difficult to find in the United States. Online sources are probably your best bet. And ask questions and read labels to be sure it's soy and gluten-free.

milk wheat eggs fish nuts

Gluten-Free Crepes

Crepes are very thin unleavened pancakes. These are savory, to be filled with meat and sauce. Use them in Ham Manicotti (page 190). Some egg replacers can contain soy.

1. In food processor or blender, combine all ingredients except rice milk; process or blend until smooth. Add enough rice milk to make a thin batter. Let stand 5 minutes.

2. Heat a nonstick 6" skillet over medium heat. Brush with a bit of oil. Using a ½ cup measure, pour about ⅓ cup of the batter into the hot pan. Immediately lift and tilt the pan so the batter coats the bottom. Cook 2–3 minutes, or until crepe is set and slightly crisp; turn and cook for 30 seconds on second side.

3. As the crepes are finished, place on kitchen towels to cool. Do not stack the crepes or they will stick together. You can freeze these, separated by parchment paper or waxed paper, up to 2 months. To thaw, let stand at room temperature.

Yields 12 crepes

Calories: 76.48
Fat: 1.95 grams
Saturated Fat: 0.27 grams
Carbohydrates: 11.82 grams
Sodium: 58.68 mg

½ cup superfine rice flour
⅓ cup potato-starch flour
¼ cup tapioca flour
½ teaspoon xanthan gum
⅛ teaspoon salt
¾ cup vegan egg replacer
1 tablespoon vegetable oil
5–8 tablespoons rice milk

**Yields 4 cups;
Serving size ½ cup**

Calories: 58.73
Fat: 0.11 grams
Saturated Fat: 0.02 grams
Carbohydrates: 12.97 grams
Sodium: 20.61 mg

1 cup rice
2 cups water
2 cups water
Pinch salt
1 teaspoon gluten-free
    vanilla
1–2 tablespoons sugar or
    honey

Rice Milk

Making your own rice milk is very simple, and the best way to control what you feed your family.

1. In small saucepan, combine rice with 2 cups water. Bring to a simmer over medium heat then cover pan, reduce heat to low, and cook 15–20 minutes, or until rice is tender.

2. Place cooked rice in a blender or food processor; puree until smooth. Add additional 2 cups water and let stand for 1 hour.

3. Strain the mixture into a clean bowl through a double layer of cheesecloth. Squeeze the cheesecloth to get all liquid possible out of rice. Flavor liquid with salt, vanilla, and sugar or honey. Cover and refrigerate up to 3 days.

Sweetness in Alternative Milks

Cow's milk is quite sweet because it contains a lot of lactose, or milk sugar. Rice doesn't have much sugar; it is made of starch and protein. You must sweeten homemade rice milk and flavor it with vanilla to make it palatable. Granulated sugar is the most reliable sweetener, but you can also use sucanat or honey.

milk wheat eggs fish nuts

Cream-Soup Mix

If you're allergic to mushrooms, just omit them. This blend is a substitute for condensed cream soups. The vegetable-soup base and dry-milk substitute probably contain soy.

1. Grind the dried mushrooms until fine. Combine with remaining ingredients in a glass jar. Seal lid; store in cool, dry place 3–4 months.

2. To use, combine ¼ cup of mix with ⅓ cup cold water; stir until blended. Add ¾ cup water and cook over low heat, stirring until thickened. Use as a substitute for canned condensed soups.

Yields 1¼ cups; Serving size 2 tablespoons

Calories: 42.69
Fat: 0.50 grams
Saturated Fat: 0.09 grams
Carbohydrates: 8.47 grams
Sodium: 65.57 mg

1 ounce dried mushrooms
½ cup dairy-free vegan dry-milk substitute
¼ cup superfine rice flour
¼ cup potato-starch flour
¼ teaspoon salt
⅛ teaspoon pepper
½ teaspoon garlic powder
½ teaspoon onion powder
1 tablespoon gluten-free powdered vegetable-soup base

milk   wheat   eggs   soy   fish   nuts

Gluten-Free Muffin Mix

Yields 12 cups; 6 batches of 12 muffins

Calories: 1371.28
Fat: 12.09 grams
Saturated Fat: 2.26 grams
Carbohydrates: 308.52 grams
Sodium: 1781.84 mg

2 cups superfine rice flour
1½ cups potato-starch four
1 cup tapioca flour
¾ cup millet flour
1 tablespoon xanthan gum
1 cup sugar
1 cup brown sugar
4 cups gluten-free oat bran
3 cups quick-cooking,
    gluten-free oatmeal
3 tablespoons gluten-free
    baking powder
2 teaspoons baking soda
2 teaspoons salt

*Store this mix in a cool, dry place in an
airtight container, and use it to make muffins.
If you can't find gluten-free oat bran, use rice polishings.*

1. In large bowl, combine rice flour, potato-starch flour, tapioca flour, millet flour, and xanthan gum; mix well. Add sugar and brown sugar; mix until evenly blended. Stir in oat bran, oatmeal, baking powder, baking soda, and salt.

2. Store in tightly covered container in dark cool place up to 1 month.

Muffin Recipe

To make the muffins, combine 2 cups of the Muffin Mix with ¾ cup rice milk, ⅓ cup vegetable oil, 1 egg or egg substitute, and ½ cup dried currants. Bake in paper-lined muffin cups at 400°F 13–18 minutes, or until golden brown. Remove from muffin cups and let cool on wire rack. Makes 12 muffins.

Chapter 5
Salads

milk wheat eggs soy fish nuts

Spinach Fruit Salad

This sweet and tangy salad dressing is good on any mixed greens; try it on coleslaw, too.

Serves 6

Calories: 135.70
Fat: 9.56 grams
Saturated Fat: 1.28 grams
Carbohydrates: 12.70 grams
Sodium: 154.65 mg

½ cup sliced strawberries
1 tablespoon lemon juice
1 tablespoon sugar
¼ teaspoon salt
1 tablespoon gluten-free mustard
1 tablespoon minced onion
¼ cup apple juice
¼ cup extra-virgin olive oil
6 cups baby spinach
2 cups watercress
2 cups sliced strawberries
1 cup raspberries

1. In food processor or blender, combine ½ cup strawberries, lemon juice, sugar, salt, mustard, minced onion, apple juice, and olive oil; process or blend until smooth. Cover and refrigerate up to 3 days.

2. In serving bowl, toss together spinach, watercress, 2 cups strawberries, and raspberries. Drizzle with half of the dressing; toss again. Serve immediately with remaining dressing on the side.

milk wheat eggs soy fish nuts

Tomato Arranged Salad

Tomatoes are so good for you, and delicious with this delicately flavored salad dressing. Serve this recipe in late summer when the fruit is at its peak.

Serves 4

Calories: 184.26
Fat: 14.15 grams
Saturated Fat: 1.99 grams
Carbohydrates: 14.83 grams
Sodium: 180.54 mg

2 red tomatoes
2 yellow tomatoes
3 plum tomatoes
1 cup grape tomatoes
¼ cup olive oil
2 tablespoons lemon juice
1 tablespoon honey
1 teaspoon gluten-free curry powder
⅛ teaspoon pepper
¼ teaspoon salt

1. Core red, yellow, and plum tomatoes and slice ½" thick. Arrange on a serving plate; top with grape tomatoes.

2. In small bowl, combine remaining ingredients and mix with wire whisk until blended. Drizzle over tomatoes and let stand 20 minutes, then serve.

milk wheat eggs soy fish nuts

Greens and Fruit Salad

This salad dressing can be used on any tossed salad. Try it the next time you make a pasta salad.

1. In serving bowl, toss together salad greens, spinach, grapes, and orange; set aside.

2. In small bottle with a screw-top lid, combine remaining ingredients. Seal lid and shake vigorously to blend salad dressing. Pour over the ingredients in serving bowl, toss lightly, and serve immediately.

Packaged Greens or Fresh?

For the freshest greens, pick those that have not been processed and packaged and are ready to use. There is less risk of cross-contamination, and you have control over exactly what is in your salad. Wash the greens by rinsing in cold water, then dry by rolling the leaves in a kitchen towel.

Serves 4

Calories: 224.31
Fat: 13.95 grams
Saturated Fat: 1.94 grams
Carbohydrates: 26.22 grams
Sodium: 204.33 mg

4 cups mixed salad greens
2 cups baby spinach
   leaves
2 cups red grapes
1 orange, peeled and
   chopped
¼ cup orange juice
2 tablespoons honey
¼ cup olive oil
1 tablespoon gluten-free
   Dijon mustard
¼ teaspoon ground ginger
¼ teaspoon salt
⅛ teaspoon white pepper

Citrus Raisin Broccoli Slaw

Serves 6

Calories: 309.51
Fat: 18.98 grams
Saturated Fat: 2.09 grams
Carbohydrates: 32.08 grams
Sodium: 297.60 mg

6 slices gluten-free bacon
1 (10-ounce) can mandarin
    oranges, drained
½ cup Eggless Mayonnaise
    (page 68)
2 tablespoons lemon juice
2 tablespoons reserved
    mandarin orange juice
½ teaspoon lemon zest
1 tablespoon sugar
2 cups shredded green
    cabbage
2 cups shredded red
    cabbage
1 (10-ounce) package
    frozen broccoli, cooked
    and drained
1 cup raisins

This flavorful salad is a takeoff on the classic broccoli-raisin salads so popular at delis.

1. Cook bacon in large skillet over medium heat until crisp. Drain on paper towel, crumble, and set aside. Drain oranges, reserving 2 tablespoons liquid.

2. In large bowl, combine Mayonnaise, lemon juice, reserved mandarin orange juice, lemon zest, and sugar; mix well. Add remaining ingredients and stir to coat. Cover and refrigerate 2–3 hours before serving.

milk   wheat   eggs   soy   fish   nuts

Garden Medley Salad

Serves 4

This salad can be served as is, or you can toss it with mixed greens or fresh spinach. Cooked chicken or ham can be added to make this a main-dish salad.

Calories: 123.54
Fat: 8.82 grams
Saturated Fat: 1.23 grams
Carbohydrates: 10.62 grams
Sodium: 147.38 mg

In medium bowl, combine all ingredients except Salad Dressing and toss to blend. Drizzle Salad Dressing over all; toss to coat. Serve immediately, or cover and chill 2–3 hours before serving to blend flavors.

1 cup sliced carrots
3 stalks celery, chopped
1 cup small cauliflower
   florets
¼ cup chopped green
   onion
1 yellow bell pepper,
   chopped
1 cup grape or cherry
   tomatoes
1 cup chopped cucumber
⅓ cup Italian Salad
   Dressing (page 93)

Vegetables for Salads

Most vegetables can be used raw in salads, as long as they are sliced thinly or broken or cut into small pieces. If you'd like, you could blanch the vegetables before adding to the salad. Drop the prepared vegetables into boiling water for 30–40 seconds, then immediately plunge into ice water to stop the cooking.

milk   wheat   eggs   soy   fish   nuts

Creamy Herb Salad Dressing

Try this dressing on spinach salad or mixed salad greens, or omit the rice milk and use it for an appetizer dip.

Yields 1¼ cups; Serving size 2 tablespoons

Calories: 100.24
Fat: 10.48 grams
Saturated Fat: 1.02 grams
Carbohydrates: 1.72 grams
Sodium: 77.43 mg

1 cup Eggless Cooked Salad Dressing (page 79)
2 tablespoons rice milk
1 tablespoon chopped fresh basil
1 tablespoon chopped fresh thyme
1 teaspoon chopped fresh oregano
⅛ teaspoon salt
⅛ teaspoon white pepper

Combine all ingredients in small bowl and mix well. Cover and chill 2–3 hours before serving. Store leftovers in refrigerator up to 3 days.

milk   wheat   eggs   soy   fish   nuts

Turkey Fruit Salad

You can serve this salad on lettuce or baby spinach leaves, or use it as a sandwich filling with raisin bread.

Serves 4

Calories: 478.11
Fat: 27.49 grams
Saturated Fat: 2.66 grams
Carbohydrates: 42.93 grams
Sodium: 173.95 mg

2 cups cubed, cooked turkey
1 apple, chopped
½ cup golden raisins
2 stalks celery, chopped
½ cup dried cherries
½ cup Eggless Mayonnaise (page 68)
2 tablespoons honey
1 tablespoon lemon juice
⅛ teaspoon pepper

1. In medium bowl, combine turkey, apple, raisins, celery, and cherries; toss to coat.

2. In small bowl, combine Mayonnaise, honey, lemon juice, and pepper and mix with wire whisk. Pour over turkey mixture and stir gently to coat. Cover and chill 2–3 hours before serving.

milk wheat eggs soy fish nuts

Italian Salad Dressing

Yields ½ cup; Serving size 2 tablespoons

You can find garlic paste in a tube at health food stores and online. It's a good way to get garlic flavoring throughout a dish without little bits of the vegetable.

Calories: 122.01
Fat: 13.51 grams
Saturated Fat: 1.85 grams
Carbohydrates: 0.15 grams
Sodium: 145.92 mg

In small bowl, combine olive oil, vinegars, and garlic paste and whisk to blend and distribute garlic paste evenly. Add remaining ingredients and whisk to blend. Store covered in refrigerator up to 4 days.

¼ cup extra-virgin olive oil
2 tablespoons gluten-free balsamic vinegar
1 tablespoon red wine vinegar
1 teaspoon garlic paste
1 teaspoon dried basil leaves
½ teaspoon dried oregano leaves
2 teaspoons dried parsley flakes
¼ teaspoon salt
⅛ teaspoon white pepper

Is Balsamic Vinegar Gluten-Free?

Not all balsamic vinegar is gluten-free. This vinegar gets its deep color and rich flavor from long aging in oak casks. The more inexpensive varieties may get that deep color from caramel coloring or other additives, which can contain gluten. To be safe, buy the most expensive balsamic vinegar you can afford, and be sure the ingredient label has only one ingredient: vinegar.

Serves 6

Calories: 334.26
Fat: 16.18 grams
Saturated Fat: 1.75 grams
Carbohydrates: 36.44 grams
Sodium: 405.88 mg

½ cup Eggless Cooked
   Salad Dressing (page 79)
2 tablespoons vegetable oil
¼ cup Mango Chutney
   (page 120)
1 tablespoon curry powder
1 (15-ounce) can cannellini
   beans, rinsed and
   drained
1 (15-ounce) can kidney
   beans, rinsed and
   drained
4 stalks celery, chopped
½ cup chopped red onion
½ cup Roasted Sweet and
   Spicy "Nuts" (page 119)
6 cups mixed salad greens

milk   wheat   eggs   fish   nuts

Greens and Beans Salad

Safe to Eat Chutney is one brand that is gluten and nut free, or you can make your own.

1. In medium bowl, combine Salad Dressing, oil, Chutney, and curry powder and blend well with wire whisk. Add all remaining ingredients except "Nuts" and salad greens and mix gently.

2. Cover and refrigerate 2–24 hours. When ready to serve, toss "Nuts" and greens with salad and serve immediately.

milk wheat eggs fish nuts

Beans and Rice Salad

You can use any chopped vegetables you'd like in this easy and hearty vegetarian main-dish salad; zucchini, summer squash, and tomatoes are all delicious.

1. Cook wild rice in water to cover, according to package directions, about 35–40 minutes. Drain if necessary and set aside.

2. In serving bowl, combine yogurt, Salad Dressing, mustard, and rice or soy milk; whisk to blend. Add cooked wild rice and remaining ingredients; stir to coat. Cover and chill 2–3 hours before serving.

Wild Rice

Wild rice is not actually rice, but a grass seed. It grows in marshy areas in the northern United States, especially Minnesota and Wisconsin. When you buy it, make sure you purchase whole grains that are about ½" long. Packages of rice with broken grains will cook up mushy.

Serves 6

Calories: 238.04
Fat: 5.61 grams
Saturated Fat: 0.62 grams
Carbohydrates: 38.83 grams
Sodium: 361.26 mg

1 cup wild rice
½ cup soy yogurt
¼ cup Eggless Cooked Salad Dressing (page 79)
2 tablespoons gluten-free Dijon mustard
2 tablespoons rice or soy milk
1 cup chopped mushrooms
1 red bell pepper, chopped
⅓ cup chopped green onions
1 (15-ounce) can black beans, rinsed and drained

Calories: 430.84
Fat: 16.98 grams
Saturated Fat: 2.50 grams
Carbohydrates: 54.65 grams
Sodium: 153.64 mg

2 (8-ounce) salmon fillets
1 tablespoon olive oil
1 teaspoon gluten-free curry powder
1 (12-ounce) box rice shell pasta
½ cup Eggless Cooked Salad Dressing (page 79)
2 tablespoons rice milk
2 teaspoons gluten-free curry powder
¼ cup gluten-free chutney
2 apples, cored and chopped
½ cup golden raisins
½ cup Roasted Sweet and Spicy "Nuts" (page 119)
6 cups mixed salad greens

milk   wheat   eggs   nuts

Curried Salmon-Apple Salad

If you aren't allergic to nuts, add some toasted pecans or walnuts to this delicious and easy main-dish salad.

1. Preheat broiler. Place salmon fillets on broiler pan; brush with olive oil; sprinkle with 1 teaspoon curry powder. Broil 6" from heat source 8–10 minutes, or until fish flakes easily when tested with fork. Remove from oven and let cool for 30–40 minutes.

2. Bring a large pot of water to a boil. Cook pasta according to package directions, until al dente.

3. While the pasta is cooking, combine Salad Dressing, rice milk, curry powder, and chutney in a large bowl. Drain pasta; add to dressing mixture. Flake salmon; add to pasta along with apples, raisins, and "Nuts"; stir to coat.

4. Cover salad and refrigerate 2–3 hours to blend flavors before serving. Serve on mixed salad greens.

wheat *eggs* *soy* *fish* *nuts*

Pasta Carrot Salad

Serves 6

This refreshing salad is great for picnics. Try the Tinkyada brand of gluten-free pasta; it's very tender and fresh tasting.

Calories: 366.77
Fat: 21.40 grams
Saturated Fat: 4.32 grams
Carbohydrates: 37.30 grams
Sodium: 259.18 mg

1. Bring a large pot of water to a boil. In medium bowl, combine Eggless Cooked Salad Dressing, sour cream, milk, and Soy Sause Substitute; mix until smooth.

2. Cook pasta until al dente, according to package directions. Drain and add to dressing in bowl; stir to coat. Stir in remaining ingredients, cover, and chill 1–2 hours to blend flavors before serving.

½ cup Eggless Cooked Salad Dressing (page 79)
¼ cup sour cream
2 tablespoons milk
2 teaspoons Soy Sauce Substitute (page 82)
1 (8-ounce) package gluten-free rice pasta
1 cup shredded carrots
¼ cup chopped green onion
½ cup diced Swiss cheese
1 cup frozen baby peas, thawed

Rice Pasta

If you've tried pasta made from rice but were unimpressed, try it again. Some brands are very improved, including Tinkyada, which was rated very highly by *Martha Stewart Living* magazine. Lundberg Family Farms has an excellent rice pasta made with brown rice. With all of these products, cook exactly as the package specifies, and drain and immediately rinse the pasta with cold water to stop the cooking process.

Crunchy Chicken-Bacon Salad

This savory and delicious salad has the best combination of fla-vors and textures. Potato sticks are a good gluten free choice for adding crunch to salads and sandwiches.

Serves 6

Calories: 371.30
Fat: 26.29 grams
Saturated Fat: 3.43 grams
Carbohydrates: 13.72 grams
Sodium: 208.18 mg

4 slices gluten-free bacon
½ cup Eggless Mayonnaise (page 68)
2 tablespoons Chicken Stock (page 137)
2 tablespoons honey
⅛ teaspoon pepper
¼ cup chopped flat-leaf parsley
⅓ cup chopped green onion
½ cup chopped celery
1 avocado, peeled and cubed
3 cups cubed, cooked chicken
4 cups mixed salad greens
1 cup crisp potato sticks

1. Cook bacon in medium skillet until crisp; remove from skillet, drain on paper towels, crumble, and set aside.

2. In large bowl, combine Mayonnaise, Chicken Stock, honey, pepper, and parsley and mix well. Add bacon, green onion, celery, avocado, and chicken; mix well.

3. Serve salad in the mixed salad greens and top with potato sticks; serve immediately.

milk   wheat   eggs   soy   fish   nuts

Southwest Potato Salad

If you like it spicy, add another jalapeno pepper and use a pob-lano pepper instead of the green bell pepper. Of course, you can also add more chili powder!

Serves 6

Calories: 317.43
Fat: 20.46 grams
Saturated Fat: 1.50 grams
Carbohydrates: 31.58 grams
Sodium: 271.79 mg

1. Scrub potatoes. If necessary, cut sweet potatoes in half so they are about the same size as the russet potatoes. Cook in a large pot of boiling water until tender when pierced with a fork, about 25–30 minutes.

2. While potatoes are cooking, combine Mayonnaise, Salad Dressing, mustard, rice milk, Chili Powder, and cayenne pepper in large bowl and blend well.

3. When potatoes are done, drain and let cool 20 minutes. Peel and cube potatoes; add to dressing while you work. Add remaining ingredients and blend well.

4. Cover and chill 2–3 hours before serving so flavors blend.

3 russet potatoes
2 sweet potatoes
½ cup Eggless Mayonnaise (page 68)
¼ cup Eggless Cooked Salad Dressing (page 79)
3 tablespoons gluten-free Dijon mustard
¼ cup rice milk
1 tablespoon Chili Powder (page 78)
⅛ teaspoon cayenne pepper
1 jalapeño pepper, minced
1 green bell pepper, chopped
1 red bell pepper, chopped

Spice Blends

Read the labels of spice blends, including curry powder and chili powder, carefully; some use gluten or wheat or egg products. Some brands do not, including Gourmet du Village and Gebrardt. Look for them in health food stores or buy them on the Internet. Or you can make your own and control every ingredient.

Calories: 482.07
Fat: 25.86 grams
Saturated Fat: 8.11 grams
Carbohydrates: 47.94 grams
Sodium: 970.49 mg

¼ pound gluten-free
   pepperoni slices
¼ pound gluten-free salami,
   cubed
1 red bell pepper, chopped
1 yellow bell pepper,
   chopped
1 green bell pepper,
   chopped
½ cup green olives
¼ cup black olives
½ cup chopped red onion
1 Focaccia Bread (page 55)
2 cups baby spinach leaves
1 cup diced Mozzarella
   cheese
3 tablespoons shredded
   Romano cheese
½ cup gluten-free tomato
   sauce
3 tablespoons extra-virgin
   olive oil
1 teaspoon dried oregano
   leaves
1 tablespoon gluten-free
   garlic paste
2 tablespoons lemon juice
1 teaspoon sugar
¼ teaspoon pepper

wheat   eggs   soy   fish   nuts

Pizza Salad

*Using toasted Focaccia Bread turns
this salad into a pizza in a bowl.*

1. Preheat oven to 400°F. In large bowl, toss together pepperoni, salami, bell peppers, olives, and onion; set aside.

2. Place Focaccia Bread on a baking sheet; bake 10–15 minutes, or until golden brown. Cool on wire rack 10 minutes; cut into 1" cubes and add to salad along with spinach leaves and cheese.

3. In small bowl, combine remaining ingredients and mix well with wire whisk. Drizzle half over salad; toss to coat. Serve with remaining dressing on the side.

milk   wheat   eggs   fish   nuts

"Ricotta" and Tomato Salad

*This beautiful arranged salad is the perfect side dish
for a summer evening.*

Serves 6

Calories: 120.04
Fat: 8.62 grams
Saturated Fat: 1.23 grams
Carbohydrates: 8.83 grams
Sodium: 109.47 mg

1. On serving plate, arrange tomatoes on salad greens. Top with dollops of soy ricotta; sprinkle all with thyme leaves.

2. Stir Pesto and drizzle over salad; serve immediately.

3 ripe red tomatoes, sliced
3 ripe yellow tomatoes, sliced
6 cups mixed salad greens
½ cup vegan, soy ricotta cheese
2 teaspoons fresh thyme leaves
½ cup Basil Pesto (page 77)

Heirloom Tomatoes

You can find far more than plain yellow and red tomatoes in the grocery store these days. Heirloom tomatoes are becoming more popular: These are tomatoes grown from seed saved from nonhybrid tomatoes, usually those developed before 1945, when horticulturists began hybridizing plants. The tomatoes are flavorful and colorful; varieties include Brandywine, Green Zebra, and Cherokee Purple.

milk　wheat　eggs　soy　fish　nuts

Spicy Roasted Corn and Bean Salad

Roasting corn brings out the flavor and adds a wonderful sweet, chewy texture to this simple salad.

1. Preheat oven to 400°F. Toss frozen corn with 2 tablespoons olive oil and place in single layer on cookie sheet. Roast 10–15 minutes, turning occasionally with a spatula, until corn begins to turn brown around edges.

2. Sprinkle with Chili Powder; toss to coat, then combine in serving bowl with black beans, red bell pepper, red onion, and cilantro.

3. In small bowl, combine remaining ingredients and stir with wire whisk to blend. Pour over vegetables and toss to coat. Cover and chill 3–4 hours before serving.

Serves 6

Calories: 292.94
Fat: 12.41 grams
Saturated Fat: 1.76 grams
Carbohydrates: 37.93 grams
Sodium: 720.55 mg

2 cups frozen corn
2 tablespoons olive oil
1 tablespoon Chili Powder (page 78)
2 (15-ounce) cans black beans, rinsed and drained
1 red bell pepper, chopped
½ cup chopped red onion
¼ cup chopped cilantro
¼ cup white gluten-free balsamic vinegar
3 tablespoons extra-virgin olive oil
⅛ teaspoon cayenne pepper
¼ teaspoon pepper
1 tablespoon gluten-free mustard

milk wheat eggs fish nuts

Creamy Fruit Salad

This salad is almost a dessert! It's creamy, sweet, and tart, with the best flavor. The kids will love it.

1. In blender or food processor, combine pudding mix and silken tofu; blend or process until smooth and creamy. Pour into serving bowl; fold in whipped topping and lemon zest.

2. Add grapes. Slice bananas, sprinkling with lemon juice as you work. Fold all fruit into pudding mixture. Cover and chill 2–3 hours before serving.

Pudding Mixes

There are some pudding mixes which are specifically formulated to use silken tofu, soy milk, or rice milk. Mori-Nu has one brand that comes in several flavors. Many pudding mixes, especially the instant type, will not thicken when mixed with soy or rice milk. The same is true with pudding recipes. Use a recipe specially formulated for soy or rice milk.

Serves 6

Calories: 230.93
Fat: 2.63 grams
Saturated Fat: 1.59 grams
Carbohydrates: 50.22 grams
Sodium: 155.40 mg

1 (4-ounce) package lemon crème soy-blend pudding mix
1 (12-ounce) container silken tofu
1 cup nondairy vegan whipped topping
½ teaspoon grated lemon zest
2 cups red grapes
1 cup green grapes
2 bananas, sliced
1 tablespoon lemon juice
2 cups sliced strawberries

milk   wheat   eggs   soy   fish   nuts

Oil and Vinegar Dressing

This simple dressing can be flavored with any herb or spice you choose. Shake it vigorously before each use.

Yields 2/3 cup; Serving size 2 tablespoons

Calories: 109.21
Fat: 12.00 grams
Saturated Fat: 1.66 grams
Carbohydrates: 0.17 grams
Sodium: 97.48 mg

⅓ cup white gluten-free balsamic vinegar
⅓ cup extra-virgin olive oil
1 clove garlic, finely minced
¼ teaspoon dried tarragon leaves
¼ teaspoon dried thyme leaves
¼ teaspoon salt
⅛ teaspoon white pepper

In jar with screw-top lid, combine all ingredients. Shake vigorously to blend. Store in refrigerator up to 2 weeks.

Olive Oil

You may be surprised to learn that Spain is the world's largest producer of olive oil and olives. Olive oil is used in all manner of cooking, from deep-frying fish, to sautéing vegetables, to drizzling over salads, or whisking into baked goods and desserts. The oils range dramatically in color and flavor, from green to golden, and they have subtle distinguishing flavors.

milk wheat eggs soy fish nuts

Thousand Island Dressing

Thousand Island Dressing got its name from the small pieces of pickle blended into the creamy sauce.

Combine all ingredients in a small bowl; mix well. Cover tightly and refrigerate up to 4 days.

Homemade Salad Dressings

It's easy to make salad dressings at home. You do have to remember that because they are not commercially made and have no preservatives, they won't last as long as commercial dressings. And they do have to be refrigerated. Use your imagination when creating dressings, and have fun with the process.

Yields ½ cup; Serving size 2 tablespoons

Calories: 159.69
Fat: 14.62 grams
Saturated Fat: 0.91 grams
Carbohydrates: 8.02 grams
Sodium: 508.88 mg

⅓ cup Eggless Mayonnaise (page 68)
3 tablespoons gluten-free ketchup
1 tablespoon gluten-free mustard
⅛ teaspoon garlic powder
½ teaspoon sugar
3 tablespoons finely chopped sweet dill pickle
¼ teaspoon salt
Pinch white pepper

milk wheat eggs soy fish nuts

Fruit Sparkle Salad

*Any canned, frozen, or fresh fruits (except fresh pineapple)
can be used in this quick and easy salad.
It's great for breakfast as well as dinner.*

Serves 9

Calories: 85.82
Fat: 0.08 grams
Saturated Fat: 0.01 grams
Carbohydrates: 20.78 grams
Sodium: 5.19 mg

2 (0.25-ounce) packages
  unflavored gelatin
⅓ cup sugar
1 (13-ounce) can pineapple
  tidbits in light syrup
Canned pineapple juice
1 cup sparkling water
1 cup sliced canned
  peaches, drained
1 cup red grapes, cut in half

1. In large bowl, combine gelatin with sugar; mix well. Drain pineapple, reserving syrup.

2. In glass measuring cup, combine reserved pineapple syrup along with enough pineapple juice and sparkling water to measure 2 cups. Pour ¾ cup of this mixture over gelatin mixture.

3. Microwave remaining liquid on 100 percent power 2–3 minutes, until it just comes to a boil. Pour over gelatin mixture; stir until gelatin and sugar dissolve completely.

4. Stir in 1 cup sparkling water along with drained pineapple, peaches, and grapes. Pour into a 2-quart, shallow glass casserole dish; refrigerate until firm. Cut into squares to serve.

milk wheat eggs fish nuts

Herbed "Feta" Salad Dressing

*The crumbled firm tofu gives you the texture
of feta cheese without the dairy.*

1. Combine olive oil, balsamic vinegar, raspberry vinegar, silken tofu, sugar, garlic, salt, pepper, and soy sauce in blender or food processor; blend or process until smooth.

2. Remove to small bowl; stir in tofu, parsley, and chives. Cover and refrigerate 2–3 hours to blend flavors. Store covered in refrigerator up to 4 days.

Flavored Vinegar

Flavored vinegars are an easy way to make a quick salad dressing with just a few ingredients. You can easily make your own. Put anything, from herbs to garlic to spices or fruit, in a very clean glass bottle. Fill bottle with gluten-free plain vinegar, cover tightly, and let stand in a cool, dark place for 1–2 weeks before using.

Yields 1 cup; Serving size 2 tablespoons

Calories: 75.81
Fat: 7.37 grams
Saturated Fat: 1.04 grams
Carbohydrates: 1.29 grams
Sodium: 185.42 mg

¼ cup olive oil
2 tablespoons gluten-free
    balsamic vinegar
2 tablespoons gluten-free
    raspberry vinegar
¼ cup silken tofu
1 teaspoon sugar
2 cloves garlic, minced
½ teaspoon salt
⅛ teaspoon white pepper
1 teaspoon soy sauce
5 tablespoons crumbled
    firm tofu
2 tablespoons chopped
    flat-leaf parsley
1 tablespoon chopped
    fresh chives

Calories: 97.38
Fat: 9.84 grams
Saturated Fat: 0.66 grams
Carbohydrates: 1.70 grams
Sodium: 175.11 mg

1 teaspoon olive oil
⅓ cup minced onion
2 cloves garlic, minced
½ cup silken tofu
½ cup Eggless Mayonnaise (page 68)
2 tablespoons rice or soy milk
2 tablespoons chopped flat-leaf parsley
2 tablespoons chopped dill weed
2 tablespoons minced chives
½ teaspoon dill seed
½ teaspoon salt
⅛ teaspoon white pepper

milk · wheat · eggs · fish · nuts

Ranch Salad Dressing

Ranch salad dressing is a classic; keep this one in the fridge for up to 3 days to use on everything from baked potatoes to salads.

1. In small saucepan, combine oil, onion, and garlic; cook and stir over medium heat until tender, about 5–6 minutes. Remove from heat; cool completely.

2. Combine onions, garlic, and all remaining ingredients in food processor or blender; process or blend until smooth. Cover and refrigerate 2–3 hours before serving.

Chapter 6
Appetizers

wheat   eggs   soy   fish   nuts

Crunchy Snack Mix

To make this recipe dairy free (but not soy-free), just use dairy-free margarine and dairy-free soy cheese. It's crisp, crunchy, and very satisfying.

**Yields 8 cups;
Serving size ½ cup**

Calories: 235.01
Fat: 14.15 grams
Saturated Fat: 5.57 grams
Carbohydrates: 23.78 grams
Sodium: 366.02 mg

*2 cups gluten-free pretzel sticks
2 cups sweet potato chips
1 cup amaranth crackers
1 cup rice chips
2 cups crisp potato sticks
½ cup butter
1 tablespoon gluten-free chili powder
½ teaspoon cumin
⅛ teaspoon pepper
½ teaspoon crushed red-pepper flakes
½ cup grated Parmesan cheese*

1. Preheat oven to 300°F. Slightly crush the pretzel sticks, sweet potato chips, amaranth crackers, and rice chips; combine in a large roasting pan with potato sticks.

2. In small saucepan, melt butter over low heat. Add chili powder, cumin, pepper, and red-pepper flakes; remove from heat. Drizzle over ingredients in roasting pan.

3. Bake 40–50 minutes, stirring twice during baking time, until snack mix is glazed and light golden brown. Sprinkle with cheese, toss to coat, and let cool.

Healthy Snacks

There are so many varieties and brands of specialty snacks available now. Gluten-free crackers, chips, and snack mixes made from rice and potatoes, as well as whole-grain snacks, are commonplace. If you can't find them at your grocery store, ask! Often, the grocer will order items for you. And of course, there's always the Internet.

milk wheat eggs soy fish nuts

Crisp Polenta Squares

Polenta is made from cornmeal that has been cooked until soft. When chilled, sliced, and fried, it becomes a crisp and delectable snack.

1. In large saucepan, combine water, tomato juice, garlic, salt, and pepper and bring to a boil. Stir in cornmeal; cook and stir over low heat until very thick, about 12–17 minutes.

2. Pour mixture into oiled baking dish; spread about ½" thick. Cover and chill until very firm.

3. When ready to eat, cut into 2" squares. Heat olive oil over medium-high heat until about 375°F. Fry polenta squares, a few at a time, until very crisp. Drain on paper towels. Serve with any spicy salsa or dip.

Serves 4–6

Calories: 115.92
Fat: 2.68 grams
Saturated Fat: 0.37 grams
Carbohydrates: 20.39 grams
Sodium: 416.89 mg

3 cups water
1 cup tomato juice
4 cloves garlic, minced
1 teaspoon salt
⅛ teaspoon pepper
1 cup cornmeal
½ cup olive oil

Crispy Rice Balls

Serves 8

Calories: 165.51
Fat: 6.03 grams
Saturated Fat: 0.82 grams
Carbohydrates: 24.58 grams
Sodium: 166.82 mg

1 cup medium-grain rice
2 cups water
1 tablespoon olive oil
½ cup minced onion
3 cloves garlic, minced
1 egg
½ teaspoon salt
⅛ teaspoon cayenne
    pepper
2 tablespoons prepared
    gluten-free horseradish
½ teaspoon dried thyme
    leaves
1 cup crushed puffed-rice
    cereal
1 cup vegetable oil

Fry these little balls as your guests arrive. They're crisp and savory, with a tender center. If you aren't allergic to cheese, try molding the rice around a tiny square of cheese before frying.

1. In medium saucepan, combine rice and water. Bring to a boil over high heat, then reduce heat to low; simmer 18–23 minutes, or until rice is tender and water is absorbed.

2. Meanwhile, heat olive oil over medium heat. Add onion; cook and stir until onion begins to brown, about 8–9 minutes. Stir in garlic for 1 minute, then stir into hot cooked rice. Let cool for 30 minutes, then add egg, salt, pepper, horseradish, and thyme.

3. Form mixture into 1" balls; roll in crushed cereal to coat.

4. Heat oil in heavy skillet over medium heat. Fry rice balls, turning carefully, until golden brown and crisp, about 4–5 minutes. Drain on paper towels to serve.

Cooking Rice

There are three main types of rice: long grain, medium grain, and short grain. They differ in the amount and kind of starch they contain. Long-grain rice cooks up fluffier because it has less amylopectin, which is the starch that makes rice sticky. Medium-grain rice has more amylopectin, so it is stickier, suitable for rice balls and risotto.

wheat · eggs · soy · fish · nuts

Pepper and Cheese Crackers

These little crackers are crisp and flaky, with an excellent spicy flavor. Serve them with hot soup for a satisfying lunch.

1. Preheat oven to 400°F. In large bowl, combine butter, oil, mustard, and Cheddar cheese; mix until combined. Add Baking Mix, pepper, and cayenne pepper; mix until crumbly. Add enough milk to make a firm, slightly crumbly dough.

2. Place dough on work surface; gently knead about 15 times. For each cracker, make three ½" diameter balls of dough; place on top of each other; flatten them all together to make one thin circle of dough. Place on Silpat-lined cookie sheets; prick with a fork. Repeat with remaining dough.

3. Bake 6–8 minutes, or until golden brown around edges. Carefully remove to wire rack to cool.

milk · wheat · eggs · fish · nuts

Dairy-Free Olive Cheese Ball

If you aren't allergic to dairy, you can make this with softened cream cheese instead. Choose your favorite olives, and serve with crisp crackers.

1. In small saucepan, heat olive oil over medium heat. Add onion and garlic; cook and stir until onion starts to brown, about 8–10 minutes. Remove from heat, place onions and garlic in small bowl, and let cool 20 minutes.

2. Add mustard and black olives and stir to combine. Add Soy-Yogurt Cheese. Cover and chill until firm, about 1–2 hours. Then form into a ball and roll in parsley to coat.

Yields 36 crackers

Calories: 101.14
Fat: 4.90 grams
Saturated Fat: 2.72 grams
Carbohydrates: 12.20 grams
Sodium: 145.58 mg

½ cup butter, softened
1 tablespoon vegetable oil
2 tablespoons gluten-free
  mustard
1½ cups shredded sharp
  Cheddar cheese
2½ cups Gluten-Free, Soy-
  Free Baking Mix (page
  67)
½ teaspoon freshly ground
  black pepper
⅛ teaspoon cayenne pepper
¼ cup milk

Serves 6–8

Calories: 125.40
Fat: 4.50 grams
Saturated Fat: 0.62 grams
Carbohydrates: 17.88
grams
Sodium: 151.15 mg

1 tablespoon olive oil
½ cup finely chopped onion
2 cloves garlic, minced
2 tablespoons gluten-free
  Dijon mustard
¼ cup finely chopped black
  olives
1½ cups Soy-Yogurt
  Cheese (page 70)
¼ cup finely chopped flat-
  leaf parsley

milk wheat eggs fish nuts

Yogurt Cheese Balls

Make your Yogurt Cheese with regular yogurt (for a soy-free recipe) or soy yogurt for a milk-free recipe, then serve these delicious little spicy balls as part of an antipasto tray.

Serves 4–6

Calories: 142.58
Fat: 8.35 grams
Saturated Fat: 1.16 grams
Carbohydrates: 14.09 grams
Sodium: 30.94 mg

1 cup Soy-Yogurt Cheese
   (page 70)
½ teaspoon paprika
⅛ teaspoon pepper
2 tablespoons minced
   cilantro
2 tablespoons fresh minced
   basil
3 tablespoons extra-virgin
   olive oil

1. Place Yogurt Cheese in a small bowl; mix in paprika and pepper. Roll mixture into 1" balls; roll in herbs; place on serving plate.

2. Drizzle with olive oil and refrigerate 1–2 hours to blend flavors before serving.

Antipasto

The word literally means "before the meal." Antipasto usually consists of smoked and brined meats, a variety of cheeses, and pickled, marinated, and raw vegetables. Yogurt Cheese Balls are a good substitute for cheeses for those allergic to dairy. You can also include breads on an antipasto platter, especially rustic Italian and French breads.

milk wheat eggs soy nuts

Grilled Shrimp Skewers

Mustard and lemon juice flavor tender shrimp in this easy recipe. You could use cubes of chicken or turkey instead of the shrimp for a fish-free recipe.

1. Place olive oil in medium pan over medium heat. Cut onions into quarters, then cut each quarter in half to make 16 wedges. Cook in oil, turning carefully to keep the wedges together, 4–5 minutes to soften.

2. Remove pan from heat, then remove onions from pan and set aside. Add lemon juice, mustard, and thyme to olive oil and mix well. Add shrimp and stir to coat.

3. String shrimp and onion wedges on skewers; brush with any remaining mustard mixture and sprinkle with salt and pepper.

4. Cook 6" from broiler or medium coals, turning once, until shrimp curl and turn pink and onions are slightly charred, about 4–5 minutes. Serve immediately.

Serves 4–6

Calories: 185.55
Fat: 6.66 grams
Saturated Fat: 1.01 grams
Carbohydrates: 6.92 grams
Sodium: 419.26 mg

2 tablespoons olive oil
2 onions
2 tablespoons lemon juice
2 tablespoons gluten-free Dijon mustard
½ teaspoon dried thyme leaves
1½ pounds large raw shrimp
½ teaspoon salt
⅛ teaspoon pepper

Corn Quesadillas

Corn tortillas are a great choice for appetizers, to make your own chips, and to use as the bread for sandwich wraps.

Serves 6

Calories: 291.05
Fat: 10.60 grams
Saturated Fat: 1.76 grams
Carbohydrates: 39.32 grams
Sodium: 565.62 mg

1 tablespoon olive oil
3 cloves garlic, minced
2 jalapeño peppers, minced
1½ cups frozen corn
1 (15-ounce) can black beans, drained and rinsed
½ cup Tomatillo Salsa (page 118)
12 (6-inch) corn tortillas
½ cup Soy-Yogurt Cheese (page 70)
1 cup shredded dairy-free Pepper Jack soy cheese

1. In small saucepan, heat olive oil over medium heat. Add garlic and jalapeños; cook and stir 2–3 minutes, until softened. Add corn; cook and stir 4–5 minutes longer, until hot. Remove from heat and stir in black beans and Tomatillo Salsa.

2. Arrange half of the tortillas on work surface. Spread each with some of the Soy-Yogurt Cheese. Divide corn mixture among tortillas, then top with the Pepper Jack cheese. Top with remaining tortillas.

3. Heat a large skillet or griddle over medium heat. Grill quesadillas, turning once, until cheese melts and tortillas are toasted. Cut into wedges and serve with more Salsa.

Soy Cheese

Soy cheeses don't melt as well as dairy cheese. They can also be rather bland. You can solve these problems by looking for flavored soy cheeses. Also, when adding the cheese to a recipe that is heated, add the cheese at the very end and cover the food while it cooks. The steam produced will help soften the cheese.

milk wheat eggs soy fish nuts

Tomato Peach Salsa

Different types of tomatoes make this salsa fresh tasting and colorful. Serve it with Crisp Polenta Squares (page 111) or Pepper and Cheese Crackers (page 113) depending on your allergy.

1. In serving bowl, combine tomatoes, peaches, jalapeño pepper, cilantro, parsley, garlic, and onion and toss to coat.

2. In small bowl, combine lemon juice, salt, pepper, and olive oil and shake until salt dissolves. Pour over fruit and toss to coat. Cover and chill 2–3 hours before serving.

Peeling Peaches

Peaches are easy to peel. Bring a large pot of water to a boil. Cut a shallow "X" in the blossom end of the fruit and boil for 10–15 seconds. Plunge the fruit into ice water until cold to the touch. The skins will slip right off. If you have a choice, buy freestone peaches, which are much easier to work with than cling peaches.

Yields 3 cups;
Serving size ½ cup

Calories: 88.95
Fat: 4.94 grams
Saturated Fat: 0.69 grams
Carbohydrates: 11.35 grams
Sodium: 208.55 mg

2 red ripe tomatoes, diced
1 yellow tomato, diced
1 cup grape tomatoes, cut in half
2 peaches, peeled and diced
1 jalapeño pepper, diced
¼ cup chopped cilantro
¼ cup chopped flat-leaf parsley
1 clove garlic, minced
½ cup minced red onion
2 tablespoons lemon juice
½ teaspoon salt
⅛ teaspoon cayenne pepper
2 tablespoons olive oil

milk   wheat   eggs   soy   fish   nuts

Tomatillo Salsa

Yields 2 cups;
Serving size ¼ cup

Calories: 40.59
Fat: 2.19 grams
Saturated Fat: 0.30 grams
Carbohydrates: 5.24 grams
Sodium: 148.16 mg

¾ pound tomatillos, husked
1 jalapeño pepper
1 habanero pepper
½ cup water
1 tablespoon olive oil
4 cloves garlic, minced
1 large onion, chopped
½ teaspoon salt
¼ teaspoon pepper
½ cup chopped cilantro
¼ cup chopped flat-leaf
    parsley

Green salsa, or salsa verde, is usually made with roasted bell peppers. This version, made with tomatillos, is tangy and spicy.

1. Rinse tomatillos and chop coarsely. Combine in a saucepan with jalapeño and habanero peppers and water and bring to a boil. Reduce heat and simmer, stirring frequently, 5 minutes. Remove from heat, drain, and set aside.

2. In medium skillet, heat olive oil over medium heat. Add garlic and onion; cook and stir until crisp-tender, about 5–6 minutes; remove from heat.

3. In blender or food processor, combine tomatillos, onion mixture, and remaining ingredients. Blend or process until desired consistency. Cover and chill 2–3 hours to blend flavors.

Tomatillos

Tomatillos are small green fruits with a papery covering. Remove the covering and rinse before using. They are not green tomatoes; in fact, they are a type of berry, related to the gooseberry. They can be eaten raw or cooked, although cooking does make them a bit less tart and crunchy.

milk wheat eggs fish nuts

Roasted Sweet and Spicy "Nuts"

Made in two steps, this wonderful recipe is a great snack for those allergic to nuts. You can flavor the "nuts" any way you'd like.

Yields 3 cups; Serves 6

Calories: 283.84
Fat: 11.72 grams
Saturated Fat: 1.70 grams
Carbohydrates: 28.93 grams
Sodium: 694.61 mg

2 cups dried soybeans
6 cups water
⅓ cup honey
1 tablespoon gluten-free
   curry powder
1 teaspoon fine salt

1. Pick over soybeans, discarding any that are shriveled, and any extraneous material. Rinse them in cold water, drain, then place in a large bowl. Cover with water and let soak 12 hours.

2. Preheat oven to 325°F. Drain soybeans and pat dry with paper towels. Place in single layer on a large cookie sheet. Roast 55–65 minutes, turning with a spatula every 10 minutes, until crisp and light golden brown. Remove from cookie sheet; let stand on paper towels 10 minutes.

3. Return soybeans to cookie sheet and drizzle with honey. Toss to coat, then sprinkle with curry powder and salt.

4. Reduce oven temperature to 275°F. Roast the seasoned soybeans another 30–40 minutes, stirring every 8 minutes, until crisp. Let cool, then store in airtight container.

milk   wheat   eggs   soy   fish   nuts

Mango Chutney

**Yields 2 pints;
Serving size ¼ cup**

Calories: 105.78
Fat: 0.28 grams
Saturated Fat: 0.07 grams
Carbohydrates: 27.15 grams
Sodium: 79.18 mg

5 mangoes, peeled and
    chopped
⅓ cup plain vinegar
¼ cup lemon juice
⅔ cup brown sugar
1 onion, finely chopped
3 cloves garlic, minced
½ cup golden raisins
¼ cup dried currants
3 tablespoons minced fresh
    ginger root
½ teaspoon salt
1 teaspoon cinnamon
1 tablespoon gluten-free
    curry powder
⅛ teaspoon white pepper

You can store this chutney in the refrigerator for up to 9 days, or process it in a hot-water bath for longer storage. The chutney can be frozen up to 3 months.

1. Combine all ingredients in a large, heavy saucepan and bring to a boil over medium-high heat. Reduce heat to medium-low; simmer, stirring frequently, until mixture thickens and becomes syrupy, about 15–25 minutes.

2. While chutney is simmering on stove, place half-pint jars or freezer containers in dishwasher and wash. Leave the containers in the dishwasher until ready to fill.

3. Ladle chutney into clean hot containers, leaving about ½" of headspace. Cover and chill in refrigerator until cold; store in refrigerator or freezer.

Preparing Mangoes

Mangoes can be tricky to peel and slice. First, be sure you have ripe mangoes that yield slightly to gentle pressure. Remove the peel with a swivel-bladed vegetable peeler or sharp knife. Then stand the mango on end and slice down, curving around the pit. If you want chopped mango, just keep paring off flesh until you reach the pit.

milk wheat eggs soy fish nuts

Spicy Fruit Salsa

Fruit salsa is a nice change from savory or tomato-based salsas. Serve this with apple and pear slices, or with water crackers.

In medium bowl, combine all ingredients and mix gently until combined. Cover and refrigerate for 2–3 hours before serving.

wheat eggs soy fish nuts

Sausage Bruschetta

For a milk-free (but not soy-free) appetizer, use Soy-Yogurt Cheese (page 70) instead of the softened cream cheese, and soy vegan shredded Muenster or Swiss cheese.

1. Preheat broiler. In medium saucepan, cook sausage, onion, and bell pepper over medium heat, stirring to break up sausage, until meat is cooked. Drain thoroughly.

2. Spread 1 ounce cream cheese on each slice of French Bread. Top with sausage mixture and sprinkle with Muenster cheese. Place Bruschetta on broiler pan. Broil 6" from heat source until cheese bubbles and begins to brown. Serve immediately.

**Yields 2 cups;
Serving size ¼ cup**

Calories: 37.12
Fat: 0.13 grams
Saturated Fat: 0.01 grams
Carbohydrates: 9.43 grams
Sodium: 146.20 mg

1 (13-ounce) can crushed
   pineapple, drained
½ cup minced red onion
1 nectarine, peeled and
   chopped
1 jalapeño pepper, minced
2 tablespoons lime juice
½ teaspoon salt
⅛ teaspoon cayenne pepper
1 tablespoon minced fresh
   ginger root

Serves 12

Calories: 346.44
Fat: 14.13 grams
Saturated Fat: 7.61 grams
Carbohydrates: 46.01 grams
Sodium: 406.86 mg

½ pound ground gluten-free
   spicy pork sausage
1 onion, chopped
½ cup chopped red bell
   pepper
1 (8-ounce) package cream
   cheese, softened
12 slices Sourdough French
   Bread (page 49), toasted
1 cup shredded Muenster
   cheese

milk   eggs   soy   fish   nuts

Chicken Mushroom Tartlets

If you're allergic to wheat, use the tartlet shells from the Spicy Sausage Tartlets recipe (page 125), and cornstarch in place of the flour used to coat the chicken.

Yields 32 tartlets

Calories: 52.88
Fat: 3.77 grams
Saturated Fat: 1.18 grams
Carbohydrates: 2.98 grams
Sodium: 73.64 mg

1 boneless, skinless chicken breast, diced
2 tablespoons flour
½ teaspoon salt
⅛ teaspoon pepper
1 tablespoon olive oil
1 onion, chopped
1 cup sliced button mushrooms
1 tablespoon lemon juice
½ teaspoon dried thyme leaves
¼ cup Eggless Mayonnaise (page 68)
½ cup chopped cherry tomatoes
32 frozen mini tartlet shells

1. Preheat oven to 375°F. Toss chicken with flour, salt, and pepper. Heat olive oil in medium skillet and add chicken; cook and stir until thoroughly cooked, about 4–6 minutes. Remove chicken from skillet with slotted spoon and set aside in medium bowl.

2. Add onion to skillet; cook and stir until it begins to brown around the edges, about 8–10 minutes. Add mushrooms; cook and stir until tender, about 4–5 minutes longer. Remove half of this mixture to food processor; process until smooth and thick.

3. Add to chicken in bowl along with unprocessed onion and mushrooms, lemon juice, thyme, Mayonnaise, and tomatoes; stir well to mix. Fill each tartlet shell with about 2 teaspoons filling; place on cookie sheet.

4. Bake 9–14 minutes, or until filling is hot and shells are golden brown. Cool for 10 minutes, then serve.

Tartlet Shells

You can sometimes find tartlet shells in the bakery or frozen foods aisle of the supermarket, but if you have a pie-crust recipe you like, use that to make the little shells. You can roll out the dough and cut 2" rounds, fit those in the miniature muffin cups, and bake or roll the dough into ¾" balls and press into the muffin cups.

milk wheat eggs fish nuts

Stuffed Cherry Tomatoes

You can flavor the basic filling any way you'd like: Add jalapeño peppers, chopped toasted nuts, tiny shrimp, cooked ground ham, or pepperoni.

1. Cut the tops off each cherry tomato; using a small serrated spoon or melon scoop, remove pulp and discard. Put tomatoes upside down on paper-towel-lined plates to drain.

2. In small bowl, combine remaining ingredients and mix well to blend. Spoon or pipe filling into each cherry tomato.

3. To serve, place curly leaf parsley on a serving plate and arrange tomatoes on top. Cover with plastic wrap and chill at least 1 hour before serving.

Yields 24 appetizers

Calories: 50.48
Fat: 3.15 grams
Saturated Fat: 0.26 grams
Carbohydrates: 4.85 grams
Sodium: 47.96 mg

2 pints cherry tomatoes
1 cup Soy-Yogurt Cheese
 (page 70)
⅓ cup Eggless Mayonnaise
 (page 68)
1 tablespoon gluten-free
 prepared horseradish
1 tablespoon lemon juice
¼ cup finely chopped ripe
 olives, if desired
⅓ cup chopped flat-leaf
 parsley
¼ cup chopped cilantro

milk   wheat   eggs   soy   fish   nuts

Spicy Guacamole

Serve this creamy, nutty dip with corn or wheat tortilla chips, depending on which one you can eat!

Yields 2 cups;
Serving size ¼ cup

Calories: 141.94
Fat: 11.52 grams
Saturated Fat: 2.25 grams
Carbohydrates: 10.14 grams
Sodium: 149.01 mg

3 ripe avocados
2 tablespoons lime juice
½ teaspoon salt
3 tablespoons chopped
   cilantro
1 ripe tomato
⅛ teaspoon cayenne
   pepper
3 drops Tabasco sauce

1. Cut avocados in half lengthwise; twist to separate, and use a chef's knife to remove the pit. Using a large spoon, scoop out flesh and place in medium bowl.

2. In small bowl, combine lime juice and salt; mix to dissolve salt. Pour over avocados and mash, using a potato masher.

3. Stir in remaining ingredients; mix well. Cover by pressing plastic wrap directly onto the surface of the dip; refrigerate 1–2 hours to blend flavors before serving.

Avocados
Ripe avocados are almost impossible to buy in the grocery store. You have to buy them a few days ahead of time. To ripen, place the hard avocados in a paper bag on the counter for 2–3 days. Check them daily; when they yield to gentle pressure, they are ready to use.

milk wheat eggs fish nuts

Spicy Sausage Tartlets

Soy cheese works really well as a binder in this spicy recipe. And the soy Pepper Jack cheese adds some heat.

1. Preheat oven to 400°F. Spray miniature muffin cups with nonstick gluten-free cooking spray. Shape Pie Crust into 1" balls. Press each ball into a miniature muffin cup, extending rim ¼" over top of tins. Bake 4–5 minutes until set; remove from oven.

2. In small skillet, brown sausage along with onion and garlic, stirring to break up meat. Remove from heat and drain well. Add Soy-Yogurt Cheese and Pepper Jack cheese and stir to mix.

3. Put about 1 tablespoon in each tartlet shell. Bake 10–15 minutes longer, or until cheese is melted and tartlet shells are golden brown. Serve immediately.

Yields 24 tartlets

Calories: 81.77
Fat: 4.63 grams
Saturated Fat: 1.82 grams
Carbohydrates: 7.11 grams
Sodium: 90.41 mg

½ recipe Cornmeal Pie
   Crust (page 289)
½ pound spicy gluten-free
   ground pork sausage
½ cup finely chopped
   onion
2 garlic cloves, minced
⅓ cup Soy-Yogurt Cheese
   (page 70)
½ cup shredded soy
   Pepper Jack cheese

wheat   eggs   soy   fish   nuts

Refried Bean Dip

Serves 8–10

Calories: 228.28
Fat: 15.28 grams
Saturated Fat: 5.99 grams
Carbohydrates: 9.41 grams
Sodium: 486.07 mg

*1 pound ground gluten-free
   spicy pork sausage*
1 onion, chopped
3 cloves garlic, minced
1 jalapeño pepper, minced
*1 (15-ounce) can gluten-free
   vegetarian refried beans*
*1 cup shredded Pepper
   Jack cheese*
1 red bell pepper, chopped
¼ cup minced cilantro

If you like it spicy, use more jalapeño peppers or add poblano or habanero peppers to this dip. Serve with blue, white, and yellow corn chips.

1. In large skillet, combine sausage, onion, and garlic. Cook and stir over medium heat until sausage is browned and vegetables are tender. Drain thoroughly and add jalapeño pepper.

2. Add refried beans; cook and stir over medium heat until hot. Spread on ovenproof serving platter. Turn oven to broil.

3. Sprinkle dip with cheese and red bell pepper. Broil 6" from heat until cheese melts and begins to brown, about 5–7 minutes. Sprinkle with cilantro and serve immediately.

Refried Beans

You can find refried beans made with oil instead of lard. Read labels: If the label says the product uses hydrogenated oils, do not buy it, as that means the product is loaded with trans fat. There are refried beans made with pinto beans and black beans, and also those spiced with garlic and peppers; take your pick!

milk eggs fish nuts

Stuffed Bacon Mushrooms

If you use gluten-free bread crumbs,
this delicious appetizer becomes gluten free!

1. Remove stems from mushrooms; trim ends of the stems and coarsely chop. Place mushrooms, gill-side up on a baking sheet and brush with olive oil. Preheat oven to 350°F.

2. Cook bacon in medium skillet over medium heat until crisp. Remove bacon to paper towels to drain and crumble; set aside. Remove all but 1 tablespoon bacon drippings from skillet.

3. Cook mushroom stems, onion, and garlic in bacon drippings until tender, about 6–7 minutes. Remove from heat and stir in reserved bacon, bread crumbs, Cheese, and cayenne pepper; mix well.

4. Stuff the mushroom caps with mixture. Bake 15–20 minutes, or until the stuffing is hot and bubbly. Sprinkle with parsley and serve immediately.

Serves 8

Calories: 88.57
Fat: 2.73 grams
Saturated Fat: 0.71 grams
Carbohydrates: 11.92 grams
Sodium: 112.75 mg

16 large button mushrooms
4 slices bacon
1 onion, chopped
4 cloves garlic, minced
½ cup seasoned bread crumbs
⅔ cup Soy-Yogurt Cheese (page 70)
⅛ teaspoon cayenne pepper
¼ cup chopped flat-leaf parsley

milk wheat eggs fish nuts

Light Fruit Dip

Serve this delicious fluffy dip with everything from pirouette cookies to strawberries and pear slices.

**Yields 2 cups;
Serving size ¼ cup**

Calories: 150.99
Fat: 1.28 grams
Saturated Fat: 0.19 grams
Carbohydrates: 32.57 grams
Sodium: 79.41 mg

*1 cup Soy-Yogurt Cheese
   (page 70)
1 (7-ounce) jar egg-
   free, rice-based, soy
   marshmallow crème
1 (8-ounce) can crushed
   pineapple, drained
1 tablespoon lemon juice
⅛ teaspoon salt
¼ teaspoon cinnamon*

1. In medium bowl, combine Soy-Yogurt Cheese and marshmallow crème and beat until fluffy.

2. Drain pineapple thoroughly. Fold pineapple, lemon juice, salt, and cinnamon into crème mixture. Cover and chill 2–3 hours before serving.

Marshmallow Crème

Marshmallow crème is an easy way to get a creamy texture into a recipe without using any milk. It's made from gelatin, egg whites, sugar, and water; that's it. There is a brand called Ricemallow that is vegan, made from brown-rice syrup, soy protein, and gums. If you're allergic to eggs, it's a great choice for dips and sweets.

milk wheat eggs fish nuts

Creamy Dill Dip

Kids love this dip, and it's a great way to get them to eat their vegetables. Use baby carrots, tiny celery sticks, bell-pepper strips, and cauliflower florets for dippers.

In small bowl, combine all ingredients and mix well to blend. Cover and chill 2–3 hours before serving.

Dill

Dill is a member of the parsley family. It is known for its powerful flavor; when you use dried dill, crush the leaves to let more of that flavor out. In addition to pairing well with vegetables, it makes a delightful addition to salmon, halibut, scallop, and other seafood dishes.

Yields 1½ cups; Serving size 2 tablespoons

Calories: 76.26
Fat: 4.63 grams
Saturated Fat: 0.35 grams
Carbohydrates: 7.26 grams
Sodium: 83.61 mg

1 cup Soy-Yogurt Cheese (page 70)
¼ cup Eggless Mayonnaise (page 68)
¼ cup finely chopped green onion
2 tablespoons chopped flat-leaf parsley
1 tablespoon dried dill weed
½ teaspoon lemon pepper
½ teaspoon gluten-free seasoned salt

Serves 6

Calories: 74.62
Fat: 4.63 grams
Saturated Fat: 0.64 grams
Carbohydrates: 7.82 grams
Sodium: 198.80 mg

2 heads garlic
2 tablespoons olive oil
2 teaspoons lemon juice
½ teaspoon salt
⅛ teaspoon pepper

Roasted Garlic

*Roasted garlic cloves are a great spread on bread.
They can be added to soy cream cheese for a
sandwich spread or to any salsa recipe.*

1. Preheat oven to 400°F. Cut garlic heads in half and place on aluminum foil, cut-side up. Drizzle with olive oil and lemon juice and sprinkle with salt and pepper.

2. Wrap foil around garlic and place on cookie sheet. Bake 35–45 minutes, or until cloves are light brown and feel soft. Cool completely, then squeeze cloves out of their papery covering; and refrigerate.

Roasted Garlic

Roasted garlic is a wonderful addition to a diet restricted by allergies. Studies have shown varied results, but the fact remains garlic is a good source of B vitamins, selenium, and manganese, and helps reduce cholesterol. When roasted, it becomes sweet and nutty. Freeze roasted garlic for up to 3 months.

Chapter 7
Soups

Calories: 243.21
Fat: 7.63 grams
Saturated Fat: 1.08 grams
Carbohydrates: 40.63 grams
Sodium: 421.37 mg

2 tablespoons olive oil
2 onions, chopped
5 cloves garlic, minced
3 carrots, sliced
1 sweet potato, peeled and
    diced
2 potatoes, peeled and
    diced
2 turnips, peeled and diced
3 cups Vegetable Broth
    (page 139)
2 cups water
½ teaspoon salt
⅛ teaspoon pepper
1 bay leaf
1 tablespoon fresh thyme
    leaves
⅛ teaspoon nutmeg
½ cup rice milk

milk wheat eggs soy fish nuts

Root Vegetable Soup

*Root vegetables are hearty and good for you.
In this soup, they become rich and sweet as well.*

1. In large soup pot, heat olive oil over medium heat. Add onion and garlic; cook and stir 4 minutes. Add carrot, sweet potato, potatoes, and turnips; cook and stir until glazed, about 5 minutes.

2. Add Broth, water, salt, pepper, bay leaf, thyme, and nutmeg. Bring to a simmer, then reduce heat and simmer until vegetables are tender, about 20–25 minutes. Remove bay leaf.

3. Using an immersion blender, puree soup. Stir in rice milk, correct seasoning if necessary, and heat until soup steams. Serve immediately.

wheat · eggs · soy · fish · nuts

Tomato Corn Soup

Serves 6

Calories: 169.05
Fat: 9.25 grams
Saturated Fat: 2.10 grams
Carbohydrates: 21.44 grams
Sodium: 327.63 mg

The butter adds a nice smoothness to this soup, but you can omit it for a milk-free recipe. Or try Ghee (page 72) if you can tolerate it.

1. In soup pot, combine olive oil and butter over medium heat. Add onion and garlic; cook and stir until tender, about 6 minutes.

2. Add tomatoes, corn, and tomato paste; cook and stir 3–4 minutes. Then add Vegetable Broth, sugar, and Chili Powder. Bring to a simmer, cover, and cook 7–10 minutes, or until soup is blended. Serve immediately.

1 tablespoon olive oil
1 tablespoon butter
1 onion, chopped
2 cloves garlic, minced
4 tomatoes, chopped
2 cups frozen corn
2 tablespoons gluten-free tomato paste
6 cups Vegetable Broth (page 139)
¼ teaspoon sugar
2 teaspoons Chili Powder (page 78)

Tomato Paste

If you're lucky enough to find tomato paste in a tube, stock up. You can keep the tube in the refrigerator and just use it as you need it. If you buy yours in a can, freeze the paste in 1 tablespoon amounts, then use what you want from the freezer. It will keep frozen up to 6 months.

wheat soy fish nuts

Sweet and Sour Meatball Stew

Rice helps thicken this stew and adds nice texture. The sweet and sour flavor is reminiscent of many Asian recipes.

Serves 6

Calories: 432.42
Fat: 13.52 grams
Saturated Fat: 4.16 grams
Carbohydrates: 42.58 grams
Sodium: 380.05 mg

1 tablespoon olive oil
1 onion, chopped
2 cloves garlic, minced
¾ cup rice
2 cups Beef Stock (page 138)
3 cups water
2 tablespoons sugar
¼ cup gluten-free apple cider vinegar
1 (13-ounce) can pineapple tidbits, undrained
1 green bell pepper, chopped
18 Meatballs (page 173), cooked
½ teaspoon salt
⅛ teaspoon pepper
2 tablespoons cornstarch
3 tablespoons orange juice
1 tablespoon Soy Sauce Substitute (page 82)

1. In large soup pot, heat olive oil over medium heat. Add onion and garlic; cook and stir until tender, about 5 minutes. Add rice; cook and stir 2–3 minutes, until rice is opaque.

2. Add Beef Stock and water and bring to a boil. Reduce heat to low, cover pan, and simmer until rice is almost tender, about 12 minutes. Add remaining ingredients, except cornstarch, orange juice, and Soy Sauce Substitute.

3. Bring to a boil again; reduce heat to low; cover; and simmer 6–8 minutes, or until bell pepper is tender and Meatballs are hot.

4. In small bowl, combine cornstarch, orange juice, and Soy Sauce Substitute and stir to combine. Add to soup; cook over medium heat until soup simmers and thickens, about 5–6 minutes. Serve immediately.

milk wheat eggs fish nuts

Creamy Beer Vegetable Chowder

Beer Chowder should always be served with popcorn. This is a meal in itself; don't serve it as a starter!

1. In large pot, heat olive oil over medium heat. Add onion and garlic; cook and stir until tender, about 5 minutes. Add carrots, celery, and potato; cook and stir for 5 minutes longer.

2. Add potato-starch flour, salt, and pepper; cook and stir until bubbly, about 3 minutes. Add beer; cook and stir until slightly thickened.

3. Add Chicken Stock and bring to a simmer. Cook, stirring occasionally, until all the vegetables are very tender, about 15–20 minutes. Using an immersion blender or potato masher, mash some of the vegetables.

4. Stir in Evaporated Rice Milk and cheese and just heat through, stirring until cheese melts; do not boil. Serve soup topped with popcorn.

Gluten-Free Beers

Many beers are made with barley, which cannot be eaten by celiacs or those allergic to gluten. There are some brands of gluten-free beers available, both to drink and use in baking and cooking. Dragon's Gold and Tavern Ale are made by Bard's Tale Beer. And Discovery Beer, Pioneer Lager, and Herald Ale are made by Green's in the UK.

Serves 6

Calories: 301.99
Fat: 14.49 grams
Saturated Fat: 2.67 grams
Carbohydrates: 26.64 grams
Sodium: 359.74 mg

2 tablespoons olive oil
1 onion, diced
3 cloves garlic, minced
½ cup diced carrots
½ cup diced celery
½ cup diced, peeled
   potato
⅓ cup potato-starch flour
½ teaspoon salt
⅛ teaspoon white pepper
1 (12-ounce) bottle gluten-
   free beer
3 cups Chicken Stock
   (page 137)
1 cup Evaporated Rice
   Milk (page 66)
1 cup shredded dairy-free,
   vegan Cheddar cheese
2 cups popped popcorn

milk wheat eggs soy fish nuts

Ham Chowder

Chowders are usually made with lots of cheese and cream. But pureeing some vegetables can create almost the same texture.

Calories: 317.88
Fat: 6.99 grams
Saturated Fat: 1.82 grams
Carbohydrates: 48.77 grams
Sodium: 840.32 mg

1 tablespoon olive oil
1 onion, diced
4 cloves garlic, minced
2 leeks, thinly sliced
½ teaspoon salt
⅛ teaspoon white pepper
½ teaspoon dried thyme
   leaves
2 (4-inch) fresh rosemary
   sprigs
4 potatoes, diced
2 cups baby carrots
1 cup frozen corn
2 cups cubed gluten-free
   ham
6 cups Chicken Stock
   (page 137)
1 cup water

1. In medium saucepan, heat olive oil over medium heat. Cook onion and garlic, stirring frequently, until crisp-tender, about 5 minutes. Place in 4- to 5-quart slow cooker. Add remaining ingredients. Cover and cook on low 8–10 hours, or until vegetables are tender.

2. Remove rosemary stems. Using a potato masher or immersion blender, mash or blend some of the vegetables in the soup, leaving others whole. Stir to blend, then serve immediately.

milk wheat eggs soy fish nuts

Chicken Stock

Chicken stock is so easy to make and so wholesome. Once you learn how to make it, this recipe will become almost second nature.

1. In large pot, heat olive oil and add chicken. Cook 10–12 minutes, or until chicken begins to brown. Add water, ginger, onion, celery, carrots, bay leaf, and cloves; bring to a boil, then reduce heat, cover, and simmer for 55 minutes. Remove chicken from bone and store for another use.

2. Strain liquid into another large pot; season to taste with salt and pepper. Place in refrigerator overnight, then remove fat that accumulates on the surface. Store stock in refrigerator 3 days or freeze for longer storage.

Stock or Broth?

Technically, stock is made from the bones of chicken, seafood, or beef, while broth is made from the meat, excluding the bones. Stock can also be referred to as the intermediate step between raw ingredients and broth, the finished product. The terms are used interchangeably.

Yields 8 cups

Calories: 98.84
Fat: 4.11 grams
Saturated Fat: 1.17 grams
Carbohydrates: 4.69 grams
Sodium: 215.94 mg

Olive oil
2 pounds chicken, cut up
8 cups water
1 tablespoon chopped fresh ginger root
1 onion, sliced
3 stalks celery, chopped
3 carrots, chopped
1 bay leaf
2 whole cloves
1 teaspoon salt
⅛ teaspoon white pepper

milk   wheat   eggs   soy   fish   nuts

Beef Stock

Yields 8 cups

Calories: 74.76
Fat: 2.00 grams
Saturated Fat: 0.74 grams
Carbohydrates: 3.84 grams
Sodium: 196.30 mg

4 pounds meaty beef bones
½ cup water
1 onion, chopped
2 carrots, chopped
1 potato, peeled and cubed
1 (14-ounce) can gluten-
    free diced tomatoes,
    undrained
1 bay leaf
1½ teaspoons salt
¼ teaspoon pepper
1 teaspoon dried marjoram
½ teaspoon dried thyme
10 cups water

*Your own beef stock is not only safe to eat, it's also delicious.
Make a batch or two and freeze in 1-cup amounts.*

1. In large soup pot, brown the bones, a couple of batches at a time, over medium-high heat, about 10–12 minutes per batch. Remove bones and set aside. Add ½ cup water to pot and bring to a boil; scrape up drippings and bits stuck to pot.

2. Return beef to pot along with all remaining ingredients. Bring to a boil over high heat. Then skim off the surface, reduce heat to low, cover, and simmer 4–5 hours.

3. Strain stock, pressing on solids to get all of the liquid possible. Cool stock in refrigerator overnight and remove excess fat. Store in refrigerator up to 2 days or freeze up to 3 months.

milk wheat eggs soy fish nuts

Vegetable Broth

*Vegetable broth can be fairly flavorless, but not this recipe!
Browning the onions and garlic first adds
great caramelized flavor.*

Yields 6 cups

Calories: 45.89
Fat: 4.65 grams
Saturated Fat: 0.63 grams
Carbohydrates: 1.34 grams
Sodium: 226.43 mg

2 tablespoons olive oil
2 onions, chopped
4 cloves garlic, chopped
4 carrots, sliced
3 stalks celery with leaves, chopped
5 tomatoes, chopped
1 teaspoon salt
¼ teaspoon pepper
¼ teaspoon ground cloves
1 bay leaf
9 cups water

1. In large soup pot, heat olive oil over medium heat. Add onion and garlic; cook and stir until onion begins to brown, about 9–11 minutes. Add carrots; cook and stir 7–8 minutes longer, until onions are brown and carrots are tender.

2. Add remaining ingredients and stir to combine. Bring to a boil, then skim surface, reduce heat, and simmer 1–2 hours, or until liquid is slightly reduced and broth tastes rich.

3. Strain broth, pressing down on vegetables to extract all the juices. Store broth covered in refrigerator up to 3 days or freeze for longer storage.

Freezing Stocks and Broths

All stocks and broths freeze very well. Cool the liquid completely, then skim off any fat that accumulates on the surface. Divide into 2-cup hard-sided freezer containers, leaving about 1" of headspace for expansion during freezing. Label the containers, seal, and freeze for up to 3 months. To use, let stand in refrigerator overnight to thaw.

Tortellini Soup

Serves 6

Calories: 381.90
Fat: 13.45 grams
Saturated Fat: 4.10 grams
Carbohydrates: 49.32 grams
Sodium: 630.03 mg

½ pound ground gluten-free
    spicy pork sausage
1 onion, chopped
3 cloves garlic, minced
4 cups Chicken Stock
    (page 137)
2 cups water
½ teaspoon salt
⅛ teaspoon white pepper
1 cup baby carrots
1½ cups sliced yellow
    summer squash
1 (14-ounce) can gluten-
    free diced tomatoes,
    undrained
½ teaspoon dried basil
    leaves
½ teaspoon dried marjoram
    leaves
1 (8-ounce) package frozen,
    gluten-free, chicken rice
    tortellini
1 cup frozen corn
¼ cup chopped flat-leaf
    parsley

If you search, you can find gluten-free tortellini. DS is one brand that makes these specialty pastas.

1. In large soup pot, cook sausage with onion and garlic until sausage is browned, stirring to break up meat. Drain mixture. Add Stock, water, salt, pepper, carrots, squash, tomatoes, basil, and marjoram. Bring to a boil, then reduce heat. Cover and simmer for 25 minutes.

2. Add tortellini and corn and bring back to a simmer. Cook until tortellini are hot and tender, about 15–20 minutes. Garnish with parsley and serve immediately.

milk wheat eggs soy fish nuts

Lentil Soup

Lentils are the fast food of the legume world; they take only about 30 minutes to cook. They're divine in this silky soup.

1. In large soup pot, heat olive oil over medium heat. Add onion, garlic, and celery; sauté for 5 minutes. Stir in lentils and potatoes; cook and stir for 1 minute longer.

2. Add water, Stock, thyme, marjoram, salt, and pepper to pot and bring to a boil. Reduce heat, cover pot, and simmer about 1 hour, until lentils are tender. Using an immersion blender or potato masher, mash some of the potatoes and lentils.

Changing Soup Recipes

Soups are probably the most tolerant of all recipes. You can add or subtract ingredients at will, and as long as you include enough water, they'll work. You can substitute beef stock, or vegetable broth for chicken stock, use all water, add carrots or zucchini or chunks of ham, and it will still be wonderful.

Serves 6

Calories: 341.77
Fat: 5.19 grams
Saturated Fat: 0.97 grams
Carbohydrates: 55.57 grams
Sodium: 402.43 mg

1 tablespoon olive oil
1 onion, chopped
2 cloves garlic, minced
3 stalks celery, chopped
2 cups lentils, sorted
1 potato, peeled and
   chopped
4 cups water
3 cups Chicken Stock
   (page 137)
½ teaspoon dried thyme
   leaves
½ teaspoon dried
   marjoram leaves
½ teaspoon salt
⅛ teaspoon pepper

Calories: 411.44
Fat: 8.07 grams
Saturated Fat: 1.70 grams
Carbohydrates: 54.63 grams
Sodium: 509.33 mg

3 slices gluten-free bacon
1 tablespoon olive oil
2 shallots, minced
2 cloves garlic, minced
2 stalks celery, chopped
2 cups frozen corn
2 potatoes, peeled and
    cubed
4 cups water
½ teaspoon salt
⅛ teaspoon white pepper
½ teaspoon dried oregano
1 pound cod or haddock
    fillets, cubed
2 tablespoons cornstarch
¼ cup rice milk

milk   wheat   eggs   soy   nuts

Seafood Corn Chowder

If you use cooked, cubed ham or chicken instead of the seafood, this rich chowder can be served to those allergic to fish. Add ham or chicken at the same time you would add the fish.

1. In large saucepan, cook bacon until crisp; drain on paper towels, crumble, and set aside. Add olive oil to bacon fat remaining in pan.

2. Cook shallots and garlic for 3 minutes, then add celery, corn and potatoes. Cook and stir for 5 minutes.

3. Add water, salt, pepper, and oregano and bring to a boil. Reduce heat to low, cover pan, and simmer 15–20 minutes, or until potatoes are tender. Using a potato masher, mash some of the potatoes.

4. Add fish and bring back to a simmer. Cook 7–10 minutes, until fish is opaque. In small bowl, combine cornstarch and rice milk. Add to soup and simmer until thickened, about 4–5 minutes. Serve immediately.

milk wheat eggs fish nuts

Savory Minestrone

Minestrone is a thick vegetable soup that contains both legumes and pasta. It's a meal all in itself; just serve with a salad and some toasted bread.

1. In large soup pot, heat olive oil over medium heat. Add onion and garlic; cook and stir 4 minutes. Then add carrots and potatoes; cook and stir 5 minutes longer.

2. Add drained beans, tomatoes, and tomato paste and stir until paste dissolves. Add Broth, water, salt, pepper, basil, and oregano and bring to a boil. Reduce heat to low and simmer 25–30 minutes, or until vegetables are tender.

3. Add pasta and cook 7–9 minutes longer, or until pasta is tender. Sprinkle with cheese, if desired, and serve immediately.

Combining Proteins

Vegetarians must learn how to combine proteins to make sure they get all the amino acids their bodies need. Grains, legumes, and nuts all have certain amino acids, but none have complete proteins. So, you must combine grains and legumes, grains and nuts or seeds, or legumes and nuts or seeds in the foods you eat.

Serves 6–8

Calories: 336.69
Fat: 6.89 grams
Saturated Fat: 1.87 grams
Carbohydrates: 59.84 grams
Sodium: 580.93 mg

2 tablespoons olive oil
1 onion, chopped
3 cloves garlic, minced
3 carrots, sliced
2 potatoes, peeled and cubed
1 (15-ounce) can Great Northern Beans, drained
2 (14-ounce) cans gluten-free diced tomatoes, undrained
1 (6-ounce) can gluten-free tomato paste
3 cups Vegetable Broth (page 139)
3 cups water
½ teaspoon salt
¼ teaspoon pepper
1 teaspoon dried basil leaves
½ teaspoon dried oregano leaves
½ cup gluten-free shell pasta
⅓ cup grated, vegan, soy Parmesan cheese

Calories: 362.63
Fat: 10.88 grams
Saturated Fat: 3.31 grams
Carbohydrates: 45.39 grams
Sodium: 428.59 mg

½ pound ground, gluten-free pork sausage
1 onion, chopped
3 cloves garlic, minced
4 carrots, sliced
1½ cups red lentils, rinsed
4 cups Beef Stock (page 138)
2 cups water
2 bay leaves
1 teaspoon dried basil leaves
1 teaspoon dried oregano leaves
½ teaspoon salt
⅛ teaspoon pepper
1 (14-ounce) can gluten-free diced tomatoes, undrained
3 tablespoons gluten-free tomato paste

 milk wheat eggs soy fish nuts

Sausage Lentil Soup

Lentil soup is soothing and delicious, and can be made while you are busy doing other things around the house.

1. In large soup pot, cook sausage with onion and garlic over medium heat until sausage is browned, stirring to break up meat. Drain well, then add carrots; cook and stir 2 minutes longer.

2. Add lentils, stock, water, bay leaves, basil, oregano, salt, and pepper. Bring to a simmer. Cover, reduce heat to low, and simmer 1 hour.

3. Add diced tomatoes and tomato paste to the soup and stir until paste dissolves. Bring back to a simmer; simmer 20–30 minutes longer, or until lentils are tender. Remove bay leaves.

milk wheat eggs soy fish nuts

Bean and Bacon Soup

*Fresh rosemary adds a wonderful flavor
to this classic soup recipe.*

Serves 6

Calories: 328.19
Fat: 6.34 grams
Saturated Fat: 1.89 grams
Carbohydrates: 50.11
grams
Sodium: 839.93 mg

6 slices gluten-free bacon
1 onion, chopped
2 cloves garlic, minced
3 stalks celery, chopped
2 cups baby carrots
*1 tablespoon chopped
   fresh rosemary*
*2 (15-ounce) cans navy
   beans, drained*
*1 (6-ounce) can gluten-free
   tomato paste*
2 cups water
*4 cups Chicken Stock
   (page 137)*
⅛ teaspoon pepper

1. In large soup pot, cook bacon until crisp. Remove, drain on paper towels, crumble, and set aside.

2. Cook onion and garlic in bacon drippings until crisp-tender, about 5 minutes. Add celery, carrots, and rosemary; cook and stir 2–3 minutes longer.

3. Mash ½ cup of navy beans and add to pot with the rest of the beans; stir. Dissolve tomato paste in water and stir into the soup pot along with Stock and pepper.

4. Bring to a boil, then cover, reduce heat to low, and simmer 20–30 minutes, until vegetables are tender. Stir in bacon and simmer 3–4 minutes longer, then serve.

Allergy Alerts

You can subscribe to allergy alerts with your e-mail. Go to *http://www.foodallergy.org/mailinglist1.html* and sign up to be informed. You can find more information about food allergies at *www.immune.com/allergy/allabc.html#food*. Sometimes, ingredients like bacon have undeclared soy and wheat or other allergenic ingredients that are inadvertently added during processing. Even if the food has been safe in the past, manufacturers sometimes change products without notice.

Lemon Chicken Soup

This simple soup is fresh tasting and comforting, good for a cool evening or for when you have a cold.

Serves 4

Calories: 466.03
Fat: 13.33 grams
Saturated Fat: 2.71 grams
Carbohydrates: 41.61 grams
Sodium: 585.33 mg

2 tablespoons olive oil
1 onion, chopped
2 cloves garlic, minced
½ teaspoon salt
⅛ teaspoon white pepper
½ cup long-grain rice
1 teaspoon dried thyme leaves
4 cups Chicken Stock (page 137)
½ teaspoon grated lemon zest
1 pound boneless, skinless chicken breasts, cubed
2 cups frozen baby peas
2 tablespoons lemon juice

1. In large saucepan, heat olive oil over medium heat. Add onion and garlic; cook and stir until crisp-tender, about 5 minutes. Sprinkle with salt and pepper. Add rice and thyme; cook and stir 3 minutes longer.

2. Add Stock and zest; bring to a simmer. Cover and simmer 10 minutes, then add chicken. Simmer 10–12 minutes longer, until chicken is cooked.

3. Add peas and lemon juice; heat through until soup is hot, but do not simmer. Serve immediately.

milk wheat eggs fish nuts

Creamy Avocado Soup

Chilled soups are perfect on hot days.
This one is creamy, nutty, and rich.

1. In food processor or blender, combine avocados, lemon juice, green onion, salt, pepper, and 1 cup Chicken Stock; process until smooth.

2. Pour into large bowl. Stir in remaining Stock and Cheese with a wire whisk until smooth. Cover by placing plastic wrap directly on the surface of soup; chill 1–2 hours to blend flavors.

3. Just before serving, stir in tomatoes. Serve in chilled soup bowls.

Chilled Soups

Chilled soups should be made several hours ahead of time so the flavors have time to blend. They should be seasoned more strongly than hot soups because the cold temperature tends to diminish the flavor. Serve them with croutons made from any gluten-free bread: Cut the bread into cubes, toss with olive oil, and bake until golden.

Serves 4

Calories: 440.78
Fat: 26.51 grams
Saturated Fat: 5.24 grams
Carbohydrates: 44.38 grams
Sodium: 472.95 mg

3 avocados, peeled and
    cubed
2 tablespoons lemon juice
¼ cup chopped green
    onions
½ teaspoon salt
⅛ teaspoon white pepper
3 cups Chicken Stock
    (page 137)
½ cup Soy-Yogurt Cheese
    (page 70)
1 (14-ounce) can gluten-
    free diced tomatoes,
    drained

Calories: 386.79
Fat: 7.31 grams
Saturated Fat: 1.72 grams
Carbohydrates: 71.91 grams
Sodium: 849.53 mg

6 gluten-free bacon slices
1 onion, chopped
2 stalks celery, chopped
6 russet potatoes, peeled
3 cups Vegetable Broth
(page 139)
3 cups water
½ cup Cream-Soup Mix
(page 85)
1 cup rice milk
½ teaspoon salt
⅛ teaspoon white pepper
¼ cup minced flat-leaf parsley

milk wheat eggs fish nuts

Smashed Potato Stew

The secret to a good potato stew is salt.
Add it, tasting, until the flavor springs to life.

1. In large soup pot, cook bacon until crisp; drain, crumble, and set aside. Drain off all but 2 tablespoons bacon fat from pot.

2. Cook onion for 3 minutes in bacon fat. Add celery and potatoes; cook and stir 4 minutes longer. Add Broth and water; bring to a simmer. Reduce heat, cover, and simmer until potatoes are tender, about 20–25 minutes.

3. In small bowl, combine Soup Mix, rice milk, salt, and pepper and mix well. Add to pot. Using a potato masher, mash some of the potatoes, leaving some texture. Heat over low heat 5–10 minutes to blend flavors. Sprinkle with parsley and serve.

Condensed Soups

Glutino and Health Valley make a large selection of gluten-free foods. Glutino has some soup bases that, when reconstituted, replicate canned "cream of whatever" soups. If you read labels carefully, you might be able to find condensed soups with no gluten. Some brands to look for include Progresso and Campbell's.

milk wheat eggs fish nuts

Broccoli Chowder

Chowder is a good choice for a cold fall night. This soup can also be packed into a warmed thermos and put in lunchboxes.

1. In large soup pot, cook sausage with onion and garlic over medium heat, stirring to break up meat. When sausage is cooked, drain off fat.

2. Add carrots; cook and stir 4–5 minutes longer. Sprinkle with salt, pepper, and marjoram, then add Stock and water. Bring to a simmer and stir in rice. Bring back to a simmer and cook 10 minutes.

3. Add broccoli and rice milk; bring to a simmer and cook 10–12 minutes longer, or until rice and broccoli are tender. In small bowl, toss cheese with cornstarch or potato-starch flour. Add to soup and melt, stirring, until smooth. Do not boil. Serve immediately.

Serves 6

Calories: 364.84
Fat: 20.38 grams
Saturated Fat: 5.98 grams
Carbohydrates: 28.94 grams
Sodium: 525.35 mg

½ pound ground gluten-free pork sausage
1 onion, chopped
2 cloves garlic, minced
1 cup shredded carrots
½ teaspoon salt
⅛ teaspoon pepper
½ teaspoon dried marjoram leaves
4 cups Chicken Stock (page 137)
2 cups water
½ cup long-grain rice
1 (16-ounce) package frozen broccoli florets
1 cup rice or soy milk
1 cup shredded, dairy-free, vegan Monterey Jack cheese
1 tablespoon cornstarch or potato-starch flour

milk · wheat · eggs · soy · fish · nuts

Creamy Tomato Bisque

A little bit of sugar takes the edge off the acidity of the tomatoes in this easy and rich soup. Serve with some rice crackers and a spinach salad.

Serves 6

Calories: 143.80
Fat: 6.92 grams
Saturated Fat: 0.98 grams
Carbohydrates: 19.63 grams
Sodium: 549.09 mg

2 tablespoons olive oil
3 cloves garlic, minced
1 leek, trimmed and chopped
1 onion, chopped
4 fresh tomatoes, peeled and chopped
1 (14-ounce) can gluten-free diced tomatoes, undrained
4 tablespoons gluten-free tomato paste
2 cups Vegetable Broth (page 139)
½ teaspoon salt
⅛ teaspoon white pepper
½ teaspoon dried basil leaves
½ teaspoon dried thyme leaves
1 tablespoon lemon juice
1 teaspoon sugar
½ cup Evaporated Rice Milk (page 66)
Fresh basil leaves

1. In large soup pot, heat olive oil. Add garlic, leek, and onion; cook and stir until tender, about 5 minutes. Add fresh tomatoes; cook and stir 5 minutes.

2. Add canned tomatoes, tomato paste, Broth, salt, pepper, basil, and thyme. Bring to a simmer, then reduce heat to low and simmer 20–25 minutes, stirring occasionally, or until soup is slightly thickened.

3. Puree soup using an immersion blender. Add lemon juice, sugar, and Rice Milk; heat through but do not boil. Serve topped with fresh basil leaves.

Bisque

A bisque is a thick and creamy French soup that has some milk added and is flavored with herbs. It usually contains seafood. You can replicate the texture by adding some cornstarch or potato-starch flour dissolved in rice or soy milk. Use lighter herbs in this type of soup; basil, thyme, and dill are good choices.

milk   wheat   eggs   soy   fish   nuts

Pork and Veggie Stew

This hearty stew is rich and well flavored. Serve it with Seasoned Breadsticks (page 48) and Greens and Fruit Salad (page 89).

1. In 4- to 5-quart slow cooker, place onion, garlic, tomatoes, mushrooms, and potatoes. In medium bowl, toss pork with salt, pepper, and potato-starch flour to coat; add to slow cooker.

2. Add Stock, water, tomato paste, bay leaf, and thyme and mix well. Cover and cook on low 7–9 hours, until pork is tender and mixture is blended. Remove bay leaf and thyme stems and serve.

Serves 8

Calories: 284.95
Fat: 7.34 grams
Saturated Fat: 2.66 grams
Carbohydrates: 27.92 grams
Sodium: 499.89 mg

1 onion, chopped
3 cloves garlic, minced
6 plum tomatoes, chopped
1 (8-ounce) package
    mushrooms, sliced
2 potatoes, cubed
1½ pounds pork loin,
    cubed
½ teaspoon salt
⅛ teaspoon pepper
2 tablespoons potato-
    starch flour
4 cups Beef Stock (page
    138)
2 cups water
1 (6-ounce) can gluten-free
    tomato paste
1 bay leaf
2 sprigs fresh thyme

Chapter 8
Poultry

Serves 4

Calories: 242.43
Fat: 12.74 grams
Saturated Fat: 1.46 grams
Carbohydrates: 2.19 grams
Sodium: 236.57 mg

½ cup Ranch Salad
　Dressing (page 108)
2 tablespoons lemon juice
⅛ teaspoon pepper
4 boneless, skinless
　chicken breasts

Grilled Ranch Chicken

*This simple recipe makes chicken
that is moist and tender, with a lot of flavor.*

1. In glass baking dish, combine Dressing, lemon juice, and pepper and mix well. Add chicken breasts and turn to coat. Cover and marinate in refrigerator 3–4 hours.

2. Prepare and preheat grill. Remove chicken from marinade. Grill 6–8 minutes per side, turning once, until chicken reaches internal temperature of 165°F. Discard any remaining marinade.

Serves 6

Calories: 182.28
Fat: 3.43 grams
Saturated Fat: 0.93 grams
Carbohydrates: 9.48 grams
Sodium: 483.29 mg

6 boneless, skinless chicken
　breasts
1 (4-ounce) can chopped
　green chilies, drained
1 cup frozen corn
2 tomatoes, chopped
2 tablespoons lime juice
¼ cup chopped cilantro
½ teaspoon salt
⅛ teaspoon cayenne pepper
1 teaspoon cumin

Green Chili Chicken

*Cooking in parchment paper ensures that the chicken will be
tender and juicy. Parchment paper also holds in all the flavors.*

1. Preheat oven to 375°F. Cut six 12" squares of parchment paper and place on work surface. Place one chicken breast in center of each.

2. In medium bowl, combine chilies, corn, tomatoes, lime juice, cilantro, salt, pepper, and cumin and mix well. Divide on top of chicken.

3. Fold edges of parchment paper over chicken and crimp to close. Place on cookie sheet and bake until chicken is cooked and parchment paper is browned, about 25–35 minutes. Serve immediately.

milk · wheat · eggs · fish · nuts

Mustard Chicken Paillards

This simple method of cooking chicken can also be used with pork chops and fish fillets, if you aren't allergic to fish.

1. Preheat broiler. Place chicken breasts, smooth-side down, between two sheets of waxed paper. Using a meat mallet or rolling pin, gently pound from the center out, until chicken is ¼" thick.

2. Carefully place chicken, smooth-side down, on broiler pan. Broil 6" from heat 3 minutes, then turn with a spatula.

3. While chicken is broiling, combine remaining ingredients in small bowl. Spoon mixture over the chicken after it has been turned. Broil 2–4 minutes longer, or until mustard mixture has brown spots and chicken is thoroughly cooked. Serve immediately.

Paillards

Paillards (pronounced "pie-yards") are thinly pounded pieces of meat, usually made of boneless chicken, veal, beef, or turkey. The meat is placed between sheets of waxed paper to help protect the flesh while it is pounded, so it won't tear. This method produces tender meat that cooks very quickly.

Serves 4

Calories: 167.07
Fat: 3.53 grams
Saturated Fat: 0.87 grams
Carbohydrates: 3.74 grams
Sodium: 192.38 mg

4 boneless, skinless chicken breasts
3 tablespoons gluten-free mustard
½ teaspoon dried thyme leaves
¼ cup vegan soy yogurt
1 tablespoon lemon juice

Poached Chicken

Serves 8

Calories: 304.09
Fat: 11.57 grams
Saturated Fat: 3.15 grams
Carbohydrates: 0.41 grams
Sodium: 194.36 mg

1 tablespoon olive oil
1 onion, chopped
3 pounds chicken parts
2 carrots, sliced
3 cups water
½ teaspoon salt
1 bay leaf
½ teaspoon dried marjoram
   leaves
½ cup chopped celery
   leaves

Poached chicken can be served on its own, diced up into broth or stock, or used in salads and sandwiches. It freezes well, too.

1. In large soup pot, heat olive oil over medium heat. Add onion; cook and stir until onion starts to turn golden, about 8 minutes. Add chicken, skin-side down. Cook until browned, then turn chicken over.

2. Add all remaining ingredients to pot. Bring to a boil, then skim surface. Reduce heat to low, cover, and cook just below a simmer until chicken is thoroughly cooked, about 30–35 minutes. Remove chicken from liquid; let cool. Remove meat from bones; refrigerate or freeze.

3. The stock can be strained, then saved for soup.

Poaching

Poaching is a cooking technique where food is cooked in a liquid at a temperature just below a simmer. The French say that the liquid or broth is "smiling." It's important to carefully regulate the heat so the exterior of the meat doesn't overcook by the time the interior comes to a safe temperature.

wheat   eggs   soy   fish   nuts

Cornmeal-Crusted Chicken

Make this dairy free by using soy milk instead of buttermilk!

Serves 8

Calories: 420.34
Fat: 23.19 grams
Saturated Fat: 6.57 grams
Carbohydrates: 7.97 grams
Sodium: 428.34 mg

3 pounds whole chicken, with skin on, cut up
2 cups buttermilk
½ cup cornmeal
¼ cup superfine rice flour
3 tablespoons cornstarch
1 teaspoon salt
1 teaspoon pepper
1 teaspoon onion powder
½ teaspoon garlic powder

1. Place chicken in large glass baking dish and pour buttermilk over. Cover and refrigerate at least 8 hours.

2. When ready to bake, preheat oven to 375°F. Line a large baking sheet with heavy-duty foil and spray the foil with nonstick gluten-free cooking spray; set aside.

3. In shallow bowl, combine all remaining ingredients and mix well. Remove chicken from buttermilk; shake off excess (discard buttermilk). Dredge chicken in the cornmeal mixture to coat.

4. Place chicken, skin-side up, on prepared baking sheet. Bake 45–55 minutes, or until chicken is thoroughly cooked and coating is deep golden brown. Let stand 5 minutes before serving.

Buttermilk

Buttermilk is a wonderful marinade for chicken; it tenderizes and adds moisture, so the chicken is juicy when cooked. Buttermilk is acidic, so it breaks down the protein bonds in the chicken. You can make vegan buttermilk by adding 1 tablespoon lemon juice to 2 cups of soy or rice milk; let stand for 10 minutes, stir, and use.

Calories: 464.30
Fat: 18.84 grams
Saturated Fat: 3.16 grams
Carbohydrates: 29.78 grams
Sodium: 469.38 mg

4 boneless, skinless chicken breasts, cubed
½ teaspoon salt
⅛ teaspoon pepper
2 tablespoons extra-virgin olive oil
1½ cups Tomato Sauce (page 81)
1 (16-ounce) package gluten-free pasta
½ cup Basil Pesto (page 77)

Calories: 251.00
Fat: 14.47 grams
Saturated Fat: 3.91 grams
Carbohydrates: 1.56 grams
Sodium: 343.49 mg

6 boneless, skinless chicken breasts
2 tablespoons lime juice
1 teaspoon dried basil leaves
½ teaspoon salt
⅛ teaspoon pepper
¼ teaspoon garlic powder
1 tablespoon olive oil
½ cup Basil Pesto (page 77)
¼ cup dairy-free vegan sour cream

milk wheat eggs fish nuts

Chicken with Penne

This well-flavored dish is quick and easy to make; it only uses five ingredients!

1. Bring a large pot of water to a boil. Sprinkle chicken with salt and pepper. In heavy skillet, heat olive oil; add chicken. Cook and stir 4–5 minutes, or until chicken is almost cooked.

2. Add Tomato Sauce to the chicken and bring to a simmer. Reduce heat and simmer while you cook pasta according to package directions.

3. When chicken is thoroughly cooked and pasta is al dente, drain pasta and add to skillet. Remove from heat; gently stir in Pesto. Serve immediately.

milk wheat eggs fish nuts

Grilled Pesto Chicken

This simple dish can be served with a fresh salsa instead of the basil mixture if you prefer.

1. Place chicken breasts in large glass dish. Sprinkle with lime juice, basil, salt, pepper, garlic powder, and olive oil; rub to coat. Let stand at room temperature 30 minutes.

2. Prepare and preheat grill. Meanwhile, in small bowl combine Pesto and sour cream; mix and refrigerate.

3. Grill chicken on oiled rack, turning once, 10–13 minutes, until chicken is thoroughly cooked with an internal temperature of 165°F. Place chicken on serving plate and top each with a spoonful of Pesto mixture. Serve with remaining Pesto mixture.

milk wheat eggs soy fish nuts

Chicken Risotto

Risotto is usually made using Arborio rice, but you can make it with plain long-grain rice if you'd like.

Serves 6

Calories: 417.55
Fat: 12.13 grams
Saturated Fat: 2.43 grams
Carbohydrates: 45.73 grams
Sodium: 400.18 mg

5 cups Chicken Stock (page 137)
3 boneless, skinless chicken breasts
½ teaspoon salt
⅛ teaspoon white pepper
3 tablespoons olive oil
1 onion, chopped
1 (8-ounce) package mushrooms, chopped
1½ cups long-grain rice
½ teaspoon dried thyme leaves
½ cup dry white wine, or more Stock

1. Place Stock in a medium saucepan and place on stove over low heat. Cut chicken into 1" pieces and sprinkle with salt and pepper. Heat olive oil in large heavy saucepan. Add chicken; cook and stir until almost cooked through, about 5–6 minutes. Remove chicken from pan and set aside.

2. Add onion and mushrooms to drippings remaining in saucepan; cook and stir until crisp-tender, about 4 minutes. Add rice and thyme leaves; cook and stir 2–3 minutes longer.

3. Add wine or Stock; cook and stir until liquid is absorbed, about 5 minutes. Add warm Stock, ½ cup at a time, stirring after each addition until rice absorbs liquid.

4. When you have added 3 cups of Stock, return chicken to saucepan. Continue adding Stock, stirring frequently, until liquid is absorbed.

5. When the mixture is creamy and rice is done, but still has a bit of texture to the center, remove from heat and serve immediately.

Mushrooms

Surprisingly, since they grow in the dark, mushrooms are a good source of Vitamin D. To prepare them, don't rinse or wash them or they will become tough. They grow in sterile soil, so just wipe them with a damp paper towel or mushroom brush. Cut off the bottoms of the stems and discard because they can be tough, then slice or chop.

milk   wheat   eggs   fish   nuts

Chicken Fried Rice

Serves 4

Calories: 417.43
Fat: 12.60 grams
Saturated Fat: 2.97 grams
Carbohydrates: 33.44 grams
Sodium: 504.75 mg

1 tablespoon olive oil
1 onion, chopped
2 cloves garlic, minced
1 tablespoon grated ginger root
2 cups cold, cooked rice
1 cup frozen baby peas
2 cups chopped Poached Chicken (page 156)
2 tablespoons low-sodium soy sauce
3 tablespoons Chicken Stock (page 137)
½ teaspoon dried thyme leaves
⅛ teaspoon white pepper

Have everything ready before you start stir-frying, as the process is very quick. All the ingredients have to be prepared ahead of time.

1. Heat olive oil in large skillet. Add onion and garlic; stir-fry 4–5 minutes, until crisp-tender. Add ginger, rice, and peas; stir-fry 3–4 minutes longer.

2. Add chicken; stir-fry until chicken is hot, about 3–5 minutes longer. Stir in soy sauce, Stock, thyme, and pepper. Stir-fry until rice absorbs the liquid and food is hot, about 3–4 minutes. Serve immediately.

Adding More Nutrients

Brown rice is higher in fiber than its processed counterpart, white rice. It might take some time to get used to the taste of brown rice, so make the change gradually. Cook brown and white rice together, and slowly increase the ratio of brown rice to white rice until you've eliminated the white rice from your diet entirely.

milk wheat eggs soy fish nuts

Chicken Paillards with Zucchini

Serves 4

Calories: 278.43
Fat: 11.25 grams
Saturated Fat: 2.15 grams
Carbohydrates: 12.97 grams
Sodium: 390.32 mg

This simple chicken dish is healthy and beautiful, too. Serve with a green salad drizzled with Ranch Salad Dressing (page 108).

1. Place chicken, smooth-side down, between sheets of plastic wrap. Using a rolling pin or meat mallet, pound chicken until about ⅓" thick. Remove plastic wrap; sprinkle chicken with cornstarch, salt, pepper, and thyme.

2. In large saucepan, heat olive oil over medium-high heat. Add chicken; cook, turning once, until cooked through, about 4–5 minutes per side. Remove chicken from pan and keep warm.

3. Add onion to saucepan; cook and stir until crisp-tender, about 4 minutes. Add zucchini; cook and stir 4 minutes longer. Return chicken to pan and add basil, Stock, and grape tomatoes. Bring to a simmer; cook 2–3 minutes. Serve immediately.

4 boneless, skinless chicken breasts
2 tablespoons cornstarch
½ teaspoon salt
⅛ teaspoon pepper
½ teaspoon dried thyme leaves
2 tablespoons olive oil
1 onion, chopped
1 zucchini, sliced
3 tablespoons torn fresh basil leaves
¼ cup Chicken Stock (page 137)
2 cups grape tomatoes

Zucchini

Zucchini is a mild vegetable with high water and fiber contents. It is delicious eaten raw with appetizer dips and on sandwiches, and good in stir-fries and soups. Look for smaller zucchini with tender skin and those that are heavy for their size. Zucchini will keep in the refrigerator for 3–4 days after purchase.

Calories: 407.84
Fat: 14.02 grams
Saturated Fat: 3.13 grams
Carbohydrates: 38.73 grams
Sodium: 526.46 mg

2 tablespoons olive oil
3 boneless, skinless chicken breasts, cubed
2 tablespoons millet flour
½ teaspoon salt
⅛ teaspoon pepper
½ teaspoon dried thyme leaves
1 onion, chopped
2 cloves garlic, minced
½ cup Chicken Stock (page 137)
½ cup rice or soy milk
1 (3-ounce) package dairy-free, vegan cream cheese, softened
1 cup frozen baby peas, thawed
¼ cup grated dairy-free, vegan Parmesan cheese
2 cups cooked brown rice

milk   wheat   eggs   fish   nuts

Creamy Chicken over Rice

This creamy main dish is pure comfort food. Serve it on a cold night with some cooked carrots and a fruit salad.

1. Place olive oil in large skillet over medium heat. Toss chicken with flour, salt, pepper, and thyme and add to skillet. Cook and stir until browned, about 4–5 minutes. Remove chicken from skillet and set aside.

2. Add onion and garlic to skillet; cook and stir until tender, about 5 minutes. Return chicken to skillet along with Stock and rice or soy milk; bring to a simmer. Cut cream cheese into cubes; add to skillet along with peas.

3. Cook and stir until cream cheese melts into the sauce, chicken is tender, and peas are hot. Add Parmesan cheese and stir. Serve immediately over brown rice.

milk wheat eggs fish nuts

Chicken Ranch Pizza

This unusual pizza has fantastic flavor. You could also use left-over Thanksgiving turkey in place of the chicken.

1. Preheat oven to 400°F. In medium bowl, combine chicken, bacon, tomatoes, peas, and Salad Dressing and mix gently.

2. Place Pizza Crust on cookie sheet. Top with chicken mixture, then sprinkle with cheeses. Bake 20–30 minutes, or until hot and bubbly. Let stand 5 minutes, then cut into wedges to serve.

Prebaking Pizza Crust

Most pizza crusts hold up better and won't get soggy if they are prebaked. This just means you bake the dough for 5–8 minutes at a fairly high temperature just until it is firm, before it starts browning. You can make several batches of pizza dough, prebake them, then freeze for later use. Just top and bake whenever you want.

Serves 6

Calories: 439.82
Fat: 18.71 grams
Saturated Fat: 3.64 grams
Carbohydrates: 48.99 grams
Sodium: 521.81 mg

2 cups cubed Poached Chicken (page 156)
3 slices gluten-free bacon, cooked crisp and crumbled
1 cup chopped tomatoes
1 cup frozen baby peas, thawed
½ cup Ranch Salad Dressing (page 108)
1 Pizza Crust (page 63), prebaked
1 cup shredded dairy-free, vegan mozzarella cheese
¼ cup grated dairy-free, vegan Parmesan cheese

Easy Chicken Spaghetti

Serves 6

Calories: 376.74
Fat: 12.25 grams
Saturated Fat: 4.29 grams
Carbohydrates: 51.22 grams
Sodium: 431.30 mg

2 tablespoons olive oil
1 leek, peeled and sliced
1 (8-ounce) package sliced mushrooms
1 yellow summer squash or zucchini, sliced
2 cups chopped cooked Brined Grilled Chicken (page 167), chopped
1 (12-ounce) package gluten-free rice spaghetti
1 (3-ounce) package dairy-free, vegan cream cheese
⅓ cup rice or soy milk
¼ cup grated gluten-free, vegan Parmesan cheese

Spaghetti without tomato sauce!
This creamy version is light and healthy, good to serve
with a fruit salad and a chocolate cake for dessert.

1. Bring a large pot of water to a boil. Meanwhile, heat olive oil in large skillet. Add leeks; cook and stir until crisp-tender, about 5 minutes. Add mushrooms and summer squash; cook and stir 3–5 minutes longer, until tender. Stir in chicken and heat, stirring frequently.

2. Cook pasta according to package directions. While chicken heats, combine cream cheese and milk in small microwave-safe bowl. Microwave on 50 percent power 2 minutes, then stir with a whisk until sauce blends. Stir into chicken mixture.

3. When pasta is al dente, drain, reserving some pasta cooking water. Add spaghetti to chicken mixture; toss to coat, adding reserved water if necessary to make a sauce. Sprinkle with Parmesan cheese and serve immediately.

milk   wheat   eggs   fish   nuts

Spicy Chicken Burgers

Adjust the cayenne pepper and chili powder in this easy recipe to your family's tastes. Serve on toasted Focaccia Rolls (page 56) or plain with whipped potatoes.

Serves 4
_____

Calories: 403.07
Fat: 21.45 grams
Saturated Fat: 5.17 grams
Carbohydrates: 13.31 grams
Sodium: 445.25 mg

1 tablespoon olive oil
½ onion, chopped
½ cup minced leek
½ cup grated carrot
1 slice French Bread,
    crumbled (page 51)
2 tablespoons mustard
½ teaspoon salt
⅛ teaspoon cayenne
    pepper
2 teaspoons chili powder
½ teaspoon cumin
1¼ pounds ground gluten-
    free chicken

1. Prepare and preheat grill. In small skillet, heat olive oil over medium heat. Add onion and leek; cook and stir until tender, about 5 minutes. Add carrot; cook and stir another 2 minutes.

2. Remove from heat and place in large bowl. Add crumbled Bread, mustard, salt, pepper, chili powder, and cumin and mix well. Add chicken; mix gently but thoroughly with hands.

3. Form into 4 patties; chill for 30 minutes. Grill patties 6" from medium coals, turning once, 10–13 minutes, or until internal temperature registers 165°F. Serve immediately.

Ground Chicken

It may be difficult to find ground chicken in your supermarket. You can buy chicken breasts and thighs and ask the butcher to grind it, or you can do it yourself in a food processor. Cut the chicken into 1" pieces and grind briefly. Do not overprocess or the finished product will be mushy. Use the ground chicken within 1 day, or freeze it.

Calories: 360.40
Fat: 15.84 grams
Saturated Fat: 4.88 grams
Carbohydrates: 30.18 grams
Sodium: 375.04 mg

1 pound boneless, skinless chicken breasts
½ teaspoon salt
⅛ teaspoon pepper
1 tablespoon potato-starch flour
2 tablespoons olive oil
1 tablespoon lemon juice
1 onion, chopped
1 yellow bell pepper, chopped
1 (15-ounce) can Great Northern beans, drained
1 cup gluten-free salsa
8 corn taco shells
2 cups shredded lettuce
1 cup grape tomatoes
½ cup dairy-free, vegan sour cream
1 cup shredded dairy-free, vegan Cheddar cheese

milk wheat eggs fish nuts

Chicken and Bean Tacos

*Read the package on the taco shells to be
sure they are gluten-free. Let your family assemble their
own tacos so they can pick their own toppings.*

1. Heat oven to 350°F. Cut chicken into 1" cubes and sprinkle with salt, pepper, and potato-starch flour. Heat olive oil in large skillet and add chicken. Cook and stir until almost cooked, about 4 minutes; remove from skillet and sprinkle with lemon juice.

2. Add onion and bell pepper to skillet; cook and stir 4–5 minutes, or until crisp-tender. Return chicken to skillet along with beans and salsa; bring to a simmer. Simmer until chicken is cooked, about 3–5 minutes longer.

3. Meanwhile, heat taco shells as directed on package. When shells are hot, make tacos with chicken mixture, lettuce, tomatoes, sour cream, and cheese. Serve immediately.

milk   wheat   eggs   soy   fish   nuts

Brined Grilled Chicken

*Brining adds great flavor to chicken breasts
and keeps them exceptionally moist.*

Serves 6

Calories: 156.04
Fat: 3.89 grams
Saturated Fat: 0.99 grams
Carbohydrates: 0.94
grams
Sodium: 364.54 mg

1. Place chicken breasts, skin-side down, in large glass baking dish. In medium bowl, combine salt and sugar. Add 1 cup water, stirring to dissolve salt and sugar. Add 2 cups more water and mix. Pour over chicken breasts; add remaining 3 cups water. Cover and refrigerate 3–4 hours.

2. When ready to cook, prepare and preheat grill. In small bowl, combine remaining ingredients and mix well. Remove chicken from brine; discard brine. Loosen skin from chicken breasts and rub half of the garlic mixture onto the flesh. Smooth skin back over chicken.

3. Rub remaining garlic mixture over chicken skin. Let stand 15 minutes. Place skin-side down on grill, 6" from medium coals. Cover and grill 8 minutes, then turn. Cover and grill 5 minutes longer, then check chicken. Rearrange on grill, cover, and grill 7–9 minutes longer, or until meat thermometer registers 170°F.

*6 bone-in, skin-on chicken
breasts
3 tablespoons salt
2 tablespoons sugar
6 cups water
2 tablespoons lemon juice
4 cloves garlic, minced
2 shallots, minced
1 teaspoon dried oregano
leaves
¼ teaspoon cayenne
pepper
3 tablespoons gluten-free
tomato paste
2 tablespoons olive oil*

Brining Chicken

Use less salt and sugar and brine for a longer time for a more evenly flavored and juicy chicken. Too much salt can result in the outer layer of flesh becoming salty and tough. Brine for only the recommended time, and do not rinse the chicken after brining. Sugar is used in brine because it helps the chicken brown when it's cooked.

Calories: 457.34
Fat: 9.43 grams
Saturated Fat: 2.19 grams
Carbohydrates: 66.94 grams
Sodium: 308.69 mg

3 boneless, skinless chicken breasts
½ teaspoon salt
⅛ teaspoon cayenne pepper
2 tablespoons potato-starch flour
2 tablespoons olive oil
⅓ cup sliced green onion
1 cup sliced mushrooms
1 pound fresh asparagus, cut into 1" pieces
1 (12-ounce) package gluten-free rice spaghetti
1 tablespoon lemon juice
⅓ cup grated dairy-free, vegan Parmesan cheese

milk wheat eggs fish nuts

Chicken Asparagus Pasta

Chicken and asparagus taste like spring, especially when flavored with lemon juice. This is a good recipe for a last-minute meal.

1. Bring a large pot of water to a boil. Meanwhile, cut chicken into 1" cubes. Toss with salt, pepper, and flour.

2. In large skillet, heat olive oil over medium heat. Add chicken; cook and stir until browned but not cooked through, about 4–5 minutes. Remove chicken from skillet and set aside.

3. Add green onions, mushrooms, and asparagus to skillet. Cook and stir until crisp-tender, about 4–6 minutes. Meanwhile, cook pasta according to package directions.

4. Return chicken to skillet along with a ladle of pasta cooking water and lemon juice. Bring to a simmer, then simmer 3–6 minutes, until chicken is thoroughly cooked and vegetables are tender.

5. Drain pasta and add to skillet. Cook and stir 1–2 minutes to blend flavors. Sprinkle with cheese and serve immediately.

milk wheat eggs fish nuts

Chicken Pesto Toss

This simple recipe is very satisfying. Keep the Pesto and Stock on hand in your freezer, and you can make this recipe in minutes.

1. Cut chicken into ½" thick strips across the breast. Toss with potato-starch flour, salt, and pepper.

2. In large skillet, heat olive oil over medium heat. Add chicken; cook, stirring occasionally, until browned, about 5–6 minutes. Remove chicken from skillet.

3. Add onion and garlic to skillet; cook and stir until crisp-tender, about 4 minutes. Add bell pepper and summer squash; cook and stir for 3 minutes longer.

4. Add green beans and chicken to skillet. Add Chicken Stock and mix well; bring to a simmer. Simmer, stirring frequently, until vegetables are tender and chicken is thoroughly cooked. Stir in Pesto and serve immediately.

Quick-Cooking Vegetables

Some quick-cooking vegetables you could substitute in many recipes include zucchini, mushrooms, bell peppers, summer squash, green onions, and dark, leafy greens. If a recipe calls for any of these, you can substitute the others, according to your taste. Make sure all of the vegetables are about the same size so they cook evenly.

Serves 4

Calories: 394.24
Fat: 21.55 grams
Saturated Fat: 3.54 grams
Carbohydrates: 20.12 grams
Sodium: 384.84 mg

4 boneless, skinless chicken breasts
2 tablespoons potato-starch flour
¼ teaspoon salt
⅛ teaspoon pepper
2 tablespoons olive oil
1 onion, chopped
2 cloves garlic, minced
1 red bell pepper, chopped
1 yellow summer squash, sliced
2 cups frozen green beans, thawed
½ cup Chicken Stock (page 137)
½ cup Basil Pesto (page 77)

Serves 6

Calories: 454.06
Fat: 17.55 grams
Saturated Fat: 4.79 grams
Carbohydrates: 3.05 grams
Sodium: 199.12 mg

1 lemon
1 (3–4 pound) whole
*   chicken*
1 teaspoon salt
¼ teaspoon white pepper
1 tablespoon honey
½ cup Chicken Stock,
*   divided (page 137)*

Roasted Lemon Chicken

*A perfectly roasted chicken is a treat any day of the week.
You can thicken the pan juices with some
cornstarch and serve it with the chicken.*

1. Cut lemon in half; remove zest and juice one half. Place unjuiced half inside chicken cavity.

2. In small bowl, combine lemon juice, zest, salt, pepper, honey, and 2 tablespoons of Stock. Pour half into the chicken cavity, and pour rest over chicken. Cover and refrigerate 2 hours.

3. Preheat oven to 350°F. Place chicken breast-side down in a roasting pan. Pour marinade over chicken, then pour rest of Stock over all. Roast 30 minutes, then turn chicken.

4. Roast, basting occasionally with pan juices, 30–40 minutes longer, or until skin is golden brown and meat thermometer inserted into thigh registers 180°F. Let chicken stand 5 minutes. Slice to serve.

Chapter 9
Beef Entrées

Mustard Steak Wraps

Mustard is a natural partner to steak. Combine that with some fresh vegetables, and you have a wonderful, easy-to-make sandwich.

Serves 4

Calories: 200.99
Fat: 6.99 grams
Saturated Fat: 2.89 grams
Carbohydrates: 17.19 grams
Sodium: 201.51 mg

2 Savory Grilled Steaks
  (page 172)
1 yellow bell pepper
1 green bell pepper
½ cup red onion, chopped
2 tomatoes, chopped
6 (6-inch) corn tortillas
3 tablespoons gluten-free
  Dijon mustard
1 (3-ounce) package dairy-
  free, vegan cream
  cheese, softened
6 lettuce leaves

1. If Steaks are cold, let stand at room temperature 30 minutes, no longer. Then slice thinly across the grain.

2. Cut bell peppers into thin strips. Combine in medium bowl with Steak slices, red onion, and tomatoes; toss to mix.

3. Place tortillas on work surface. In small bowl, combine mustard and cream cheese and mix well. Spread onto tortillas.

4. Top with lettuce leaves, then Steak mixture. Roll up. Serve immediately.

Savory Grilled Steaks

Marinating steaks adds to their flavor and helps tenderize the meat by breaking down fibers with acidic ingredients.

Serves 6

Calories: 275.32
Fat: 10.38 grams
Saturated Fat: 3.46 grams
Carbohydrates: 1.60 grams
Sodium: 183.54 mg

2 garlic cloves, minced
2 tablespoons gluten-free
  tomato paste
1 tablespoon olive oil
3 tablespoons gluten-free
  balsamic vinegar
¼ teaspoon pepper
1 tablespoon Soy Sauce
  Substitute (page 82)
6 (6-ounce) sirloin steaks

1. In large zip-top, heavy-duty food-storage bag, combine all ingredients except steaks; seal and knead to blend. Add steaks and turn to coat. Place bag in glass bowl; refrigerate 3–4 hours.

2. When ready to eat, prepare and preheat grill. Remove steaks from marinade; discard marinade. Grill steaks 6" from medium coals 4–8 minutes on each side, until food thermometer registers at least 145°F, turning once.

3. Remove steaks from grill and cover with foil. Let stand 5–10 minutes before serving.

wheat soy fish nuts

Meatballs

Make a batch or two of these meatballs and freeze them to make your own submarine sandwiches, or add them to pasta sauce.

1. Preheat oven to 350°F. In small saucepan, heat olive oil over medium heat. Add onion and garlic; cook and stir until tender, about 6 minutes. Place in large bowl and let stand 10 minutes.

2. Add basil, oregano, thyme, Stock, and Bread crumbs; mix well. Add beef; mix gently but thoroughly with hands until combined. Form into 18 meatballs.

3. Place meatballs on a cookie sheet with sides. Bake 25–35 minutes, or until meatballs are browned and cooked through.

Freezing Meatballs

Meatballs freeze very well, before or after cooking. Make a batch or two to have on hand so you can have spaghetti and meatballs at a moment's notice. If cooked, cool the meatballs completely and freeze in a single layer on a cookie sheet. Pack in hard-sided freezer containers, label, seal, and freeze up to 6 months.

Yields 18 meatballs

Calories: 91.19
Fat: 3.45 grams
Saturated Fat: 1.18 grams
Carbohydrates: 4.94 grams
Sodium: 38.81 mg

1 tablespoon olive oil
1 onion, finely minced
2 cloves garlic, minced
½ teaspoon dried basil leaves
½ teaspoon dried oregano leaves
½ teaspoon dried thyme leaves
½ cup Beef Stock (page 138)
2 slices Light White Batter Bread, crumbled (page 50)
1¼ pounds 90 percent lean ground beef

milk   wheat   eggs   soy   fish   nuts

Beef Piccata

Piccata is usually made with chicken or veal,
but beef is a nice twist on a classic.

Serves 4

Calories: 392.51
Fat: 16.86 grams
Saturated Fat: 4.60 grams
Carbohydrates: 13.94 grams
Sodium: 396.36 mg

4 (6-ounce) top round steaks
3 tablespoons rice milk
2 tablespoons potato-starch flour
2 tablespoons cornstarch
½ teaspoon pepper
½ teaspoon salt
½ teaspoon paprika
2 tablespoons olive oil
1 (8-ounce) package mushrooms, sliced
3 cloves garlic, minced
1 cup Beef Stock (page 138)
¼ cup dry red wine, if desired
3 tablespoons water
1 tablespoons cornstarch

1. Place beef between sheets of waxed paper and pound gently with meat mallet or rolling pin to slightly flatten. Place rice milk in a shallow bowl. In another shallow bowl, combine potato-starch flour, cornstarch, pepper, salt, and paprika.

2. Dip beef into milk, then into flour mixture to coat. In large saucepan, heat olive oil over medium-high heat. Add beef; brown on both sides, turning once, about 5–6 minutes. Remove from pan.

3. Add mushrooms and garlic to pan; cook and stir until tender, about 5–6 minutes. Add Stock and wine and bring to a simmer. Return steaks to pan; simmer 15–25 minutes, or until beef is tender.

4. In small bowl, combine water and cornstarch and mix well. Add to saucepan; cook and stir until sauce is slightly thickened. Serve immediately.

milk wheat eggs fish nuts

Taco Pasta

This hearty and flavorful dish can be made spicier if you add more jalapeño peppers or chili powder. Season to taste!

Serves 6–8

Calories: 372.24
Fat: 10.78 grams
Saturated Fat: 4.97 grams
Carbohydrates: 47.40 grams
Sodium: 438.90 mg

1. Bring a large pot of water to a boil. In large saucepan, cook ground beef with onion and garlic, stirring to break up meat, until beef is browned. Drain thoroughly. Add bell pepper and jalapeño peppers to saucepan; cook and stir 1 minute longer.

2. Add tomatoes, tomato sauce, tomato juice, and Seasoning Mix to the saucepan; stir to combine. Bring to a boil, reduce heat to low, and simmer 15–20 minutes.

3. When sauce is almost cooked, cook spaghetti in the water according to package directions until al dente. Drain well and place on serving plate. Top with beef mixture. Sprinkle with corn chips and cheese; serve with sour cream.

1 pound gluten-free ground beef
1 onion, chopped
4 cloves garlic, minced
1 green bell pepper, chopped
1–2 jalapeño peppers, minced
1 (14-ounce) can gluten-free diced tomatoes, undrained
1 (8-ounce) can gluten-free tomato sauce
½ cup tomato juice
2 tablespoons Taco Seasoning Mix (page 80)
1 (12-ounce) package gluten-free rice spaghetti
½ cup crushed corn chips
½ cup shredded dairy-free, vegan extra-sharp Cheddar cheese
½ cup vegan sour cream

Make It Spicy

For spicier foods, use habanero or Scotch Bonnet peppers instead of jalapeños. The smaller the pepper, the more heat it has. The heat of the pepper, called capsaicin, is mostly contained in the membranes and seeds of the peppers. For a milder taste, remove the membranes and seeds before chopping or mincing.

Microwave Meatloaf

Serves 4

Calories: 286.19
Fat: 9.65 grams
Saturated Fat: 3.97 grams
Carbohydrates: 15.32 grams
Sodium: 546.17 mg

3 slices gluten-free bacon
½ cup Tomato Sauce (page 81), divided
2 tablespoons gluten-free apple cider vinegar
2 tablespoons brown sugar
1 tablespoon gluten-free mustard
½ cup cooked rice
¼ cup minced green onion
¼ teaspoon salt
⅛ teaspoon pepper
½ teaspoon dried basil leaves
1 pound gluten-free ground beef

Making meatloaf in the microwave is fun and easy.
You can flavor this basic recipe any way you'd like.

1. Place bacon on microwave-safe plate and top with a paper towel. Microwave on 100 percent power 4 minutes, then rotate and microwave 1–2 minutes longer. Let bacon stand 2 minutes; drain and crumble.

2. In medium bowl, combine crumbled bacon with ¼ cup Tomato Sauce, vinegar, brown sugar, and mustard and mix well. Add rice, green onion, salt, pepper, and basil, and stir. Let stand 10 minutes. Then add beef; mix with hands until combined.

3. Form into a loaf and place in a 1½ quart microwave-safe dish. Microwave on high 10 minutes, then carefully drain off fat. Return to microwave and cook on high 5–7 minutes longer, until internal temperature registers 160°F.

4. Remove from microwave, add remaining ¼ cup Tomato Sauce for glaze, cover with foil, and let stand on solid surface 5 minutes. Slice and serve.

milk　wheat　eggs　soy　fish　nuts

Marinated Flank Steak

Flank steak is tender, juicy, and succulent when marinated and cooked until medium or medium-well.

1. In large zip-top food-storage bag, combine all ingredients except flank steak. Add steak, seal bag, and knead bag gently to mix.

2. Place bag in large pan and refrigerate 18–24 hours, turning bag occasionally.

3. When ready to eat, prepare and preheat grill. Remove steak from marinade; discard marinade. Grill steak 6" from medium coals 12–16 minutes, turning once, until desired doneness. Cover and let stand 5 minutes. Slice across grain to serve.

Flank Steak

Flank steak has a clearly defined grain running through the meat. This looks like fine lines in the flesh. When you cut flank steak, whether you're cutting it before cooking or after, it must be cut against the grain. That means you should make your cuts perpendicular to the lines in the meat.

Serves 4

Calories: 302.20
Fat: 11.55 grams
Saturated Fat: 4.79 grams
Carbohydrates: 1.50 grams
Sodium: 135.92 mg

⅓ cup dry red wine
2 tablespoons brown sugar
1 tablespoon honey
2 tablespoons Beef Stock (page 138)
2 cloves garlic, minced
1 onion, minced
1 jalapeño pepper, minced, if desired
⅛ teaspoon pepper
½ teaspoon salt
1½ pounds flank steak

milk wheat eggs soy fish nuts

Grilled Steak Salad

Any fresh vegetable adds flavor, nutrition, and color to this pretty salad; use sliced mushrooms or sugar snap peas if you'd like.

Serves 4

Calories: 272.54
Fat: 17.51 grams
Saturated Fat: 3.44 grams
Carbohydrates: 5.69 grams
Sodium: 222.56 mg

2 Savory Grilled Steaks
   (page 172)
1 red bell pepper, chopped
1 cucumber, peeled and
   sliced
4 cups baby spinach leaves
2 cups watercress
½ cup Oil and Vinegar
   Dressing (page 104)

1. If Steaks are cold, let stand at room temperature 30 minutes, no longer. Slice Steaks thinly against the grain. Combine in serving bowl with bell pepper, cucumber, spinach, and watercress.

2. Drizzle half of the Dressing over the salad and toss to coat. Serve with remaining Dressing on the side.

milk wheat eggs soy fish nuts

Tomato Beef Burgers

Tomatoes in the burgers add great flavor and moisture. Serve these with plenty of ketchup and mustard.

Serves 4

Calories: 416.54
Fat: 12.11 grams
Saturated Fat: 3.94 grams
Carbohydrates: 44.06 grams
Sodium: 737.33 mg

¼ cup cooked rice
¼ cup chopped tomatoes
2 tablespoons gluten-free
   ketchup
1 tablespoon water
½ teaspoon salt
⅛ teaspoon cayenne pepper
1 pound gluten-free ground
   beef
4 Focaccia Rolls (page 56)
4 slices tomato
4 slices butter lettuce

1. In medium bowl, combine rice, tomatoes, ketchup, water, salt, and cayenne pepper and mix well. Let stand 10 minutes.

2. Add beef and mix lightly but thoroughly. Shape into 4 patties and refrigerate. Prepare and preheat grill. Cook burgers 6" from medium coals, turning once, 9–14 minutes, or until well done.

3. Serve on toasted Focaccia Rolls with tomato slices and lettuce. Add any condiment you'd like, including pickles, ketchup, mustard, and Eggless Mayonnaise (page 68).

milk wheat eggs soy fish nuts

Asian Steaks

Asian flavors infuse this tender steak. Serve it with some fried rice, a napa cabbage salad, and fresh fruit for dessert.

1. In large zip-top food-storage bag, combine all ingredients except flank steak. Add steak, seal bag, and knead bag gently to mix.

2. Place bag in large pan and refrigerate 18–24 hours, turning bag occasionally.

3. When ready to eat, prepare and preheat grill. Remove steak from marinade; discard marinade. Grill steak 6" from medium coals 12–16 minutes, turning once, until desired doneness. Cover and let stand 5 minutes, then slice across the grain to serve.

Cutting Steaks

When cutting steaks after they are cooked, you have to wait. If steaks are cut into right off the grill or griddle, the juice will run all over your serving plate. Let the steaks stand, covered, for 5–10 minutes to allow the juices to redistribute. Then serve or slice the meat.

Serves 4

Calories: 282.05
Fat: 15.89 grams
Saturated Fat: 4.36 grams
Carbohydrates: 2.99 grams
Sodium: 61.57 mg

1 tablespoon minced ginger root
2 cloves garlic, minced
1 shallot, minced
½ teaspoon five spice powder
2 tablespoons rice wine vinegar
1 tablespoon lime juice
2 teaspoons Soy Sauce Substitute (page 82)
2 tablespoons vegetable oil
1/8 teaspoon cayenne pepper
1 pound flank steak

milk wheat eggs soy fish nuts

Beef and Pea Stir-Fry

Two kinds of peas make this stir-fry special.
Serve with hot cooked rice and a salad made
with lettuce and mandarin oranges.

Serves 4

Calories: 353.99
Fat: 14.39 grams
Saturated Fat: 3.70 grams
Carbohydrates: 21.02 grams
Sodium: 440.13 mg

1 pound boneless beef sirloin tip steak
⅓ cup Beef Stock (page 138)
1 teaspoon sugar
2 tablespoons cornstarch
2 tablespoons apple juice
2 tablespoons Soy Sauce Substitute (page 82)
⅛ teaspoon pepper
2 tablespoons olive oil
1 onion, sliced
2 cloves garlic, minced
2 cups snow peas
1 cup frozen baby peas

1. Cut beef into ¼" × 4" strips against the grain. In medium bowl, combine Stock, sugar, cornstarch, apple juice, Soy Sauce Substitute, and pepper; mix well. Add beef and let stand 15 minutes.

2. Drain beef, reserving marinade. Heat olive oil in wok or large skillet over medium-high heat. Add beef; stir-fry until browned, about 3–4 minutes. Remove beef from wok and set aside.

3. Add onion and garlic to wok; stir-fry 4–5 minutes until crisp-tender. Add snow peas and baby peas to wok; stir-fry 2 minutes.

4. Stir marinade and add to wok along with beef. Stir-fry until sauce bubbles and thickens, about 4–5 minutes. Serve immediately over hot cooked rice.

milk wheat eggs fish nuts

Spaghetti Bolognese

Spaghetti Bolognese is a rich and thick meat sauce well flavored with onion and herbs.

1. In large skillet, cook ground beef over medium heat, stirring to break up meat, until partially cooked. Drain beef. Add onions and garlic; continue cooking until beef is browned.

2. Add bell pepper, tomatoes, and canned tomatoes; cook and stir 5 minutes. In small bowl, combine Stock, wine, and tomato paste; stir with wire whisk until tomato paste dissolves.

3. Add to skillet with bay leaf, sugar, salt, pepper, oregano, and basil; bring to a simmer. Lower heat; and simmer 15–20 minutes.

4. Bring a large pot of water to a boil. Cook pasta until al dente, then drain, reserving ⅓ cup pasta cooking water. Stir pasta into meat sauce along with water, if necessary, if sauce is too thick. Remove and discard bay leaf, top with cheese, and serve immediately.

Spaghetti Bolognese

This dish is very popular in Europe, especially the Scandinavian countries and England. It's traditionally made from prosciutto, beef, carrots, onions, celery, wine, and milk, but different variations abound. You can make your own version by adding bacon or prosciutto, using celery instead of bell pepper, and changing the herbs.

Serves 6–8

Calories: 447.54
Fat: 8.47 grams
Saturated Fat: 3.66 grams
Carbohydrates: 61.88 grams
Sodium: 390.32 mg

1½ pounds lean gluten-free ground beef
2 onions, chopped
4 cloves garlic, minced
1 green bell pepper, chopped
6 plum tomatoes, chopped
1 (14-ounce) can gluten-free diced tomatoes, undrained
1 cup Beef Stock (page 138)
½ cup red wine
1 (6-ounce) can gluten-free tomato paste
1 bay leaf
1 teaspoon sugar
½ teaspoon salt
⅛ teaspoon pepper
½ teaspoon dried oregano leaves
½ teaspoon dried basil leaves
1 (16-ounce) package gluten-free rice spaghetti
½ cup grated dairy-free, vegan Parmesan cheese

Beef and Bean Enchiladas

Enchiladas are spicy and rich, with a wonderful combination of flavors. You can make this casserole ahead of time and refrigerate, baking it for 10–15 minutes longer.

Serves 8

Calories: 478.32
Fat: 22.93 grams
Saturated Fat: 8.81 grams
Carbohydrates: 33.44 grams
Sodium: 920.33 mg

1 pound lean gluten-free ground beef
1 onion, chopped
2 cloves garlic, minced
3 tablespoons Taco Seasoning Mix (page 80)
½ cup tomato juice
1 (8-ounce) can gluten-free tomato sauce
¼ cup gluten-free tomato paste
1 cup dairy-free vegan sour cream
1 (4-ounce) can green chilies, drained
2 cups shredded dairy-free, vegan Monterey Jack cheese, divided
12 (6-inch) corn tortillas
1 (15-ounce) can vegetarian refried beans
1 cup shredded dairy-free, vegan Cheddar cheese

1. Preheat oven to 375°F. In large skillet, cook ground beef with onion and garlic until beef is browned, stirring to break up meat. Drain well, then stir in Seasoning Mix, tomato juice, tomato sauce, and tomato paste. Cook, stirring occasionally, until sauce bubbles and thickens, about 10 minutes.

2. In small bowl, combine sour cream, chilies, and 1 cup of the Monterey Jack cheese; mix well.

3. Spread ½ cup of meat sauce in bottom of 13" × 9" glass baking dish. Arrange tortillas on work surface. Divide refried beans among the tortillas, then top with a spoonful of meat sauce and a spoonful of sour cream mixture.

4. Roll up and place, seam-side down, in prepared dish. Pour remaining meat sauce over all, then top with remaining Monterey Jack cheese and Cheddar cheese. Bake 30–40 minutes, or until casserole is bubbling and cheese melts and begins to brown.

milk wheat eggs soy fish nuts

Mom's Meatloaf

Serves 6

If you don't have leftover mashed potatoes, make some from dried potato flakes; they're fine to use in this tender meatloaf.

Calories: 340.82
Fat: 16.88 grams
Saturated Fat: 6.11 grams
Carbohydrates: 17.57 grams
Sodium: 473.94 mg

1. Preheat oven to 375°F. In medium skillet, heat olive oil over medium heat. Add onions and mushrooms; cook and stir until tender, about 6 minutes. Add hash brown potatoes; cook until liquid evaporates. Remove from heat.

2. Place onion mixture in large bowl; add Mashed Potatoes, salt, pepper, marjoram, and ¼ cup ketchup and mix well. Add beef and pork; work gently but thoroughly with hands until combined.

3. Shape into a loaf on a broiler pan. In small bowl, combine 2 tablespoons ketchup, honey, and mustard; spread over loaf. Bake 65–75 minutes, or until internal temperature reaches 165°F. Let stand for 5 minutes. Slice to serve.

1 tablespoon olive oil
1 onion, chopped
1 cup chopped mushrooms
1 cup shredded gluten-free hash brown potatoes
½ cup Mashed Potatoes (page 242)
½ teaspoon salt
⅛ teaspoon pepper
½ teaspoon dried marjoram leaves
6 tablespoons gluten-free ketchup, divided
1 pound gluten-free ground beef
½ pound ground pork
1 tablespoon honey
1 tablespoon gluten-free mustard

Meatloaf Tips

There are some tricks for making the best meatloaf. Overhandling the meat will make the meatloaf tough, so don't mix more than necessary. Combine all the other ingredients first and mix, then add the meat. Adding a glaze will help hold in moisture. And let meatloaf stand for 5–10 minutes after baking before slicing.

Pesto Beef Stir-Fry

Serves 4

Pesto adds bright flavor and color to this classic stir-fry. You could also make it with chicken and chicken stock.

Calories: 431.39
Fat: 21.35 grams
Saturated Fat: 4.59 grams
Carbohydrates: 24.50 grams
Sodium: 315.58 mg

1 tablespoon cornstarch
1 teaspoon brown sugar
1 tablespoon gluten-free apple cider vinegar
½ cup Beef Stock (page 138)
2 tablespoons olive oil
1 pound boneless sirloin steak
1 onion, chopped
2 cups broccoli florets
3 carrots, sliced
2 cups baby frozen peas
⅓ cup Basil Pesto (page 77)

1. In small bowl, combine cornstarch, sugar, vinegar, and Beef Stock; mix well. Cut steak into ¼" × 3" pieces against the grain and add to cornstarch mixture. Let stand for 10 minutes.

2. In wok or large skillet, heat olive oil. Drain meat, reserving marinade. Add meat to wok; stir-fry until browned, about 3–4 minutes. Remove from wok and set aside.

3. Add onion, broccoli, and carrots to wok. Stir-fry until crisp-tender, about 5–7 minutes. Return beef to wok along with frozen peas.

4. Stir Stock mixture and add to wok. Stir-fry until peas are hot and sauce bubbles and thickens slightly. Stir in Pesto. Serve immediately.

milk   wheat   eggs   soy   fish   nuts

Lean Beef Stroganoff

Serves 6

Calories: 443.10
Fat: 13.43 grams
Saturated Fat: 2.99 grams
Carbohydrates: 55.27 grams
Sodium: 357.02 mg

This rich recipe is wonderful for entertaining. Serve with a spinach and pea salad and some garlic bread made with Sourdough French Bread (page 49).

1. Bring a large pot of water to a boil. Meanwhile, in small saucepan heat 2 tablespoons olive oil over medium heat. Add potato-starch flour; cook and stir with a wire whisk until bubbly. Add rice milk, 1 cup Stock, and lemon juice and bring to a simmer. Reduce heat to low and simmer 5 minutes, stirring frequently, until thick. Set aside.

2. Cut steak into ¼" × 4" strips. Toss with 1 tablespoon potato-starch flour, salt, and pepper. In large skillet, heat 1 tablespoon olive oil over medium heat. Add steak; brown, stirring occasionally, 4–5 minutes. Add onion, garlic, mushrooms, and thyme; cook and stir 5–6 minutes.

3. Cook egg noodles as directed on package until al dente. Add Stock mixture and mustard to steak mixture in skillet; simmer 5–6 minutes to blend flavors. When noodles are cooked, drain and add to skillet. Stir to coat noodles. Serve immediately.

2 tablespoons olive oil
2 tablespoons potato-starch flour
½ cup rice milk
1 cup Beef Stock (page 138)
1 tablespoon lemon juice
1 pound sirloin steak
1 tablespoon potato-starch flour
½ teaspoon salt
1/8 teaspoon pepper
1 tablespoon olive oil
1 onion, chopped
3 cloves garlic, minced
1 (8-ounce) package sliced mushrooms
½ teaspoon dried thyme leaves
1 (12-ounce) package gluten-free rice noodles
1 tablespoon gluten-free Dijon mustard

Stroganoff

Beef Stroganoff is a dish from Russia that is typically made of steak or other beef cuts simmered in sour cream, served over noodles. If you use vegan products in place of the sour cream, and alternatives to pasta, this dish can be enjoyed by everyone. Adding vegetables adds nutrition, texture, and flavor to this classic recipe.

Calories: 463.53
Fat: 15.80 grams
Saturated Fat: 3.12 grams
Carbohydrates: 53.48 grams
Sodium: 539.92 mg

1 pound lean gluten-free
    ground beef
1 onion, chopped
1 jalapeño pepper, minced
1 red bell pepper, chopped
1 (8-ounce) package sliced
    mushrooms
2 plum tomatoes, chopped
1 cup Tomato Sauce (page
    81)
⅛ teaspoon cayenne
    pepper
1 teaspoon cumin
1 Pizza Crust, prebaked
    (page 63)
1 cup shredded dairy-
    free, vegan mozzarella
    cheese
¼ cup grated dairy-free,
    vegan Parmesan cheese

Spicy Beef and Veggie Pizza

This hearty pizza is really a meal in one. Serve with a gelatin fruit salad and some cooked green beans.

1. Preheat oven to 400°F. In large skillet, cook ground beef with onion until meat is browned, stirring to break up beef. Drain, then add jalapeño, red bell pepper, mushrooms, and plum tomatoes. Cook and stir 5 minutes.

2. Add Tomato Sauce, cayenne pepper, and cumin; bring to a simmer. Reduce heat to low and simmer 10–15 minutes to blend flavors.

3. Place Pizza Crust on cookie sheet. Top with beef mixture, then sprinkle with cheeses. Bake 20–25 minutes, or until crust is golden brown and cheese is melted and starts to brown.

Ground Beef

The best buy in ground beef is 80 percent lean to fat ratio. When beef is on sale, buy a bunch and freeze it. But don't freeze it as it came from the store; divide each pound into four patties and stack with waxed paper in between each patty. Then wrap, label, and freeze up to 3 months. The beef will thaw in the refrigerator in a few hours.

milk   wheat   eggs   soy   fish   nuts

Beef Paillards with Lemon Salad

Filet mignon are a splurge, but there is really no waste, and no more tender cut of meat. This recipe is really good for company.

1. Using a sharp knife, cut each steak horizontally into two pieces. Place on plastic wrap, cover with more plastic wrap, and pound gently until ¼" thick. Sprinkle steak with salt and pepper.

2. Heat olive oil in large skillet over medium-high heat. Add steaks; cook for 1 minute, then turn and cook 1–2 minutes longer. Transfer to warm plate and cover.

3. Toss spinach, lettuce, basil, and green onion together; set aside. Add shallots to skillet; cook and stir until tender. Add lemon juice and Stock; bring to a boil. Return steaks to skillet and cook 30 seconds.

4. Place steaks on serving plate, top with lettuce mixture, and pour juice from skillet over all. Serve immediately.

Serves 4

Calories: 390.45
Fat: 28.45 grams
Saturated Fat: 10.58 grams
Carbohydrates: 4.88 grams
Sodium: 385.45 mg

2 (8-ounce) filet mignon steaks
½ teaspoon salt
⅛ teaspoon pepper
1 tablespoon olive oil
2 cups baby spinach leaves
1 cup torn butter lettuce leaves
½ cup torn fresh basil leaves
⅓ cup sliced green onion
2 shallots, minced
3 tablespoons lemon juice
2 tablespoons Beef Stock (page 138)

Spicy Meatball Stew

Serves 6

Calories: 492.53
Fat: 13.87 grams
Saturated Fat: 4.09 grams
Carbohydrates: 55.39 grams
Sodium: 694.34 mg

1 tablespoon olive oil
1 onion, chopped
1 jalapeño pepper, minced
4 cloves garlic, minced
3 carrots, sliced
⅛ teaspoon pepper
1 tablespoon chili powder
4 cups Beef Stock (page 138)
2 cups water
1 (14-ounce) can gluten-free diced tomatoes, undrained
1 recipe Meatballs, cooked (page 173)
1 (9-ounce) package frozen green beans
1 cup brown rice orzo or small rice shell pasta
2 tablespoons cornstarch or potato-starch flour

You can leave out the cornstarch at the end for a soup. But if you like thick stew, be sure to use it.

1. In large pot, heat olive oil over medium heat. Add onion, jalapeño pepper, and garlic; cook and stir 4 minutes. Add carrot, pepper, and chili powder; cook and stir 2 minutes longer.

2. Add Stock, water, and tomatoes and bring to a simmer. Simmer 10 minutes. Add Meatballs, green beans, and orzo or pasta; bring to a simmer. Simmer 10–12 minutes, or until orzo or pasta is cooked and Meatballs and beans are hot.

3. Scoop out a small amount of the liquid and combine in small bowl with cornstarch or potato-starch flour; mix well. Add to pot and simmer until thickened, about 4–5 minutes longer. Serve immediately.

Reheating Soup

When you reheat soup that uses rice pasta, you may need to add more liquid. The pasta can absorb a lot of the liquid in the soup while it is refrigerated. Add more of the liquid you used to make the soup so the flavor is not diluted. You may want to cook more pasta separately and add it to the soup if the original falls apart when reheated.

Chapter 10
Pork Entrées

Ham Manicotti

Serves 6

Calories: 435.26
Fat: 19.22 grams
Saturated Fat: 3.21 grams
Carbohydrates: 41.27 grams
Sodium: 830.23 mg

12 Gluten-Free Crepes
   (page 83)
1 tablespoon olive oil
1 onion, chopped
1 green bell pepper,
   chopped
2 cups diced ham
½ cup shredded vegan soy
   cheese
2½ cups Tomato Sauce
   (page 81)

This is the way authentic manicotti is made in Italy. Make a bunch of Crepes and freeze them, and you can get this dish ready in minutes.

1. Preheat oven to 350°F. Spray a 2-quart, shallow casserole with nonstick gluten-free cooking spray and set aside. Make Gluten-Free Crepes and let cool. Do not stack Crepes.

2. In medium skillet, heat olive oil over medium heat. Add onion and bell pepper; cook and stir until tender, about 5–6 minutes. Add ham and cook 2 minutes longer. Remove from heat.

3. Add cheese and ½ cup of Tomato Sauce and mix well. Divide mixture among the Crepes and roll up. Place ½ cup Tomato Sauce in bottom of prepared pan.

4. Place Crepes, seam-side down, in Sauce in the dish. Spoon remaining Sauce over Crepes. Bake 25–30 minutes, until thoroughly heated. Serve immediately.

Crepes

Crepes are easy to make and store well. You can keep them in the refrigerator up to 3 days; freeze them for longer storage. To thaw, just put them in the refrigerator for 3–5 hours until pliable. You can fill them with everything from meatballs to chocolate mousse. They are a good substitute for pasta when making manicotti and cannelloni.

milk wheat eggs soy fish nuts

Sausage and Broccoli Stir-Fry

Stir-frying is a very quick cooking technique that preserves vitamins and minerals. You don't need a wok to stir-fry, but you do need a very sturdy spatula.

1. In small bowl, combine red pepper flakes, Soy Sauce Substitute (or real soy sauce if you aren't allergic), cornstarch or potato-starch flour, ginger, and water; mix well and set aside.

2. In large wok or skillet, stir-fry pork sausage with onion until sausage is browned, stirring to break up meat. Remove meat and onions from wok, leaving about 1 tablespoon of drippings.

3. Add mushrooms, broccoli, and bell pepper to wok; stir-fry until crisp-tender, about 4–5 minutes. Stir cornstarch or potato-starch flour mixture and add to wok along with sausage and onions. Stir-fry until sauce thickens and boils, about 2–3 minutes. Serve immediately over hot cooked rice.

Serves 4

Calories: 394.19
Fat: 26.31 grams
Saturated Fat: 8.14 grams
Carbohydrates: 12.73 grams
Sodium: 805.34 mg

⅛ teaspoon crushed red
    pepper flakes
1 tablespoon Soy Sauce
    Substitute (page 82)
2 tablespoons cornstarch
    or potato-starch flour
¼ teaspoon ginger
½ cup water
1 pound spicy ground
    gluten-free pork
    sausage
1 onion, chopped
1 cup sliced fresh
    mushrooms
2 cups fresh broccoli
    florets
1 red bell pepper, sliced

Calories: 396.64
Fat: 8.37 grams
Saturated Fat: 1.56 grams
Carbohydrates: 67.68 grams
Sodium: 623.42 mg

2 tablespoons garlic olive oil
2 onions, chopped
4 cloves garlic, minced
½ teaspoon salt
¼ teaspoon pepper
1 teaspoon dried basil leaves
2 cups cubed gluten-free ham
1 cup Chicken Stock (page 137)
1 (16-ounce) package gluten-free rice spaghetti
½ cup chopped flat-leaf parsley

milk   wheat   eggs   soy   fish   nuts

Spaghetti with Ham Sauce

This is the same basic formula used for spaghetti with clam sauce, but it can be eaten by those with fish allergies.

1. Bring a large pot of salted water to a boil. Meanwhile, in large saucepan, heat olive oil over medium heat. Add onion and garlic; cook and stir until tender, about 6–7 minutes.

2. Sprinkle with salt, pepper, and basil leaves. Add ham and Chicken Stock; bring to a simmer.

3. Cook pasta according to package directions until almost al dente. Drain and add to saucepan with ham mixture. Cook and stir 2–3 minutes, until pasta is al dente. Sprinkle with parsley and serve immediately.

Flavored Oils

Flavored oils are a good way to add flavor with fewer ingredients. But please don't make your own. The combination of an anaerobic environment (the oil) with ingredients that can contain bacteria and spores (herbs and garlic) can result in botulism. There are many commercially produced flavored oils to choose from, including basil, garlic, and onion.

milk wheat eggs fish nuts

Chimichangas

Chimichangas are usually deep fried, but this baked version is easier, and better for you, too.

Serves 6–8

Calories: 422.12
Fat: 25.95 grams
Saturated Fat: 6.51 grams
Carbohydrates: 27.98 grams
Sodium: 669.45 mg

1. Preheat oven to 375°F. In large saucepan, cook sausage with onion and garlic, stirring to break up meat. Drain well. Return pan to heat. Add jalapeño and green bell pepper; cook and stir 3 minutes.

2. Add refried beans, tomato paste, Chili Powder, salt, and pepper and mix well. Bring to a simmer; simmer, stirring frequently, 10 minutes.

3. Arrange tortillas on work surface. Place about ¼ cup sausage mixture on each, then top with cheese. Roll up and place seam-side down on cookie sheet. Repeat with remaining tortillas, cheese, and filling.

4. Brush Chimichangas with oil and bake 25–35 minutes, or until tortillas are crisp and cheese is melted. Serve immediately with salsa and avocado.

1 pound spicy ground gluten-free pork sausage
1 onion, chopped
3 cloves garlic, minced
1 jalapeño pepper, minced
1 green bell pepper, chopped
1 (15-ounce) can refried beans
1 (6-ounce) can gluten-free tomato paste
1 tablespoon Chili Powder (page 78)
¼ teaspoon salt
¼ teaspoon white pepper
12 (6-inch) corn tortillas
1½ cups shredded dairy-free, vegan Monterey Jack cheese
2 tablespoons vegetable oil
Salsa
Avocado

Tortilla Stack

Crisp tortillas are layered with a rich bean and sausage mixture, then baked with cheese. Yum!

Serves 6–8

Calories: 411.03
Fat: 23.75 grams
Saturated Fat: 6.11 grams
Carbohydrates: 27.48 grams
Sodium: 804.03 mg

1 pound gluten-free ground pork sausage
1 red bell pepper, chopped
1 (4-ounce) can chopped green chilies, drained
2 (15-ounce) cans kidney beans, drained
2 tablespoons Taco Seasoning Mix (page 80)
1 (8-ounce) can gluten-free tomato sauce
3 tablespoons vegetable oil
9 (6-inch) corn tortillas
1 cup shredded dairy-free, vegan Cheddar cheese
½ cup shredded dairy-free, vegan Monterey Jack cheese

1. In large saucepan, cook pork sausage over medium heat, stirring to break up meat, until browned. Drain well. Add red bell pepper; cook and stir 3 minutes longer. Add chilies, beans, Seasoning Mix, and tomato sauce and bring to a simmer. Simmer, stirring frequently, 10 minutes.

2. In another large saucepan, heat vegetable oil over medium-high heat. Fry the tortillas, one at a time, until crisp, turning once, about 2–3 minutes. Drain on paper towels.

3. On a large cookie sheet with sides, place one tortilla. Top with one-sixth of the pork mixture and one-sixth of the cheese. Repeat layers, using 3 tortillas, ending with tortilla and cheese. Repeat with remaining tortillas, pork mixture, and cheese, making three stacks.

4. Bake 25–35 minutes, or until cheese is melted and bubbly. Let stand 5 minutes. Cut each stack in thirds to serve.

Corn Tortillas

Corn tortillas are made of corn, right? Not always. You must read the label every single time you buy a package of corn tortillas. Once you're sure they are wheat free, you can choose from many varieties, colors, and flavors. Blue corn tortillas, spicy tortillas made with red pepper, and white corn tortillas are all delicious.

milk   wheat   eggs   soy   fish   nuts

Grilled Pork Tenderloin

This simple yet flavorful recipe is a good choice for an outdoor cookout. Serve with fresh fruit and potato salad.

1. Combine honey, jelly, mustard, Stock, salt, pepper, and marjoram in a small saucepan. Heat over low heat until jelly melts and mixture is blended.

2. Place tenderloins in a glass dish and pour marinade over. Cover and refrigerate 4–6 hours.

3. When ready to eat, prepare and preheat grill. Drain pork, reserving marinade. Place pork on grill 6" from medium coals; cover and grill 15 minutes.

4. Brush pork with marinade as it grills for another 15–25 minutes, turning occasionally, or until an instant read meat thermometer registers 155°F. Let pork stand, covered, for 5 minutes before slicing. Discard remaining marinade.

Serves 6

Calories: 355.68
Fat: 8.95 grams
Saturated Fat: 3.11 grams
Carbohydrates: 25.44 grams
Sodium: 339.54 mg

¼ cup honey
⅓ cup apple jelly
2 tablespoons gluten-free Dijon mustard
¼ cup Chicken Stock (page 137)
½ teaspoon salt
⅛ teaspoon pepper
½ teaspoon dried marjoram leaves
2 (1-pound) pork tenderloins

Serves 4

Calories: 287.59
Fat: 15.45 grams
Saturated Fat: 5.25 grams
Carbohydrates: 8.95 grams
Sodium: 198.52 mg

1 tablespoon olive oil
2 cloves garlic, minced
1 jalapeño pepper, minced
1 tablespoon Chili Powder
   (page 78)
2 tablespoons gluten-free
   apple cider vinegar
¼ teaspoon salt
⅛ teaspoon pepper
¼ cup pineapple juice
2 tablespoons sugar
⅛ teaspoon cayenne pepper
4 boneless loin pork chops

Serves 6

Calories: 404.44
Fat: 21.11 grams
Saturated Fat: 6.99 grams
Carbohydrates: 32.58
grams
Sodium: 590.30 mg

3 cups Chicken Stock (page
   137)
1 pound spicy ground
   gluten-free Italian pork
   sausage
1 onion, chopped
1 cup Arborio rice
1 tablespoon fresh chopped
   sage leaves
¼ cup grated dairy-free,
   vegan Parmesan cheese

milk · wheat · eggs · soy · fish · nuts

Spicy Grilled Pork Chops

Spicy, tender, juicy, and savory pork chops are a real treat. Serve these with potato salad and a fruit pie for dessert.

1. In heavy-duty, plastic food-storage bag, combine all ingredients except the chops; mix well. Add chops, seal bag, place in a bowl, and refrigerate 3–4 hours.

2. When ready to eat, prepare and preheat grill. Drain chops, reserving marinade. Grill chops 6" from medium coals 10–12 minutes, basting occasionally with reserved marinade, until meat thermometer registers 155°F. Discard remaining marinade. Serve immediately.

milk · wheat · eggs · fish · nuts

Sausage Risotto

This simple dish can be ready in about half an hour, even though you have to stir and stir!

1. Place Stock in a small saucepan over low heat. In large saucepan, cook sausage and onion over medium heat until browned, stirring to break up meat. When pork is cooked, drain, leaving a few spoonfuls of liquid in saucepan.

2. Add rice; cook and stir until rice turns light gold. Add the Stock, ½ cup at a time, stirring constantly, until rice is al dente. This should take about 20 minutes.

3. Stir in sage leaves and cheese; cover, remove from heat, and let stand 5 minutes before serving.

milk *wheat* *eggs* *fish* *nuts*

Sausage Mini Pizzas

These little pizzas are fun to make and eat. You can top them with anything you'd like, including pepperoni or cooked chicken.

Serves 8

Calories: 531.33
Fat: 22.89 grams
Saturated Fat: 6.72 grams
Carbohydrates: 57.86 grams
Sodium: 608.44 mg

1. Preheat oven to 400°F. In large skillet, cook sausage, onion, and jalapeño pepper until sausage is done, stirring to break up meat. Drain thoroughly.

2. Add bell pepper and mushrooms; cook and stir 4 minutes longer. Add Tomato Sauce and bring to a simmer. Lower heat and simmer 4 minutes.

3. Arrange Pizza Crusts on two cookie sheets. Top with pork mixture, then cheeses. Bake 10–15 minutes, or until Crusts are golden brown and cheese is melted and beginning to brown. Serve immediately.

1 pound gluten-free ground pork sausage
1 onion, chopped
1 jalapeño pepper, minced
1 green bell pepper, chopped
1 cup sliced mushrooms
1 cup Tomato Sauce (page 81)
8 Mini Pizza Crusts, prebaked (page 61)
1 cup shredded dairy-free, vegan mozzarella cheese
¼ cup grated dairy-free, vegan Parmesan cheese

Jalapeño Peppers

Jalapeño peppers, with their fiery kick, are quite mild as peppers go. They are used most often in recipes. To make them milder, just remove the membranes and seeds. That's where the capsaicin, the compound that provides the heat, resides. And be careful when handling hot peppers; don't touch your eyes until you've thoroughly washed your hands.

milk   wheat   eggs   soy   fish   nuts

Ham Hash

*Make this delicious hash with leftovers from
Easter or Christmas dinner. If you aren't allergic to eggs,
top each serving with a crisp fried egg.*

Serves 4

Calories: 368.02
Fat: 9.31 grams
Saturated Fat: 2.09 grams
Carbohydrates: 53.04 grams
Sodium: 787.49 mg

1 tablespoon vegetable oil
2 cloves garlic, minced
1 onion, diced
3 russet potatoes, diced
⅓ cup Chicken Stock (page 137)
2 cups diced gluten-free ham
1 tablespoon lemon juice
1 tablespoon gluten-free mustard
¼ teaspoon salt
⅛ teaspoon pepper

1. In large skillet, heat oil over medium heat. Add garlic, onion, and potatoes; cook and stir until potatoes start to brown, about 7–8 minutes. Add Stock and bring to a simmer. Cover and simmer 5–6 minutes, until potatoes are almost tender.

2. Add ham, lemon juice, mustard, salt, and pepper. Cook and stir another 6–8 minutes, stirring frequently, until potatoes are tender. Serve immediately.

Cooking Potatoes

When cooking potatoes in a skillet, stir just enough so the potatoes don't stick, but don't stir too much or they will start to break up. In hash and other casseroles, you do want some brown bits on the potatoes. Leave the skin on, because this adds nutrients and fiber to the finished dish.

milk   wheat   eggs   soy   fish   nuts

Roasted Apricot Pork Tenderloin

Pork tenderloin is, as the name says, tender and juicy. It's a very low-fat cut of pork that is easy to prepare and serve.

1. Combine all ingredients except tenderloin in a small bowl. Place pork in a glass baking dish and pour apricot mixture over all. Cover and refrigerate 8–24 hours.

2. When ready to eat, preheat oven to 325°F. Roast pork with marinade 40–50 minutes, basting occasionally with marinade, until meat thermometer registers 155°F. Cover pork and let stand for 5 minutes. Slice to serve.

Serves 6

Calories: 330.05
Fat: 9.05 grams
Saturated Fat: 3.19 grams
Carbohydrates: 15.82 grams
Sodium: 105.96 mg

¼ cup gluten-free apricot
    preserves
¼ cup apricot nectar
2 tablespoons brown sugar
2 tablespoons gluten-free
    apple cider vinegar
2 tablespoons Chicken
    Stock (page 137)
3 cloves garlic, minced
2 pounds pork tenderloin

milk   wheat   eggs   soy   fish   nuts

Roasted Pork Tenderloin

Pork tenderloin is low fat and tender, and is one of the easiest cuts of pork to prepare.

1. Combine all ingredients except pork in small bowl and mix until blended. Place pork in a 13" × 9" glass baking dish and pour wine mixture over. Cover and refrigerate 3–4 minutes, turning pork occasionally.

2. When ready to eat, preheat oven to 325°F. Add ¼ cup water to dish with pork and bake 40–50 minutes, basting occasionally with juices, or until meat thermometer inserted into pork registers 155°F. Let stand 10 minutes. Slice to serve.

Serves 6

Calories: 279.51
Fat: 9.02 grams
Saturated Fat: 3.18 grams
Carbohydrates: 2.64 grams
Sodium: 208.04 mg

¼ cup red wine
1 shallot, minced
2 cloves garlic, minced
2 tablespoons sugar
1 tablespoon gluten-free
    mustard
½ teaspoon salt
⅛ teaspoon pepper
½ teaspoon dried marjoram
    leaves
2 pounds pork tenderloin

milk   wheat   eggs   fish   nuts

Ham Pizza

Ham and pineapple are natural partners. Paired with a spicy-sweet sauce and baked on a pizza, they're even more delicious.

Serves 8

Calories: 466.97
Fat: 17.51 grams
Saturated Fat: 3.35 grams
Carbohydrates: 59.59 grams
Sodium: 903.24 mg

1 (8-ounce) can crushed
    pineapple
1 tablespoon olive oil
1 onion, chopped
1 cup Tomato Sauce (page
    81)
2 tablespoons gluten-free
    chili sauce
1 tablespoon honey
1 (4-ounce) can chopped
    green chilies, drained
1 Pizza Crust, prebaked
    (page 63)
1½ cups ham, diced
1½ cups shredded dairy-
    free, vegan mozzarella
    cheese

1. Preheat oven to 400°F. Thoroughly drain pineapple, pressing down on fruit in sieve; reserve juice.

2. In medium skillet, heat olive oil over medium heat. Add onion; cook and stir until tender, about 7 minutes. Add Tomato Sauce, ¼ cup reserved pineapple juice, chili sauce, honey, and green chilies; simmer 10 minutes.

3. Remove sauce from heat and stir in drained pineapple and chiles. Spread sauce over Pizza Crust. Top with ham and mozzarella cheese.

4. Bake 20–30 minutes, or until crust is golden brown and cheese melts and begins to brown.

Ham

Ham can be found in many forms. You can buy whole hams, sliced ham, ham steaks, or thin slices of boiled ham. If ham is diced or sliced in a recipe, you can use any form you'd like. Hams are dry cured or wet cured, then usually smoked or dried. Canadian bacon can be substituted for ham.

milk   wheat   eggs   fish   nuts

Pork and Bean Tacos

Serves 6

Calories: 429.32
Fat: 23.89 grams
Saturated Fat: 6.79 grams
Carbohydrates: 26.70 grams
Sodium: 642.07 mg

Tacos made with pork instead of beef are a nice change of pace. You can add more chili powder and jalapeños if you like it spicy.

1. Preheat oven to 350°F. In large skillet, cook pork, onion, garlic, and jalapeño, stirring to break up meat, until pork is done. Drain thoroughly.

2. Add Taco Seasoning Mix, tomato sauce, and kidney beans and bring to a simmer. Lower heat and simmer 5–10 minutes to blend flavors.

3. Heat taco shells as directed on package. Make tacos using shells, lettuce, pork filling, and cheese. Serve immediately.

1 pound gluten-free ground pork
1 onion, chopped
2 cloves garlic, minced
1 jalapeño pepper, minced
3 tablespoons Taco Seasoning Mix (page 80)
1 (8-ounce) can gluten-free tomato sauce
1 (15-ounce) can kidney beans, drained
6–8 corn taco shells
3 cups shredded lettuce
1 cup shredded dairy-free, vegan Cheddar cheese

Tacos

There are two kinds of tacos: soft and crisp. Soft tacos are also called burritos; they are made of soft corn or flour tortillas filled with a spicy meat or bean mixture and rolled up. Crisp tacos have taco shells made by bending and deep-frying corn or flour tortillas into a "U" shape. Either way, they're delicious.

Calories: 303.56
Fat: 14.51 grams
Saturated Fat: 4.63 grams
Carbohydrates: 29.10 grams
Sodium: 690.93 mg

½ pound gluten-free ground pork sausage
1 cup shredded red cabbage
2 sliced carrots
¼ cup chopped green onion
2 cups cold, cooked rice
3 tablespoons soy sauce or Soy Sauce Substitute (page 82)
3 tablespoons Vegetable Broth (page 139)
⅛ teaspoon pepper

Fried Rice

You can omit the sausage if you'd like and use a tablespoon of vegetable oil instead. If you're not allergic to eggs, add two with the rice and cook until done.

1. In wok or large skillet, stir-fry pork until browned, breaking up meat as it cooks. Drain almost all fat out of wok. Add cabbage and carrots; stir-fry 4 minutes.

2. Add green onions and rice; stir-fry until rice starts to brown, about 5–7 minutes. Add soy sauce or Soy Sauce Substitute, Broth, and pepper; stir-fry until rice absorbs liquid and mixture is hot. Serve immediately.

Veggies Galore!
Fried rice is a great way to use up your leftover vegetables. Clean out your fridge, and throw in those extra mushrooms, peppers, onions, and peas you have lying around. They'll enhance the flavor, and you'll never have the same dish twice!

milk   wheat   eggs   fish   nuts

Ham Risotto

Risotto is a classic Italian dish that isn't difficult to make, but it does take time. Serve this with a fresh green salad and some Seasoned Breadsticks (page 48).

1. In a medium saucepan, place Chicken Stock over low heat. Meanwhile, in large saucepan, heat olive oil over medium heat. Add onion and garlic; cook and stir until crisp-tender, about 4 minutes. Sprinkle with salt, pepper, and thyme.

2. Add ham and rice; cook and stir 3 minutes. Add warm Stock, ½ cup at a time, stirring constantly, until liquid is absorbed. Continue adding Stock, cooking and stirring, for about 20 minutes.

3. Add the pineapple juice with the last ½ cup of Stock; cook and stir until sauce is very creamy and rice is al dente. Stir in cheese. Serve immediately.

Versatile Risotto

Risotto can be made with any meat, or with no meat at all. The only rules are to toast the rice in the fat before the liquid is added, to keep the liquid warm while the risotto is cooking, and to stir pretty much constantly. And make sure to add the cheese at the very end of the cooking time.

Serves 4

Calories: 421.22
Fat: 13.98 grams
Saturated Fat: 3.51 grams
Carbohydrates: 54.05 grams
Sodium: 910.89 mg

4 cups Chicken Stock (page 137)
2 tablespoons olive oil
1 onion, chopped
2 cloves garlic, minced
¼ teaspoon salt
⅛ teaspoon white pepper
½ teaspoon dried thyme leaves
1 cup chopped ham
1 cup Arborio rice
3 tablespoons pineapple juice
¼ cup grated dairy-free, vegan Parmesan cheese

milk wheat eggs soy fish nuts

Skillet Chops and Veggies

This easy one-dish meal is pure comfort food. Serve with a butter lettuce salad mixed with mushrooms and green peppers.

Serves 4

Calories: 620.58
Fat: 14.35 grams
Saturated Fat: 3.50 grams
Carbohydrates: 83.34 grams
Sodium: 516.32 mg

4 (4-ounce) boneless loin pork chops
2 tablespoons potato-starch flour
½ teaspoon salt
⅛ teaspoon pepper
2 tablespoons olive oil
1 onion, chopped
3 cloves garlic, minced
4 russet potatoes, thinly sliced
3 carrots, sliced
1 cup Chicken Stock (page 137)
1 tablespoon lemon juice

1. Sprinkle chops with flour, salt, and pepper; set aside. In large skillet, heat olive oil over medium heat. Add chops; brown 2–3 minutes on each side. Remove from heat and set aside.

2. Add onion and garlic to skillet; cook and stir until crisp-tender, about 5 minutes. Add potatoes to pan; cook and stir until potatoes are coated. Top with carrots, then add browned pork chops.

3. Add Stock and lemon juice and bring to a simmer. Cover skillet tightly, reduce heat to medium-low, and simmer 35–45 minutes, or until potatoes are tender and chops are cooked, shaking pan occasionally. Serve immediately.

Chapter 11
Vegetarian and Fish Entrées

Spaghetti Sauce

A combination of fresh and canned tomatoes creates a real depth of flavor in this simple recipe. Serve it with pasta, or use it to make Pizza Wraps (page 224). It freezes very well.

**Yields 1½ quarts;
Serving size ½ cup**

Calories: 76.57
Fat: 2.52 grams
Saturated Fat: 0.35 grams
Carbohydrates: 12.27 grams
Sodium: 417.67 mg

2 tablespoons olive oil
1 onion, chopped
3 cloves garlic, minced
1 cup chopped mushrooms
1 cup shredded carrots
2 (14-ounce) cans diced tomatoes, undrained
1 (6-ounce) can gluten-free tomato paste
6 plum tomatoes, chopped
1½ cups water
1 teaspoon dried basil leaves
½ teaspoon dried oregano leaves
½ teaspoon salt
¼ teaspoon pepper
1 bay leaf

1. Heat olive oil in large heavy saucepan; cook onion and garlic over medium heat until tender, 5–6 minutes. Add mushrooms and carrots; cook 4–5 minutes longer.

2. Add canned tomatoes, tomato paste, plum tomatoes, water, and remaining ingredients to saucepan. Bring to a boil, then reduce heat to low, cover pan, and simmer 45–50 minutes, until sauce is blended and slightly thickened. Remove bay leaf and discard.

3. Serve immediately with cooked pasta, or cover and refrigerate up to 4 days. Freeze for longer storage.

milk wheat eggs soy fish nuts

Fresh Tomato Rotini

This recipe should be made with tomatoes picked from the garden, but you can also make it with tomatoes from the farmer's market.

1. Bring a large pot of water to a boil. Meanwhile, in serving bowl, combine tomatoes, cherry tomatoes, basil, olive oil, and garlic. Sprinkle with salt and pepper; toss gently. Set aside.

2. Cook pasta as directed on package until al dente. Drain and immediately add to tomato mixture. Toss to coat. Serve immediately.

Preparing Tomatoes

If the tomatoes you are using are tender and thin skinned, you don't need to peel them. If the skins are thicker or a bit tough, peel them by cutting an "X" into the blossom end. Drop them into a pot of boiling water for 15 seconds, then plunge into ice water; the skins will peel off. Then cut the tomatoes in half and slice or chop.

Serves 4

Calories: 394.20
Fat: 8.85 grams
Saturated Fat: 1.27 grams
Carbohydrates: 74.14 grams
Sodium: 301.77 mg

2 tomatoes, chopped
2 cups cherry tomatoes, cut in half
¼ cup torn fresh basil leaves
2 tablespoons olive oil
1 clove garlic, minced
½ teaspoon salt
⅛ teaspoon pepper
1 (12-ounce) package gluten-free rice Rotini pasta

Serves 6

Calories: 233.28
Fat: 6.13 grams
Saturated Fat: 0.88 grams
Carbohydrates: 37.77 grams
Sodium: 583.02 mg

1 tablespoon olive oil
1 onion, chopped
3 cloves garlic, minced
1 (8-ounce) package button mushrooms
1 (15-ounce) can black beans, drained
1 cup Tomato Sauce (page 81)
4 cups Vegetable Broth (page 139)
1 cup yellow cornmeal
½ teaspoon salt
⅛ teaspoon pepper

Black Beans and Polenta

Polenta is cooked cornmeal. It's easy to make, and provides complete protein when eaten with black beans.

1. Preheat oven to 350°F. In large skillet, heat olive oil over medium heat. Add onion and garlic; cook and stir until crisp-tender, about 6 minutes. Add mushrooms; cook and stir 5 minutes longer.

2. Add beans and Tomato Sauce; bring to a simmer. Reduce heat and simmer while preparing polenta.

3. In large pot, bring Broth to a boil over high heat. Stir in cornmeal, salt, and pepper. Reduce heat to medium and cook, stirring constantly, until mixture is thick. Pour into prepared dish and smooth into an even layer.

4. Top with black bean mixture. Bake 20–30 minutes, or until food is hot. Spoon out of casserole dish to serve.

milk wheat eggs soy fish nuts

Risotto Curry

*Combining Italian and Indian cuisines,
this recipe is a delightful change of pace. You could add chicken
or shrimp to it for a nonvegetarian version.*

1. Place Broth in small saucepan over low heat. In large saucepan, heat olive oil over medium heat. Add onion and mushrooms; cook and stir until tender, about 7 minutes.

2. Add rice and curry powder to large saucepan; cook and stir until rice turns golden, about 3–4 minutes. Add wine; cook and stir until wine is absorbed.

3. Add warm Broth, about ½ cup at a time, stirring almost constantly, until liquid is absorbed. This should take about 20 minutes. When done, the rice should be tender but still slightly firm in the center, and the sauce creamy and thick. Serve immediately.

Arborio Rice

Risotto is a classic Italian dish that purists say must be made with Arborio rice. Arborio is a short-grain rice that has a higher content of amylopectin, a branched starch molecule that is released from the rice when it is stirred, making the liquid creamy. You must stir risotto frequently as it cooks. Cook only until the rice is al dente.

Serves 4

Calories: 271.06
Fat: 6.56 grams
Saturated Fat: 0.95 grams
Carbohydrates: 45.67 grams
Sodium: 191.28 mg

2½ cups Vegetable Broth (page 139)
1 tablespoon olive oil
1 onion, chopped
1 cup chopped portabella mushrooms
1 cup Arborio rice
2 teaspoons Curry Powder (page 79)
¼ cup dry white wine

milk   wheat   eggs   fish   nuts

Apple Sandwiches

Serves 4

Calories: 428.18
Fat: 15.94 grams
Saturated Fat: 3.34 grams
Carbohydrates: 72.15 grams
Sodium: 340.26 mg

1 large Granny Smith apple, very thinly sliced
2 tablespoons apple jelly
8 slices French Bread (page 51)
½ cup Not Peanut Butter (page 73)
3 tablespoons dairy-free, vegan margarine

These delicious sandwiches have wonderful flavor and texture. For a nice nonvegetarian twist, add some crisp bacon slices.

1. In small saucepan, combine apple slices and apple jelly; heat over low heat until apple jelly melts and apple slices start to cook, about 4–6 minutes. Remove from heat.

2. Slice Bread on the diagonal to get larger slices. Spread one side of each piece with Not Peanut Butter. Top with apple mixture, then remaining Bread slices. Spread outsides of sandwich with margarine.

3. Preheat griddle of indoor dual-contact grill. Grill sandwiches, covered, until bread is toasted and filling is hot, about 4–6 minutes total. Serve immediately.

milk   wheat   eggs   fish   nuts

Stuffed Potatoes

Ranch Salad Dressing (page 108) is so full of fresh herbs, you don't need to add any more to this excellent recipe. But you could if you wanted to!

Serves 6

Calories: 270.89
Fat: 19.30 grams
Saturated Fat: 2.79 grams
Carbohydrates: 18.43 grams
Sodium: 625.00 mg

3 large russet potatoes
1 tablespoon solid
   shortening
2 tablespoons olive oil
½ teaspoon salt
¼ teaspoon white pepper
⅓ cup chopped green
   onions
½ cup Ranch Salad
   Dressing (page 108)
1 cup shredded nondairy,
   vegan soy Cheddar
   cheese

1. Preheat oven to 400°F. Scrub potatoes and dry. Rub with solid shortening and prick with a fork. Place directly on oven rack; bake 50–60 minutes, or until potatoes are tender when pierced with fork.

2. Remove from oven and let cool 15 minutes. Then cut potatoes in half lengthwise. Carefully scoop out the flesh, leaving about ¼" shell. Place flesh in large mixing bowl; add olive oil, salt, and pepper and mash until smooth.

3. Beat-in green onions, Salad Dressing, and cheese until smooth. Fill shells with this mixture, mounding the tops. Place on cookie sheet.

4. Return to oven and bake 20–25 minutes, or until filling starts to brown and crisp. Serve immediately.

Baking Potatoes

You can bake potatoes in the oven or the microwave. To cook 3 potatoes in the microwave, cook on high for 4 minutes, then turn over. Microwave for 3 minutes longer, then let stand for 2 minutes; check for doneness. If necessary, microwave for 1–2 minutes longer. Let stand for 4 minutes longer before you use or eat them.

milk   wheat   eggs   soy   fish   nuts

Tomato Avocado Spaghetti

Serve this delicious dish when tomatoes and basil are in season.

Serves 6

Calories: 464.92
Fat: 15.22 grams
Saturated Fat: 2.83 grams
Carbohydrates: 59.33 grams
Sodium: 228.93 mg

2 tomatoes, chopped
2 cups grape tomatoes
¼ cup sliced green onion
2 avocadoes, peeled and diced
½ teaspoon salt
⅛ teaspoon pepper
½ cup chopped fresh basil
2 tablespoons olive oil
1 (16-ounce) package gluten-free rice spaghetti

1. Bring a large pot of water to a boil. Meanwhile, in serving bowl, combine tomatoes, grape tomatoes, green onion, avocado, salt, pepper, basil, and olive oil; mix gently.

2. Cook pasta according to package directions until al dente. Drain and immediately toss with tomato mixture. Serve at once.

milk   wheat   eggs   soy   nuts

Glazed Fish

A sweet and tart glaze coats tender fish fillets in this super-easy recipe. Serve with green beans and Honey Rolls (page 59).

Serves 6

Calories: 414.72
Fat: 25.54 grams
Saturated Fat: 2.82 grams
Carbohydrates: 0.54 grams
Sodium: 182.20 mg

½ cup Eggless Mayonnaise (page 68)
2 tablespoons honey
½ teaspoon dried thyme leaves
1 tablespoon lemon juice
⅛ teaspoon white pepper
6 (6-ounce) fillets red snapper

1. Preheat oven to 350°F. In small bowl, combine all ingredients except fish; mix well. Place fish on cookie sheet. Divide Mayonnaise mixture among fillets, spreading gently to cover.

2. Bake fish 20–30 minutes, or until flesh flakes when tested with a fork. Serve immediately.

milk   wheat   eggs   nuts

Fisherman's Stew

This hearty and flavorful stew can also be made with chicken or ham instead of seafood. Serve it with biscuits and a fruit salad.

1. In large soup pot, heat olive oil over medium heat. Add onion and celery; cook and stir 5 minutes. Add carrots and potatoes; cook and stir 3 minutes longer.

2. Add rice; cook and stir 2 minutes. Add Broth, water, salt, pepper, and tarragon and bring to a simmer. Reduce heat, cover, and simmer about 15 minutes, or until rice is almost tender.

3. Cut snapper into 1" pieces. Add to pot along with shrimp and scallops; stir to blend. Cover, and simmer for 5–8 minutes, until fish flakes and shrimp and scallops are opaque.

4. In small bowl, toss cheese with cornstarch. Stir into soup; cook and stir until cheese melts. Serve immediately.

Fish for Stew

If you're allergic to some fish but not others, you can pick and choose the ones you want to include in this recipe. Remember that some fish cook faster than others. The general rule is to cook for 10 minutes per inch of thickness. In a stew, shrimp cook in about 3–5 minutes; mussels and clams take 6–8; and white fish cooks in 5–9 minutes.

Serves 6

Calories: 359.75
Fat: 12.94 grams
Saturated Fat: 2.22 grams
Carbohydrates: 24.85 grams
Sodium: 684.24 mg

1 tablespoon olive oil
1 onion, chopped
1 cup chopped celery
3 carrots, sliced
2 potatoes, peeled and cubed
⅓ cup long-grain rice
3 cups Vegetable Broth (page 139)
2 cups water
½ teaspoon salt
⅛ teaspoon pepper
1 teaspoon dried tarragon leaves
1 pound red snapper fillets
½ pound peeled shrimp
½ pound bay scallops
1 cup shredded dairy-free, vegan Cheddar cheese
1 tablespoon cornstarch

Calories: 300.51
Fat: 5.23 grams
Saturated Fat: 0.90 grams
Carbohydrates: 59.41 grams
Sodium: 660.39 mg

1 tablespoon olive oil
1 onion, chopped
2 cloves garlic, minced
3 russet potatoes, peeled and chopped
2 cups apple juice
1 cup Vegetable Broth (page 139)
½ teaspoon salt
⅛ teaspoon white pepper
½ teaspoon dried thyme leaves
2 apples, peeled and chopped
1 (3-ounce) package dairy-free, vegan cream cheese
1 tablespoon cornstarch
½ cup apple cider
1 tablespoon lemon juice

 milk wheat eggs fish nuts

Creamy Potato Apple Soup

Apple juice, apple cider, and apples add sweet and tart flavor to this rich and homey soup.

1. In large soup pot, heat olive oil over medium heat. Add onion and garlic; cook and stir until tender, about 6 minutes. Add potatoes; cook and stir 4 minutes longer.

2. Add apple juice, Broth, salt, pepper, and thyme leaves and bring to a boil. Cover pan, reduce heat to low, and simmer 12–16 minutes, or until potatoes are tender.

3. Puree soup using an immersion blender. Add apples; cook and stir 4 minutes, until tender. Cube cream cheese and add to soup; cook and stir until melted.

4. In small bowl, combine cornstarch, cider, and lemon juice; mix well. Add to soup; cook and stir until soup just comes to a simmer and thickens, about 3–4 minutes. Serve immediately.

milk wheat eggs fish nuts

Vegetarian Quiche

This quiche can also be made with broccoli or mixed vegetables instead of spinach.

1. Preheat oven to 350°F. In large skillet, heat 2 tablespoons olive oil over medium heat. Add onion and garlic; cook and stir until tender, about 6 minutes. Add bell pepper; cook and stir 3 minutes longer.

2. Add spinach, salt, pepper, and nutmeg; cook and stir until moisture evaporates. Set aside.

3. In food processor, combine ¼ cup olive oil with tofu, cream cheese, vinegar, lemon juice, mustard, oregano, and basil; process until smooth.

4. Sprinkle Cheddar cheese in Cornmeal Pie Crust. Top with spinach mixture, then slowly pour tofu mixture over all. Shake pie gently so the tofu filling settles into it. Sprinkle with Parmesan cheese.

5. Bake 40–50 minutes, or until quiche is set and crust is browned. Cool 5 minutes. Cut into wedges to serve.

Vegan Quiches

Vegan quiches aren't going to have quite the same texture as those made with eggs or milk, but they can be delicious. You can vary the filling as you'd like, as long as the volume is about the same. Choose different soy or rice cheeses, and different herbs and spices, too.

Serves 6

Calories: 421.10
Fat: 25.30 grams
Saturated Fat: 6.39 grams
Carbohydrates: 29.02 grams
Sodium: 683.23 mg

2 tablespoons olive oil
1 onion, finely chopped
3 cloves garlic, minced
1 red bell pepper, chopped
1 cup frozen spinach, thawed and well drained
½ teaspoon salt
⅛ teaspoon pepper
Pinch nutmeg
3 tablespoons olive oil
12 ounces firm tofu, crumbled
1 (3-ounce) package dairy-free, vegan cream cheese
1 tablespoon apple cider vinegar
1 tablespoon lemon juice
1 tablespoon gluten-free Dijon mustard
½ teaspoon dried oregano leaves
1 teaspoon dried basil leaves
1 cup shredded dairy-free, vegan Cheddar cheese
1 Cornmeal Pie Crust (page 289)
¼ cup grated dairy-free, vegan Parmesan cheese

milk   wheat   eggs   fish   nuts

Garlic Lover's Pizza

If you love garlic, this is the pizza for you. You could also add cooked chicken or pork sausage for a meat pizza.

Serves 6

Calories: 468.18 grams
Fat: 16.66 grams
Saturated Fat: 3.01 grams
Carbohydrates: 64.96 grams
Sodium: 841.48 mg

1 head Roasted Garlic
    (page 130)
1 tablespoon olive oil
1 onion, chopped
1 cup shredded carrots
½ teaspoon salt
⅛ teaspoon pepper
1 (8-ounce) package dairy-
    free, vegan, soy cream
    cheese, softened
1 Pizza Crust, prebaked
    and cooled (page 63)
1 cup shredded dairy-
    free, vegan mozzarella
    cheese

1. Preheat oven to 400°F. Squeeze cloves out of the garlic head and place in small bowl and set aside.

2. In small saucepan, heat olive oil over medium heat. Add onion and carrot; cook and stir until tender, about 6 minutes. Sprinkle with salt and pepper; add to garlic in bowl. Stir to combine.

3. Spread cream cheese on Pizza Crust; top with garlic mixture. Sprinkle with mozzarella cheese. Bake 20–25 minutes, or until crust is deep golden brown and cheese is melted and beginning to brown. Cut into wedges to serve.

milk wheat eggs fish nuts

Broccoli Penne

*This green pasta sauce looks like pesto,
but it's full of broccoli, vitamins, and minerals.*

1. Bring a large pot of water to a boil. In large saucepan, heat 1 tablespoon olive oil over medium heat. Add onion, garlic, and ginger; cook and stir until crisp-tender, about 5 minutes. Add broccoli; cook and stir 4 minutes longer.

2. Add water, bring to a simmer, cover pan, and cook 3–5 minutes, until broccoli is tender. Drain and place in food processor.

3. Add lemon juice, salt, pepper, basil, and remaining 3 tablespoons olive oil; process until smooth. Return to saucepan over low heat.

4. Cook pasta according to package directions; drain; add to saucepan with sauce. Toss to coat over low heat, then sprinkle with cheese. Serve immediately.

Al Dente

Al dente is an Italian term which means "to the tooth." It describes how pasta should feel when it's properly cooked. Never cook pasta until it's very soft or it will lose its character. When you taste cooked pasta, there should be a little bit of resistance at the center. When you look at the bitten end, you should see a small opaque line.

Serves 4

Calories: 508.48
Fat: 17.54 grams
Saturated Fat: 3.27 grams
Carbohydrates: 79.86 grams
Sodium: 411.99 mg

4 tablespoons olive oil, divided
1 onion, chopped
4 cloves garlic, minced
1 tablespoon grated ginger root
1 (16-ounce) package frozen broccoli florets
¼ cup water
2 tablespoons lemon juice
½ teaspoon salt
⅛ teaspoon cayenne pepper
¼ cup fresh basil leaves
1 (12-ounce) package gluten-free rice penne pasta
⅓ cup grated dairy-free, vegan Parmesan cheese

milk   wheat   eggs   fish   nuts

Pesto Pasta

For a nonvegetarian dish, add some cooked chicken or ham to this easy recipe.

Serves 6

Calories: 341.97
Fat: 11.90 grams
Saturated Fat: 2.12 grams
Carbohydrates: 52.63 grams
Sodium: 258.36 mg

1 tablespoon olive oil
1 onion, chopped
1 (8-ounce) package sliced
    mushrooms
1 (12-ounce) package
    gluten-free rice pasta
    shells
1 cup frozen baby peas
½ cup Vegetable Broth
    (page 139)
½ cup Basil Pesto (page
    77)
¼ cup grated dairy-free,
    vegan Parmesan cheese

1. Bring a large pot of water to a boil. Meanwhile, in large saucepan, heat olive oil over medium heat. Add onion; cook and stir until tender, about 5 minutes. Add mushrooms; cook and stir 3 minutes longer.

2. Cook pasta according to package directions until al dente. Meanwhile, add peas and Broth to saucepan and bring to a simmer. Simmer until peas are hot, about 3–5 minutes.

3. Drain pasta and add to saucepan along with Pesto. Cook and stir 2–3 minutes. Sprinkle with cheese and serve.

milk *wheat* *eggs* *fish* *nuts*

Veggie Enchiladas

Cooking vegetables until they brown caramelizes the sugars, creating rich and complex flavor. These enchiladas are different and delicious.

Serves 8

Calories: 331.47
Fat: 13.88 grams
Saturated Fat: 2.38 grams
Carbohydrates: 39.67 grams
Sodium: 649.03 mg

1. Preheat oven to 375°F. In large skillet, heat olive oil over medium heat. Add onion; cook and stir until onion starts to brown, about 8–10 minutes. Add mushrooms; cook and stir until tender, about 8 minutes longer.

2. Add squash and bell peppers. Cook and stir until liquid evaporates and vegetables begin to brown, about 7–9 minutes longer.

3. Place sweet potatoes in medium bowl; add basil, thyme, salt, pepper, and Vegetable Broth. Mash using a potato masher until smooth. In medium bowl, combine Tomato Sauce and Taco Seasoning Mix; stir until blended. Place ½ cup Sauce mixture in bottom of 13" × 9" baking dish.

4. Arrange tortillas on work surface. Spread with potato mixture, then divide vegetable mixture on top. Roll up and place seam-side down in sauce in baking dish. Pour remaining Tomato Sauce mixture over all and top with cheese. Bake 30–40 minutes, or until casserole is bubbling.

1 tablespoon olive oil
1 onion, chopped
1 (8-ounce) package sliced mushrooms
2 yellow summer squash, chopped
1 green bell pepper, chopped
1 red bell pepper, chopped
1 (17-ounce) can sweet potatoes, drained
1 teaspoon dried basil leaves
1 teaspoon dried thyme leaves
½ teaspoon salt
⅛ teaspoon pepper
½ cup Vegetable Broth (page 139)
3 cups Tomato Sauce (page 81)
2 tablespoons Taco Seasoning Mix (page 80)
12 (6-inch) corn tortillas
2 cups shredded dairy-free, vegan Cheddar cheese

Enchiladas and Burritos

Enchiladas and burritos are similar, but differ in preparation. The fillings can be the same, but enchiladas are usually baked in a sauce and covered with cheese, while burritos are just filled and rolled corn or flour tortillas, baked or deep fried until crisp. They can be made with just about any filling—vegetarian, beef, chicken, or fish.

Mini Cheese Pizzas

You can leave off the tomatoes or add more vegetables to this simple recipe. Kids love to make and eat these pizzas.

Serves 6

Calories: 424.70
Fat: 16.39 rams
Saturated Fat: 2.82 grams
Carbohydrates: 49.20 grams
Sodium: 456.92 mg

1 (3-ounce) package dairy-free, vegan cream cheese, softened
5 tablespoons Basil Pesto (page 77)
¼ cup chopped green onion
6 Mini Pizza Crusts, prebaked (page 61)
2 tomatoes, chopped
1 cup shredded dairy-free, vegan mozzarella cheese

1. Preheat oven to 400°F. In small bowl, combine cream cheese, Pesto, and green onion and mix well.

2. Spread over the Crusts and top with tomatoes and mozzarella cheese. Bake 10–15 minutes, or until crust is golden brown and cheese is melted and beginning to brown. Serve immediately.

Grilled Salmon

Salmon is marinated for a while, then grilled to perfection in this delicious and easy recipe. Serve with roasted potatoes and steamed veggies.

Serves 4

Calories: 352.92
Fat: 22.62 grams
Saturated Fat: 4.37 grams
Carbohydrates: 3.92 grams
Sodium: 295.30 mg

¼ cup orange juice
1 tablespoon lemon juice
2 tablespoons olive oil
1 tablespoon gluten-free Dijon mustard
2 cloves garlic, minced
½ teaspoon dried dill weed
4 (6-ounce) salmon steaks

1. In 13" × 9" glass baking dish, combine orange juice, lemon juice, olive oil, mustard, garlic, and dill. Add salmon steaks; turn to coat. Cover and refrigerate 1–2 hours.

2. Prepare and preheat grill. Make sure grill is clean. Lightly oil the grill rack with vegetable oil. Add salmon and grill 6" from medium coals 9–12 minutes, turning once, until fish flakes easily when tested with fork. Discard remaining marinade.

milk wheat eggs fish nuts

Veggie Pizza

Let your kids chop the vegetables and assemble this quick pizza.

1. Preheat oven to 400°F. In skillet, heat olive oil over medium heat. Add onion and garlic; cook and stir 3 minutes. Add bell pepper, squash, and mushrooms; cook and stir for 3 minutes longer.

2. In small bowl, combine cream cheese and Salad Dressing; mix well. Spread on Pizza Crust. Top with vegetable mixture, then sprinkle with mozzarella cheese.

3. Bake 20–30 minutes, or until crust is deep golden brown and cheese is melted and starts to brown. Let cool 5 minutes. Cut into wedges to serve.

Salad Dressing as Pizza Sauce

Most salad dressings will work well as a pizza sauce. It helps to combine them with some type of vegan sour cream or cream cheese so they have more body and don't soak into the crust. For non vegetarian pizzas, top with cooked chicken or pork sausage, then pile on the vegetables. When you make your own pizza, you can be adventurous.

Serves 8

Calories: 378.27
Fat: 17.30 grams
Saturated Fat: 3.30 grams
Carbohydrates: 47.43 grams
Sodium: 340.93 mg

1 tablespoon olive oil
1 onion, sliced
2 cloves garlic, sliced
1 red bell pepper, sliced
1 yellow summer squash, sliced
1 cup sliced mushrooms
1 (3-ounce) package dairy-free, vegan cream cheese, softened
½ cup Ranch Salad Dressing (page 108)
1 Pizza Crust (page 63)
1 cup shredded dairy-free, vegan mozzarella cheese

Chapter 12
Sandwiches

Cheesy Apple Melts

*This crunchy and cheesy sandwich melt is just delicious. Keep
the spread in the refrigerator for up to 3 days.*

Serves 4

Calories: 530.08
Fat: 29.34 grams
Saturated Fat: 4.08 grams
Carbohydrates: 54.18 grams
Sodium: 490.49 mg

1 apple, diced
½ cup chopped celery
1 tablespoon lemon juice
⅓ cup Eggless Mayonnaise
  (page 68)
½ cup chopped red onion
1 cup diced dairy-free,
  vegan Cheddar cheese
¼ cup shredded dairy-free,
  vegan Parmesan cheese
8 slices French Bread (page
  51)
2 tablespoons olive oil

1. In small bowl, combine all ingredients except Bread and olive oil. Mix well.

2. Slice the Bread on an angle to make larger slices. Make sandwiches with the filling. Brush outsides of sandwiches with olive oil. Cook in covered preheated skillet 5–7 minutes, turning once, until bread is crisp and golden and filling is hot. Serve immediately.

Pizza Wraps

*Other ingredients can be used instead of the bell pepper;
use sautéed onions, canned mushrooms,
cooked sausage, or just leave it out.*

Serves 6

Calories: 208.08
Fat: 13.43 grams
Saturated Fat: 3.25 grams
Carbohydrates: 11.92
grams
Sodium: 367.72 mg

½ cup Spaghetti Sauce
  (page 206)
½ cup gluten-free pepperoni
  slices
1 green bell pepper,
  chopped
6 (6-inch) corn tortillas
1 cup shredded dairy-free,
  vegan Cheddar cheese

1. Preheat oven to 350°F. In medium bowl, combine Sauce, pepperoni, and bell pepper; mix well.

2. Arrange tortillas on work surface and divide Sauce mixture among them. Top with cheese, then fold in sides and roll up like a burrito. Place seam-side down on ungreased cookie sheet.

3. Bake 12–18 minutes, or until wraps are hot and tortillas are slightly toasted. Cut in half and serve immediately.

milk wheat eggs fish nuts

Grilled Cheese Sandwiches

Grilled cheese sandwiches are an American classic. You can make this with real American cheese and butter if you aren't allergic to dairy.

1. Slice Focaccia into 6 wedges. Carefully slice each wedge in half, making 12 thinner wedges. Make sandwiches using the cheese and tomato.

2. In small bowl, combine margarine and oil; beat to combine. Spread this mixture on outside of Focaccia.

3. Heat a griddle over medium-low heat. Add sandwiches and cook, turning once and pressing down with spatula occasionally, until bread is toasted and cheese is melted, about 5–6 minutes. Serve immediately.

Soy Cheese Varieties

You may have to try several varieties of soy cheese before you find one you like. The cheese works best when it's used as "glue" in a recipe, as in the Grilled Cheese Sandwiches or Pizza Wraps (page 224); it also melts better when diced or shredded. Some good brands include Soymage, Vegan Gourmet, Sheese, and Galaxy Nutritional Foods Vegan Soy.

Serves 6

Calories: 435.92
Fat: 18.45 grams
Saturated Fat: 5.66 grams
Carbohydrates: 56.20 grams
Sodium: 839.93 mg

1 recipe Focaccia Bread (page 55)
12 slices vegan, soy American cheese, diced
6 slices tomato
2 tablespoons dairy-free vegan margarine
1 tablespoon extra-virgin olive oil

Fruity Ham Sandwiches

Serves 6

Calories: 280.93
Fat: 6.93 grams
Saturated Fat: 2.92 grams
Carbohydrates: 38.02 grams
Sodium: 470.95 mg

1½ cups chopped gluten-free ham
½ cup Eggless Mayonnaise (page 68)
1 (8-ounce) can crushed pineapple, drained
½ cup chopped celery
¼ cup dried cherries, chopped
2 tablespoons chopped cilantro
6 gluten-free hoagie buns, split
6 leaves butter lettuce

Instead of the dried cherries, use fresh when they are in season, or use chopped strawberries or blueberries. Yum!

1. In medium bowl, combine ham, Mayonnaise, pineapple, celery, cherries, and cilantro and mix well.

2. Toast hoagie buns and place lettuce leaf on bottom half of each. Top with ham mixture, then top half of buns. Serve immediately.

The Many Cuisines of Cilantro

Cilantro, or coriander, is among the most popular herbs in the world. It is used in a host of cuisines, including Mexican, Chinese, Thai, Indian, Vietnamese, and Central American. It is usually added to dishes at the last minute or eaten raw in salads and sandwiches because of its delicate nature.

milk wheat eggs fish nuts

Turkey Wraps

Serves 6

Calories: 249.31
Fat: 11.28 grams
Saturated Fat: 4.49 grams
Carbohydrates: 14.00 grams
Sodium: 143.01 mg

These flavorful wrap sandwiches are really delicious. If you like your food spicy, add another jalapeño or two.

1 tablespoon olive oil
½ cup chopped red onion
1 red bell pepper, chopped
1 jalapeño pepper, minced
2 cups cubed cooked
    turkey
1 tablespoon lemon juice
2 tablespoons chopped
    flat-leaf parsley
6 (8-inch) corn tortillas
2 (3-ounce) packages
    dairy-free, vegan cream
    cheese, softened
1 cup baby spinach leaves

1. In medium saucepan, heat olive oil over medium heat. Add red onion; cook and stir 2 minutes. Add bell pepper and jalapeño pepper; cook and stir 3-4 minutes longer.

2. Remove from heat and stir in turkey, lemon juice, and parsley.

3. Soften tortillas as directed on package. Arrange on work surface; spread each with 1 ounce of soy cream cheese. Layer spinach leaves on top of the cream cheese, and divide turkey mixture over.

4. Roll up the tortillas, enclosing filling. Cut in half. Serve immediately.

Leftover Turkey

When you roast a turkey for Thanksgiving or other holidays, remove the meat within 2 days. Chop or dice, then package into hard-sided freezer containers. Label, seal, and freeze up to 3 months. To use, let stand in refrigerator overnight, then use in recipes from casseroles to sandwich spreads. Use the bones to make stock.

Serves 4

Calories: 228.09
Fat: 10.51 grams
Saturated Fat: 3.65 grams
Carbohydrates: 3.40 grams
Sodium: 403.85 mg

1 tablespoon olive oil
1 cup finely chopped
    mushrooms
½ cup finely chopped onion
½ teaspoon salt
⅛ teaspoon pepper
1 tablespoon mustard
1 pound lean gluten-free
    ground beef

Vegetable Beef Burgers

Serve these burgers on top of some mashed or hash brown potatoes, or on gluten-free hamburger buns with ketchup and mustard.

1. In small skillet, heat olive oil over medium heat. Add mushrooms and onion; cook and stir until tender, about 5–6 minutes. Remove from heat and add salt, pepper, and mustard; mix well. Let cool 20 minutes.

2. Add the beef and mix gently with your hands. Form into 4 patties. Cook under the broiler or over charcoal until beef is well done, with internal temperature reading of 160°F. Serve immediately.

Serves 6

Calories: 183.93
Fat: 6.30 grams
Saturated Fat: 1.38 grams
Carbohydrates: 19.43 grams
Sodium: 288.23 mg

1/3 cup vegan soy
    mayonnaise
½ cup Tomatillo Salsa (page
    118)
2 tomatoes, chopped
1 cup frozen corn, thawed
    and drained
1 jalapeño pepper, minced
2 cups cooked, cubed
    gluten-free turkey
6 butter lettuce leaves
6 (6-inch) corn tortillas

Turkey Enchilada Wraps

These simple wrap sandwiches are good to tuck into lunchboxes.

1. In small bowl, combine mayonnaise with Salsa; mix well. Stir in remaining ingredients except tortillas.

2. Place tortillas on work surface; line with lettuce. Top with turkey mixture and roll up to serve.

milk   wheat   eggs   soy   fish   nuts

Chicken Lettuce Wraps

These simple sandwiches can be prepared in minutes, if you use the shredded carrots you can buy them in the produce aisle at your grocery store.

1. Drain peppers on paper towel and chop into small pieces. In medium bowl, combine peppers with chicken, Mayonnaise, basil, green onions, and carrots.

2. Spread this mixture on lettuce leaves; roll up. Serve immediately.

Sandwich Spreads

Sandwich spreads are a wonderful thing to have in the refrigerator. Kids with allergies can make snacks from them without fear. They can be used as appetizer dips as well. Cover them with foil and store for 3–4 days. You could add any type of vegetable to these spreads, including chopped bell peppers, zucchini, and celery.

Serves 4

Calories: 342.11
Fat: 24.99 grams
Saturated Fat: 2.18 grams
Carbohydrates: 4.90 grams
Sodium: 630.94 mg

1 (7-ounce) jar roasted red peppers, drained
2 cups chopped cooked chicken
½ cup Eggless Mayonnaise (page 68)
½ teaspoon dried basil leaves
¼ cup chopped green onions
½ cup shredded carrots
4–6 large lettuce leaves

milk   wheat   eggs   fish   nuts

Steak Wraps

Ribeye steaks are tender and flavorful without much fat. If you can't find boneless steaks, just use bone-in and cut around it.

Calories: 314.56
Fat: 18.08 grams
Saturated Fat: 4.80 grams
Carbohydrates: 18.46 grams
Sodium: 548.22 mg

1 tablespoon olive oil
1 onion, sliced
1 cup sliced mushrooms
1 (8-ounce) boneless ribeye
    steak, sliced thin
½ teaspoon salt
⅛ teaspoon pepper
⅓ cup Basil Pesto (page
    77)
½ cup grated dairy-free,
    vegan Parmesan cheese
4–6 (6-inch) corn tortillas
4–6 lettuce leaves

1. Heat olive oil in large skillet over medium heat. Add onion and mushrooms; cook and stir until tender, about 5 minutes.

2. Add steak; sprinkle with salt and pepper. Stir-fry until steak is just cooked, about 2–3 minutes.

3. Remove skillet from heat and drain thoroughly. Stir in Pesto and cheese. Line tortillas with lettuce and add steak mixture. Roll up and serve immediately.

milk wheat eggs soy fish nuts

Chicken à la King Wraps

Instead of serving over biscuits, make your next Chicken à la King into a wrap sandwich!

Serves 4

Calories: 270.48
Fat: 10.66 grams
Saturated Fat: 2.27 grams
Carbohydrates: 17.38 grams
Sodium: 422.15 mg

1. In medium skillet, heat olive oil over medium heat. Add mushrooms and bell pepper; cook and stir until tender, about 5 minutes. Add chicken, salt, pepper, marjoram, and pimento; cook 3 minutes.

2. In small bowl, combine cornstarch and rice milk and mix well. Add to skillet; cook and stir until sauce thickens, about 3–5 minutes. Make wrap sandwiches with the tortillas. Serve immediately.

1 tablespoon olive oil
1 cup sliced mushrooms
1 green bell pepper, chopped
2 cups chopped Poached Chicken (page 156)
½ teaspoon salt
⅛ teaspoon pepper
½ teaspoon dried marjoram leaves
2 tablespoons diced pimento
2 tablespoons cornstarch
⅔ cup rice milk
4 (6-inch) corn tortillas

Chicken à la King

The origins of Chicken à la King are murky. It was invented a long time ago, but could have been at the Brighton Beach Hotel in New York City, or Claridge's in London. It is made of chicken, mushrooms, pimentos, and green peppers in a cream sauce flavored with sherry, usually served on toast. There are many variations of it, but not as a sandwich until now!

Calories: 493.23
Fat: 21.04 grams
Saturated Fat: 3.40 grams
Carbohydrates: 56.90 grams
Sodium: 672.33 mg

3 slices gluten-free bacon
1 onion, chopped
1 cup sliced mushrooms
1 green bell pepper, chopped
1 (3-ounce) package vegan, soy cream cheese, softened
⅓ cup Ranch Salad Dressing (page 108)
½ loaf French Bread (page 51)
2 tomatoes, sliced
4 slices vegan, soy mozzarella cheese

milk wheat eggs fish nuts

Bacon Veggie Sub Sandwich

Use any fresh vegetable you'd like in this excellent sandwich.

1. In large skillet, cook bacon until crisp. Remove bacon from pan, drain on paper towel, crumble, and set aside.

2. Use bacon drippings to cook onion, mushrooms, and bell pepper until tender, about 5–6 minutes. Drain well and place in medium bowl. Add bacon.

3. In small bowl, combine cream cheese and Salad Dressing; beat until smooth. Stir into bacon mixture.

4. Cut French Bread in half lengthwise. Spread bacon mixture over bottom half, and top with tomatoes and mozzarella cheese. Replace top half of bread. Slice to serve.

wheat   eggs   soy   fish   nuts

Roasted Red Pepper Pressed Sandwiches

The whole point of a pressed sandwich is to let the juices from vegetables and the dressing soak into the bread. It's perfect for a picnic.

1. Cut loaf in half lengthwise. Scoop out some of the inside of the Bread with your fingers, leaving a 1" shell.

2. In small bowl, combine Mayonnaise and pimento. Spread on inside of both halves of Bread. Fill one half with red pepper, basil, tomatoes, mushrooms, and avocado. Sprinkle with lemon juice. Place Bread halves together to form a sandwich.

3. Wrap sandwich tightly in foil and place in a baking dish. Weigh down the sandwich with cans of food; refrigerate 1–2 hours to blend flavors. Slice to serve.

Vegetables for Sandwiches

You can use just about any vegetable in a sandwich, but some are better cooked than raw. Broccoli is best cooked, as are mushrooms, because cooked (or canned) mushrooms won't darken. You can also sneak vegetables into sandwiches; stir shredded cucumber, zucchini, or carrots into cream cheese or mayonnaise and spread on the bread.

Serves 4

Calories: 476.40
Fat: 20.23 grams
Saturated Fat: 2.72 grams
Carbohydrates: 70.10 grams
Sodium: 901.92 mg

½ loaf Sourdough French Bread (page 49)
¼ cup Eggless Mayonnaise (page 68)
2 tablespoons minced pimento
1 (7-ounce) jar gluten-free roasted red peppers, drained
1 cup fresh basil leaves
2 tomatoes, sliced
1 (7-ounce) jar gluten-free sliced mushrooms, drained
1 avocado, thinly sliced
1 tablespoon lemon juice

Wild Rice Sandwich Spread

Yields 4 cups;
Serving size ½ cup

Calories: 127.14
Fat: 5.24 grams
Saturated Fat: 1.10 grams
Carbohydrates: 11.65 grams
Sodium: 349.03 mg

⅓ cup silken tofu
2 tablespoons gluten-free mustard
1 tablespoon soy or rice milk
½ teaspoon dried thyme leaves
½ teaspoon salt
⅛ teaspoon pepper
2 cups cooked wild rice
1 red bell pepper, chopped
¼ cup chopped green onion
1 (4-ounce) can sliced mushrooms, drained
¼ cup shredded dairy-free, vegan soy Parmesan cheese
1 cup diced dairy-free, vegan soy Monterey Jack cheese

Cook wild rice according to package directions. Look for long, whole grains of rice; do not buy packages that have broken grains.

1. In medium bowl, combine tofu, mustard, soy or rice milk, thyme, salt, and pepper and mix well.

2. Add all remaining ingredients and stir to coat. Cover and chill 2 hours before serving. Use to make sandwiches. Spread can be stored covered in refrigerator up to 3 days.

milk wheat soy fish nuts

Beef and Avocado Bagels

Bagels make a satisfying and filling sandwich, even open-faced. This one should be eaten as soon as it's made.

Serves 4

Calories: 523.00
Fat: 31.02 grams
Saturated Fat: 7.02 grams
Carbohydrates: 35.95 grams
Sodium: 252.66 mg

½ pound sliced gluten-free deli roast beef
1 avocado
⅓ cup Eggless Mayonnaise (page 68)
1 red bell pepper, chopped
1 cup sliced yellow summer squash
2 Bagels, split (page 64)
4 leaves red lettuce

1. Cut beef into small pieces and place in medium bowl. Peel avocado, remove pit, and dice; add to beef along with Mayonnaise. Stir to coat, then add bell pepper and summer squash.

2. Place Bagels in microwave. Microwave on high 40 seconds, then turn Bagels ½ turn. Microwave on high 15 seconds longer, then remove and cut in half. Top the Bagel halves with lettuce, then add the beef filling. Serve immediately.

Avocados

It's next to impossible to find ripe avocados in the grocery store. To ripen, buy avocados that are firm but not rock hard. Place them in a paper bag with a red apple, close the bag, and let stand on the counter for 1–3 days. Check the avocados every day. When they yield to gentle pressure, they're ready to use.

Asian Veggie Wraps

*You could add cooked pork or chicken
to this simple wrap recipe if you'd like.*

Serves 6

Calories: 138.33
Fat: 2.64 grams
Saturated Fat: 0.39 grams
Carbohydrates: 25.14 grams
Sodium: 465.72 mg

1 tablespoon olive oil
1 onion, chopped
1 shallot, minced
2 tablespoons minced ginger root
2 cups shredded cabbage
½ cup shredded carrot
2 tablespoons Soy Sauce Substitute (page 82)
2 tablespoons Vegetable Broth (page 139)
3 tablespoons gluten-free, soy-free plum sauce
⅛ teaspoon white pepper
2 cups cooked rice
6–8 romaine lettuce leaves

1. In large skillet, heat olive oil over medium heat. Add onion, shallot, and ginger; stir-fry 4 minutes.

2. Add cabbage and carrot; stir-fry 4–5 minutes longer, until crisp-tender. In small bowl, combine Soy Sauce Substitute, Broth, plum sauce, and pepper; mix well. Add to skillet along with rice; stir-fry until hot.

3. Divide rice mixture among the lettuce leaves; roll up. Serve immediately.

milk *wheat* *eggs* *fish* *nuts*

Cheesy Pear Ham Wraps

*Simmering pears in pear nectar really enhances
and strengthens the sweet flavor.*

Serves 4

Calories: 220.03
Fat: 6.26 grams
Saturated Fat: 2.05 grams
Carbohydrates: 27.73
grams
Sodium: 901.93 mg

1. In small saucepan over medium-low heat, simmer pears in pear nectar and lemon juice until tender, about 5–7 minutes. Remove from heat and let pears cool in the nectar.

2. Remove pears from nectar and drain on paper towel. In small bowl, beat cream cheese with salt, pepper, and thyme leaves until blended. Spread on boiled ham slices and top with pears; fold over.

3. Line tortillas with lettuce leaves and top with ham bundles; roll up. Serve immediately.

2 pears, sliced
½ cup pear nectar
1 tablespoon lemon juice
*1 (3-ounce) package dairy-
free, vegan cream
cheese*
¼ teaspoon salt
⅛ teaspoon pepper
*½ teaspoon dried thyme
leaves*
*4 thin slices boiled gluten-
free ham*
4 (6-inch) corn tortillas
4 leaves lettuce

Pears

Ripe pears can be difficult to find in the supermarket. You may find that they're ripe one day and overripe the next. You can use under-ripe pears in cooked recipes, like Pear Crisp and this sandwich recipe. Keep the skin on for more fiber and to help the pears hold their shape when they're cooked.

Sausage Sandwiches

*This recipe is similar to sausage sandwiches
you can buy at street fairs.*

Serves 6

Calories: 549.12
Fat: 25.72 grams
Saturated Fat: 7.32 grams
Carbohydrates: 82.00
grams
Sodium: 1140.93 mg

*1 pound spicy gluten-free
    Italian sausage
1 onion, chopped
2 cloves garlic, minced
1 green bell pepper,
    chopped
1 cup sliced mushrooms
1 cup Spaghetti Sauce,
    divided (page 206)
1 Focaccia Bread (page 55)*

1. Preheat oven to 400°F. In large skillet, brown sausage with onion and garlic, stirring to break up meat, until sausage is cooked. Drain well, then add green bell pepper and mushrooms. Cook and stir 4–5 minutes longer, until vegetables are tender. Remove from heat; stir in ½ cup Spaghetti Sauce.

2. Cut Focaccia in half lengthwise. Spread both halves with Spaghetti Sauce. Top one half with the sausage filling, then top with other half of Bread. Wrap loosely in foil and place on cookie sheet.

3. Bake 15–20 minutes, or until sandwich is hot. Slice into wedges to serve.

milk   wheat   eggs   soy   fish   nuts

Cranberry Chicken Sandwiches

You can make this recipe using leftover Thanksgiving turkey as well as poached chicken. It's delicious and colorful.

1. In medium bowl, combine all ingredients except Focaccia; mix well. Cover and refrigerate 2–3 hours to blend flavors.

2. Make sandwiches using Focaccia Bread; grill until bread is toasted and filling is hot, turning once.

Dried Cranberries

Dried cranberries are a delicious snack. They usually contain sugar, as plain cranberries are very tart. Dried cranberries contain 300 calories per cup, so they aren't a diet food, but they have a good amount of fiber. Stir them into homemade snack mixes, add to muffins, and use in salads.

Serves 4

Calories: 545.60
Fat: 22.06 grams
Saturated Fat: 3.04 grams
Carbohydrates: 58.65 grams
Sodium: 752.32 mg

2 cups Poached Chicken, cubed (page 156)
⅓ cup Eggless Mayonnaise (page 68)
¼ cup gluten-free whole berry cranberry sauce
½ cup gluten-free dried cranberries
½ cup chopped red onion
½ cup chopped celery
½ teaspoon salt
⅛ teaspoon white pepper
4 wedges Focaccia Bread, split (page 55)

Chicken Apple Sandwiches

Grilled sandwiches make an excellent quick lunch. You can keep this filling in the refrigerator, covered, for up to 3 days.

Serves 4

Calories: 483.75
Fat: 23.28 grams
Saturated Fat: 4.21 grams
Carbohydrates: 35.45 grams
Sodium: 648.22 mg

2 cups cubed cooked chicken
1 Granny Smith apple, peeled and diced
1 cup shredded carrot
½ cup vegan mayonnaise
½ teaspoon dried thyme leaves
⅛ teaspoon pepper
1 cup shredded dairy-free, vegan mozzarella cheese
8 slices gluten-free bread
2 tablespoons olive oil

1. In medium bowl, combine chicken, apple, and carrot and mix gently. Add mayonnaise, thyme, and pepper and mix well. Stir in cheese.

2. Make sandwiches using the bread. Brush outsides of sandwiches with the olive oil.

3. Cook in covered preheated skillet 5–6 minutes, turning once, or in a Panini maker 3–4 minutes, until bread is toasted and filling is hot. Serve immediately.

Soy Cheese Safety

Make sure that your soy cheese does not include any milk proteins. Even the words "milk free" or "dairy free" do not always mean that the product is safe for those with milk allergies. The words to look out for include "casein," "rennet," and "hydrosalates." Vegan brands may be your best bet, but be sure you still read the label carefully.

Chapter 13
Side Dishes

Mashed Potatoes

Mashed potatoes are true comfort food, and with this recipe anyone can eat them, no matter what allergies they have.

Serves 6

Calories: 204.96
Fat: 5.00 grams
Saturated Fat: 0.75 grams
Carbohydrates: 37.09 grams
Sodium: 508.73 mg

6 russet potatoes, peeled
2 tablespoons olive oil
1 onion, chopped
½–1 cup Chicken Stock
*   (page 137)*
½ teaspoon salt
⅛ teaspoon white pepper

1. Cut potatoes into chunks and place in large pot. Cover with water and bring to a boil over high heat. Reduce heat to low, cover pot, and simmer 9–15 minutes, or until potatoes are tender when tested with knife.

2. Meanwhile, in small saucepan, heat olive oil over medium heat. Add onion; cook and stir until onions start to brown and caramelize, about 10–12 minutes.

3. When potatoes are cooked, drain and return to the hot pot. Set over medium heat and shake a few minutes to dry potatoes. Add onion mixture and mash with a potato masher.

4. Gradually beat in enough Stock until the potatoes are light and fluffy. Add salt and pepper to taste. Serve immediately.

Chopped Veggie Couscous

Use your favorite combination of vegetables in this easy side dish. To make it gluten free, see the sidebar below.

1. In large skillet, heat olive oil over medium heat. Add onion and garlic; cook and stir 4 minutes. Add bell pepper and mushrooms; cook and stir 4–5 minutes longer, until crisp-tender.

2. Meanwhile, bring Broth to a boil in large saucepan. Add couscous, cover pan, remove from heat, and let stand 5 minutes.

3. Add peas, salt, pepper, and thyme to vegetables in skillet; cook and stir 4–5 minutes longer, until vegetables are tender.

4. Fluff couscous with a fork and add to skillet along with vinegar; stir gently to blend. Serve immediately.

Couscous

You could substitute cooked millet or quinoa for the couscous in this recipe to make it gluten free. And be sure the balsamic vinegar is pure. Be sure that you can tolerate these grains, and that you buy them from an organic purveyor with a dedicated mill. Couscous itself is a coarsely ground pasta made from semolina wheat, so it does contain gluten.

Serves 8

Calories: 243.04
Fat: 5.52 grams
Saturated Fat: 0.78 grams
Carbohydrates: 40.86 grams
Sodium: 284.40 mg

2 tablespoons olive oil
1 onion, chopped
4 cloves garlic, minced
1 yellow bell pepper, chopped
1 cup chopped mushrooms
3 cups Vegetable Broth (page 139)
2 cups couscous
1 cup frozen baby peas
½ teaspoon salt
⅛ teaspoon pepper
1 teaspoon dried thyme leaves
1 tablespoon balsamic vinegar

Sautéed Peas

Baby peas are tender and sweet. Frozen peas can actually have more nutrients than fresh because they're processed right in the field.

Serves 6

Calories: 65.89
Fat: 2.45 grams
Saturated Fat: 0.35 grams
Carbohydrates: 8.20 grams
Sodium: 248.65 mg

1 tablespoon olive oil
2 shallots, minced
3 cloves garlic, minced
1 (16-ounce) bag frozen peas
2 tablespoons Vegetable Broth (page 139)
½ teaspoon salt
⅛ teaspoon pepper
½ teaspoon dried thyme leaves

1. In large skillet, heat olive oil over medium heat. Add shallots and garlic; cook and stir until crisp-tender, about 4 minutes. Add peas and remaining ingredients and bring to a simmer.

2. Cover skillet and cook, stirring occasionally, until peas are hot and tender, about 8–11 minutes. Serve immediately.

Citrus Carrots

Citrus, in the form of juices and zest, brighten up carrots and mushrooms to turn this side dish into one worthy of company.

Serves 6

Calories: 75.02
Fat: 4.66 grams
Saturated Fat: 0.65 grams
Carbohydrates: 8.14 grams
Sodium: 254.55 mg

1 (16-ounce) package baby carrots
2 tablespoons olive oil
3 cloves garlic, minced
1 cup chopped mushrooms
½ teaspoon salt
⅛ teaspoon white pepper
1 tablespoon lemon juice
2 tablespoons orange juice
1 teaspoon grated orange zest

1. Place carrots in a skillet; cover with cold water. Bring to a boil, cover, reduce heat to low, and simmer 3–4 minutes, until crisp-tender. Drain carrots and reserve; return skillet to heat.

2. Add olive oil to skillet along with garlic and mushrooms. Cook and stir 4–5 minutes, until crisp-tender. Return carrots to skillet along with remaining ingredients.

3. Bring to a simmer; simmer 2–3 minutes, or until vegetables are tender. Serve immediately.

wheat eggs soy fish nuts

Cheesy Spinach

Make sure you buy the cut-leaf spinach, not the frozen chopped blocks. It has a better texture than the chopped product.

1. Preheat oven to 375°F. In large skillet, heat olive oil over medium heat. Add onion and garlic; cook and stir 3 minutes. Add drained tomatoes; cover and bring to a simmer.

2. Remove cover, add spinach, increase heat, and cook, stirring frequently, until liquid has evaporated. Sprinkle with salt, pepper, and basil leaves. Spoon into 1½ quart casserole and sprinkle with Cheddar cheese.

3. In small bowl, combine Bread crumbs, olive oil, and Parmesan cheese and mix well. Sprinkle over casserole. Bake 25–35 minutes, or until topping is browned and casserole is bubbling. Serve immediately.

Check all Recipes!

When recipes call for other recipes in the ingredient list, be sure you check the ingredient recipe for any allergenic foods. For instance, the French Bread in the Cheesy Spinach recipe contains milk, so even if you substitute vegan cheese for the Cheddar and Parmesan, milk proteins are still lurking in the recipe.

Serves 6

Calories: 236.63
Fat: 14.12 grams
Saturated Fat: 5.35 grams
Carbohydrates: 20.47 grams
Sodium: 630.17 mg

2 tablespoons olive oil
1 onion, chopped
3 cloves garlic, minced
1 (14-ounce) can gluten-free diced tomatoes, drained
1 (16-ounce) bag frozen cut-leaf spinach
½ teaspoon salt
⅛ teaspoon pepper
½ teaspoon dried basil leaves
1 cup shredded, extra-sharp Cheddar cheese
1 slice Sourdough French Bread, crumbled (page 49)
1 tablespoon olive oil
2 tablespoons grated Parmesan cheese

milk wheat eggs soy fish nuts

Apricot Glazed Beans

Serves 4

Calories: 159.64
Fat: 3.74 grams
Saturated Fat: 0.54 grams
Carbohydrates: 31.24 grams
Sodium: 156.74 mg

1 pound green beans
1 tablespoon olive oil
1 shallot, minced
¼ cup apricot nectar
⅓ cup gluten-free apricot preserves
2 teaspoons fresh chopped rosemary leaves
¼ teaspoon salt
Pinch white pepper

Green beans are often served plain; this recipe is a nice change of pace. It's a good side dish to serve with simple broiled chicken or pork chops.

1. Cook beans in a steamer until crisp-tender, about 4–5 minutes. Drain and set aside.

2. In large saucepan, heat olive oil over medium heat. Add shallot; cook and stir until crisp-tender, about 4 minutes.

3. Add apricot nectar and beans; bring to a simmer. Cover pan and simmer 3–4 minutes, until beans are tender. Uncover and add preserves, rosemary, salt, and pepper. Cook and stir 1–2 minutes, until beans are glazed.

milk wheat eggs soy fish nuts

Rice Pilaf

Serves 8

Calories: 232.03
Fat: 5.99 grams
Saturated Fat: 0.88 grams
Carbohydrates: 40.10 grams
Sodium: 448.92 mg

2 tablespoons olive oil
1 onion, chopped
3 cloves garlic, minced
½ cup chopped celery
2 cups uncooked long-grain rice
1 teaspoon salt
⅛ teaspoon pepper
4 cups Vegetable Broth (page 139)

If you aren't allergic to dairy, add a tablespoon or two of butter to this pilaf just before serving.

1. In heavy saucepan, combine olive oil, onion, garlic, and celery. Cook and stir over medium heat until crisp-tender, about 5 minutes.

2. Add rice; cook and stir 2 minutes longer. Sprinkle with salt and pepper and add Broth.

3. Bring to a boil, then reduce heat to low, cover saucepan, and cook 15–20 minutes, or until rice is tender and Broth is absorbed. Cover and remove from heat; let stand 5 minutes. Fluff pilaf with fork and serve.

milk wheat eggs soy fish nuts

Sautéed Yellow Squash and Carrots

When the food on your plate is colorful, you know you're eating well. This side dish is a good example of a colorful recipe.

1. In large saucepan, heat olive oil over medium heat. Add shallot; cook and stir 2 minutes. Add carrot; cook and stir 2 minutes. Add water and bring to a simmer. Cover saucepan; simmer 3 minutes.

2. Add squash, stir, and raise heat. Simmer until liquid evaporates, stirring occasionally. Add salt, pepper, and sage leaves; cover and let stand off heat 3 minutes. Stir and serve.

Summer Squash

There are two basic kinds of squash: summer and winter. Summer squash are thin skinned and tender, cook quickly, and can be served raw. They include yellow squash and zucchini. Winter squash are hard, with thick shells, and they must be cooked before eating, like pumpkins, butternut squash, and acorn squash.

Serves 6

Calories: 83.86
Fat: 4.88 grams
Saturated Fat: 0.70 grams
Carbohydrates: 9.67 grams
Sodium: 215.07 mg

2 tablespoons olive oil
2 shallots, minced
2 carrots, sliced
¼ cup water
3 yellow summer squash, sliced
½ teaspoon salt
⅛ teaspoon white pepper
½ teaspoon dried sage leaves

milk   wheat   eggs   fish   nuts

Pesto Potatoes

This flavorful side dish is delicious served with a steak or some grilled chicken or fish.

1. Preheat oven to 400°F. Scrub potatoes and cut into 1" pieces. Combine in large roasting pan with olive oil, onion, and garlic. Roast 30 minutes, then turn with a spatula. Roast 30–40 minutes longer, or until potatoes are tender and turning brown on the edges.

2. In serving bowl, combine Pesto and yogurt and mix well. Add the hot potato mixture and toss to coat. Serve immediately.

milk   wheat   eggs   soy   fish   nuts

Pea Sauté

Who doesn't love peas? This simple side dish takes just minutes to make.

1. In medium saucepan, heat olive oil over medium heat. Add shallot and garlic; cook and stir 4–5 minutes, until crisp-tender.

2. Add peas and water; bring to a simmer. Cover and cook, shaking pan occasionally, until peas are hot and tender, about 4–6 minutes. Drain, then sprinkle with salt and pepper. Serve immediately.

milk wheat eggs soy fish nuts

Fried Rice

Fried rice doesn't have to contain egg! If you add some chicken or ham to this easy recipe, you've created a main dish.

Serves 6

Calories: 201.68
Fat: 4.95 grams
Saturated Fat: 0.74 grams
Carbohydrates: 35.15 grams
Sodium: 544.08 mg

¼ cup Vegetable Broth
   (page 139)
1 tablespoon Soy Sauce
   Substitute (page 82)
1 tablespoon minced fresh
   ginger root
⅛ teaspoon pepper
2 tablespoons olive oil
1 onion, chopped
3 cloves garlic, minced
½ cup shredded carrot
½ cup chopped green
   onions
4 cups long-grain rice,
   cooked and cooled

1. In small bowl, combine Broth, Soy Sauce Substitute, ginger root, and pepper and mix well and set aside.

2. In wok or large skillet, heat olive oil over medium-high heat. Add onion and garlic; stir-fry 3 minutes. Add carrot and green onion; stir-fry 2–3 minutes longer.

3. Add rice; stir-fry until rice is hot and grains are separate, about 4–5 minutes. Stir Broth mixture and add to wok; stir-fry until hot, about 3–4 minutes. Serve immediately.

Cooking Rice

If you have trouble cooking rice, get a rice cooker. This inexpensive appliance cooks rice to fluffy perfection every time. Another option is to cook rice like you cook pasta—in a large pot of boiling water. Keep tasting the rice; when it's tender, thoroughly drain and use in a recipe or serve.

Hash Brown Casserole

Serves 8–10

*This recipe makes a huge amount,
so it's perfect for entertaining or holidays.*

Calories: 346.10
Fat: 18.79 grams
Saturated Fat: 4.55 grams
Carbohydrates: 36.23 grams
Sodium: 438.18 mg

1 (32-ounce) package
   frozen hash brown
   potatoes, thawed
1 onion, minced
2 cloves garlic, minced
1 teaspoon salt
¼ teaspoon white pepper
1 cup Soy-Yogurt Cheese
   (page 70)
⅓ cup soy or rice milk
2 cups shredded nondairy,
   vegan mozzarella
   cheese

1. Preheat oven to 375°F. Spray a 13" × 9" baking dish with nonstick gluten-free cooking spray and set aside.

2. In large bowl, combine all ingredients and mix well. Spoon into baking dish and spread into an even layer. Cover and bake 30 minutes, then uncover and bake 30–40 minutes longer, or until casserole is bubbly and starting to brown. Serve immediately.

Hash Brown Potatoes

You can find hash brown potatoes in the refrigerated and freezer sections of your local grocery store. Read labels to learn which one has the fewest additives and other ingredients. To thaw the frozen potatoes, just let the bag stand in the refrigerator overnight. Drain the potatoes well before using in recipes.

Risotto Cakes

You can serve these little cakes as a side dish for fried chicken. Top with some fresh salsa for a great contrast.

1. In medium bowl, combine all ingredients except olive oil. Form the mixture into small cakes.

2. In large skillet, heat olive oil over medium heat. Add cakes; sauté on one side until golden brown, about 3–5 minutes. Carefully turn and cook on second side until browned. Serve immediately.

Part-Skim Mozzarella Cheese

Most low-fat cheeses do not melt as well as their full-fat counterparts. Part-skim mozzarella cheese is the exception to this rule. Fresh, or full-fat mozzarella contains a lot of water, so it doesn't melt well. Part-skim mozzarella is firmer and melts beautifully. It also shreds more easily.

Serves 6

Calories: 241.21
Fat: 9.57 grams
Saturated Fat: 1.56 grams
Carbohydrates: 30.38 grams
Sodium: 272.85 mg

2 cups Veggie Risotto (page 255), chilled
1 slice Light White Batter Bread, crumbled (page 50)
1 egg, beaten
½ cup shredded part-skim mozzarella cheese
2 tablespoons olive oil

milk   wheat   eggs   fish   nuts

Smashed Potatoes

These rustic potatoes aren't smashed perfectly smooth. The skins are left on, which adds nutrients and fiber.

Calories: 333.76
Fat: 7.35 grams
Saturated Fat: 1.06 grams
Carbohydrates: 60.99 grams
Sodium: 226.04 mg

6 Yukon Gold potatoes
3 tablespoons olive oil
3 garlic cloves, minced
2 shallots, minced
1 (3-ounce) package dairy-free, vegan cream cheese, softened
2–4 tablespoons soy milk
½ teaspoon salt
⅛ teaspoon pepper

1. Scrub potatoes and cut into 1" pieces. Bring a large pot of water to a boil. Add potatoes; bring back to a simmer. Simmer 10–20 minutes, or until potatoes are tender when pierced with a fork. Drain, then return potatoes to hot pot.

2. Meanwhile, in small saucepan, heat olive oil over medium heat; cook garlic and shallots. Place pot with hot potatoes over medium heat and, using a fork, mash in the garlic mixture. Leave some pieces of the potato whole.

3. Stir in the cream cheese, 2 tablespoons soy milk, salt, and pepper; add enough milk for desired consistency. Serve immediately. Or you can keep these potatoes warm in a double boiler over simmering water for about an hour.

milk wheat eggs soy fish nuts

Sparkly Carrots

*Use your favorite clear carbonated soda in this easy recipe.
It adds a slightly sweet crispness to this side dish.*

1. In large skillet, heat olive oil over medium heat. Add shallots; cook and stir until crisp-tender, about 2 minutes. Add carrots; cook and stir 2–3 minutes.

2. Add soda, salt, and pepper to skillet and bring to a boil. Reduce heat, cover, and simmer 4–5 minutes, or until carrots are tender. Serve immediately.

Baby Carrots

Baby carrots aren't just ordinary carrots cut down to size. Ordinary carrots have a clear orange center that isn't as sweet as the rest of the carrot. If made from regular carrots, baby carrots would consist of mostly the center. They are made from a special variety of carrot that is cut down to the baby carrot size. They're delicious eaten cooked or raw.

Serves 4

Calories: 69.52
Fat: 3.52 grams
Saturated Fat: 0.49 grams
Carbohydrates: 9.34 grams
Sodium: 235.41 mg

1 tablespoon olive oil
2 shallots, minced
2 cups baby carrots
½ cup gluten-free lime carbonated soda
¼ teaspoon salt
⅛ teaspoon pepper

Citrus Squash

Serves 4–6

Calories: 89.60
Fat: 0.19 grams
Saturated Fat: 0.04 grams
Carbohydrates: 23.05 grams
Sodium: 201.78 mg

2 acorn squash, cut in half
1 tablespoon olive oil
1 onion, chopped
2 cloves garlic, minced
2 tablespoons lemon juice
2 tablespoons orange juice
1 tablespoon grapefruit
   juice
2 tablespoons brown sugar
½ teaspoon cinnamon
½ teaspoon salt
⅛ teaspoon pepper

In the fall, baked squash is a wonderful side dish that you can flavor many ways. Try baking it with onion and hot chili peppers instead of the juices, sugar, and cinamon!

1. Preheat oven to 375°F. Remove seeds from squash and discard. Place squash in a baking dish large enough to hold the halves snugly, cut-side up. Cover tightly with foil; bake 20 minutes.

2. In small saucepan, cook onion and garlic in olive oil until tender, about 5 minutes. Remove from heat and stir in juices, sugar, cinnamon, salt, and pepper, and mix well. Spoon mixture into squash halves, making sure to baste the flesh with the liquid.

3. Return to the oven and bake, uncovered, 20–30 minutes longer, or until squash is very tender, basting occasionally with the liquid. Serve immediately.

milk wheat eggs soy fish nuts

Veggie Risotto

*Since there's no butter or cheese in this recipe,
as there is in classic risotto, you really need to use
Arborio rice for the creamiest texture.*

1. Place Broth in medium saucepan; heat over low heat. Meanwhile, in large skillet, heat olive oil over medium heat. Add onion and garlic; cook and stir until crisp-tender, about 4 minutes.

2. Add mushrooms, carrot, salt, pepper, thyme, and rice; cook and stir 2–3 minutes. Add wine or Broth; cook and stir until absorbed.

3. Slowly add the warm Broth, ½ cup at a time, stirring constantly. Add the peas with the last ½ cup of Broth. The rice should be tender yet firm in the center, with a creamy sauce. Serve immediately.

Is Wine Gluten-Free?

Wine should be gluten-free because it is made from grapes. But that isn't necessarily the case. On some celiac message boards, people have complained that certain brands of wine have made them sick. If your allergy to gluten is severe, make sure that the casks used to age the wine are gluten-free and that the wine is free from additives.

Serves 8

Calories: 289.64
Fat: 6.70 grams
Saturated Fat: 0.97 grams
Carbohydrates: 48.82 grams
Sodium: 375.23 mg

5 cups Vegetable Broth (page 139)
2 tablespoons olive oil
1 onion, chopped
2 cloves garlic, minced
1 (8-ounce) package mushrooms, sliced
3 large carrots, sliced
½ teaspoon salt
⅛ teaspoon pepper
½ teaspoon dried thyme leaves
2 cups Arborio rice
½ cup dry white wine or more Vegetable Broth
1 cup frozen baby peas, thawed

Calories: 163.42
Fat: 4.69 grams
Saturated Fat: 0.69 grams
Carbohydrates: 28.52
grams
Sodium: 238.17 mg

4 large sweet potatoes
1 (6-ounce) can gluten-free
   pineapple-orange juice,
   divided
2 tablespoons olive oil
1 tablespoon minced fresh
   ginger root
½ teaspoon salt
⅛ teaspoon pepper

milk   wheat   eggs   soy   fish   nuts

Mashed Sweet Potatoes

*This is the perfect dish for Thanksgiving dinner.
Make it about an hour ahead of time and keep the
potatoes warm in a slow cooker.*

1. Peel the sweet potatoes and cut into 1" chunks. Place in a large pot full of cold water; add half of the juice. Bring to a boil, then reduce heat, cover, and simmer 10–20 minutes, or until sweet potatoes are soft.

2. Drain and return to hot pot. Add olive oil and ginger root; mash using a potato masher. Add remaining pineapple-orange juice along with salt and pepper; stir until combined. Serve immediately or hold on warm in a slow cooker.

Sweet Potato or Yam?

Yams are not commonly sold in the United States; what we see in the market are two varieties of sweet potatoes. There's a pale-skinned variety that is not sweet, and one with an orange skin and flesh that is sweet and moist when cooked. It's the latter type that is used for Thanksgiving side dishes and mashed sweet potatoes.

milk   wheat   eggs   soy   fish   nuts

Baked Rice Pilaf

For a vegetarian side dish, use Vegetable Broth (page 139) or water instead of the chicken stock.

1. Preheat oven to 350°F. Combine Chicken Stock and water in a small saucepan and place over medium heat.

2. Meanwhile, heat olive oil in ovenproof, 2-quart skillet over medium heat. Add onion; cook and stir until crisp-tender, about 4 minutes. Add carrots, salt, pepper, and marjoram; cook and stir 2 minutes longer.

3. Stir in rice; cook and stir 3 minutes longer. Pour hot Chicken Stock mixture over all and stir.

4. Cover and bake 35–45 minutes, or until rice is tender and liquid is absorbed; fluff with fork. Serve.

Serves 6

Calories: 213.02
Fat: 5.74 grams
Saturated Fat: 0.95 grams
Carbohydrates: 34.52 grams
Sodium: 316.53 mg

2 cups Chicken Stock
   (page 137)
½ cup water
2 tablespoons olive oil
1 onion, chopped
½ cup shredded carrots
½ teaspoon salt
⅛ teaspoon pepper
½ teaspoon dried
   marjoram leaves
1¼ cups long-grain white
   rice

milk   wheat   eggs   soy   fish   nuts

Zucchini Stir-Fry

If you have a garden, you know August and September can mean bumper crops of zucchini and tomatoes. Use the proceeds in this easy side dish recipe.

1. In wok or large skillet, heat olive oil over medium-high heat. Add zucchini and shallot; stir-fry until crisp-tender, about 5–7 minutes.

2. Add grape tomatoes, salt, pepper, and thyme leaves; stir-fry until hot and all vegetables are tender, about 3–5 minutes longer. Serve immediately.

Serves 4

Calories: 82.12
Fat: 7.00 grams
Saturated Fat: 0.99 grams
Carbohydrates: 4.81 grams
Sodium: 300.20 mg

2 tablespoons olive oil
2 cups sliced zucchini
2 shallots, minced
2 cups grape tomatoes,
   halved
½ teaspoon salt
⅛ teaspoon pepper
½ teaspoon dried thyme
   leaves

Chapter 14
Cookies, Candies, and Cakes

Fudge Frosting

**Yields 2 cups;
Serving size ¼ cup**

Calories: 392.36
Fat: 14.14 grams
Saturated Fat: 10.88 grams
Carbohydrates: 70.87
grams
Sodium: 31.63 mg

⅓ cup extra-virgin coconut
  oil
3 tablespoons Lyle's Golden
  Syrup
2 (1-ounce) squares gluten-
  free unsweetened
  chocolate, chopped
1 (1-ounce) square
  gluten-free semisweet
  chocolate, chopped
4 cups gluten-free
  powdered sugar
Pinch salt
1 teaspoon gluten-free
  vanilla
¼ cup rice milk

Lyle's Golden Syrup is an English product you can find in large grocery stores or online. It's similar to corn syrup, but is gluten, fish, and gelatin free with Kosher Certification.

1. In large microwave-safe bowl, combine coconut oil, Golden Syrup, and chocolates. Melt on 50 percent power 2 minutes; remove and stir. Repeat process, microwaving for 1 minute intervals, until mixture is melted and smooth.

2. Beat in 2 cups of the powdered sugar, the salt, and vanilla until smooth. Then alternately add the rest of the powdered sugar along with the rice milk, beating until fluffy. You may need to add more sugar or rice milk to get desired consistency. Fills and frosts 2 8" cake layers.

wheat eggs soy fish

Best Cookie Bars

These delicious bars are rich and decadent and take about 5 minutes to put together. They're perfect for packing into lunchboxes or filling a cookie jar.

1. Preheat oven to 325°F. Line a 13" × 9" baking pan with parchment paper; lightly grease with unsalted butter.

2. Layer coconut, white chocolate chips, dark chocolate chips, cashews, and pecans in pan in that order. In small bowl, combine condensed milk, cocoa powder, and vanilla; mix with wire whisk until blended. Drizzle this mixture evenly over ingredients in pan.

3. Bake 22–26 minutes, or until the bars are set and are bubbly all over the surface. Cool completely in pan. Then remove the bars with the parchment paper from pan, peel off paper, and cut into bars. Store tightly covered at room temperature.

Be an Alert Label Reader!

When baking for celiac patients and others who are allergic to gluten, be sure to read every single label on everything you buy. Some chocolates and even some canned milks can contain gluten. Look for mention of any type of flour or gluten, including wheat, rye, barley, wheat germ, couscous, seitan, or cereal extract.

Yields 36 bars

Calories: 148.76
Fat: 8.89 grams
Saturated Fat: 3.73 grams
Carbohydrates: 16.61 grams
Sodium: 48.51 mg

Unsalted butter
1 cup coconut
1 cup gluten-free white chocolate chips
1 cup special dark, gluten-free chocolate chips
1 cup chopped salted cashews
1 cup chopped pecans
1 (14-ounce) can gluten-free, sweetened condensed milk
3 tablespoons gluten-free cocoa powder
1 teaspoon gluten-free vanilla flavoring

wheat soy fish nuts

Decadent Cinnamon Chocolate Bars

Yields 16 bars

Calories: 239.85
Fat: 11.97 grams
Saturated Fat: 6.68 grams
Carbohydrates: 30.89 grams
Sodium: 105.93 mg

Unsalted butter
1 cup superfine rice flour
½ cup brown sugar
½ cup sugar
1 teaspoon cinnamon
½ teaspoon gluten-free
    baking powder
½ teaspoon baking soda
¼ teaspoon salt
¼ teaspoon xanthan gum
⅓ cup chilled butter
1 egg
1 cup sour cream
1½ teaspoons gluten-free
    vanilla
1½ cups gluten-free milk
    chocolate chips

These bars have a chewy texture, almost like a chocolate chip cookie, but are slightly more crumbly. The rice flour creates a finer crumb and adds a bit of crispness.

1. Preheat oven to 350ºF. Grease a 9" × 9" pan with unsalted butter and set aside. In medium bowl, combine rice flour, brown sugar, sugar, cinnamon, baking powder, baking soda, salt, and xanthan gum, and mix well. Cut butter into small pieces and add to flour mixture; cut in using 2 knives or a pastry blender until particles are fine.

2. In small bowl, combine egg, sour cream, and vanilla and mix well. Stir into flour mixture until combined, then stir in milk chocolate chips. Spread evenly into prepared pan.

3. Bake 20–30 minutes, or until bars are golden brown and set. Cool in pan on wire rack; cut into bars. Store bars tightly covered at room temperature.

eggs soy fish nuts

Rich Chocolate Caramel Cake

Serves 16

Using sweetened condensed milk adds a great caramel flavor to this simple cake. Bake it in two 9" pans about 25 minutes, then layer with the frosting for a birthday cake!

Calories: 526.61
Fat: 20.85 grams
Saturated Fat: 12.93 grams
Carbohydrates: 81.67 grams
Sodium: 331.57 mg

1. Preheat oven to 350°F. Spray a 13" × 9" pan with nonstick baking spray containing flour and set aside. In large bowl, combine butter and brown sugar and beat until light and fluffy. Gradually add condensed milk; beating until smooth.

2. In medium bowl, combine flour, cocoa, baking powder, baking soda, and salt and mix to combine. In small bowl, combine vinegar, chocolate milk, sparkling water, and vanilla. Add flour, alternately with milk mixture, to butter mixture, beginning and ending with dry ingredients.

3. Stir in the melted chocolate; pour into prepared pan. Bake 30–40 minutes, or until top springs back when lightly touched in center and cake begins to pull away from sides of pan. Cool completely on wire rack. Frost with Caramel Frosting.

¾ cup butter, softened
½ cup brown sugar
1 (14-ounce) can sweetened condensed milk
2½ cups all-purpose flour
⅓ cup cocoa powder
2 teaspoons baking powder
1 teaspoon baking soda
½ teaspoon salt
2 tablespoons apple cider vinegar
1 cup chocolate milk
¼ cup sparkling water
1 teaspoon vanilla
2 (1-ounce) squares semisweet chocolate, melted
1 recipe Caramel Frosting (page 265)

Egg-Free Recipes

Egg-free cakes were common during World War II when rationing forced housewives to adapt. If someone in your family has an egg allergy, look for cookbooks from that time to find tried-and-true egg-free recipes. You can usually find them in used bookstores and on the Web, particularly abebooks.com and alibris.com.

Serves 12

Calories: 406.18
Fat: 13.40 grams
Saturated Fat: 7.19 grams
Carbohydrates: 69.49 grams
Sodium: 299.62 mg

Unsalted butter
1½ cups superfine rice flour
1 cup chocolate milk
¾ cup tapioca flour
1 teaspoon xanthan gum
½ teaspoon salt
2 teaspoons gluten-free baking powder
1 teaspoon baking soda
¾ cup cocoa powder, divided
1 cup brown sugar, divided
1 cup sugar
4 eggs
⅓ cup gluten-free mayonnaise
⅓ cup butter, softened
2 teaspoons gluten-free vanilla
½ cup superfine white rice flour
¼ cup butter, melted

Crunchy Streusel Chocolate Cake

Superfine rice flour is the secret to most recipes if you're avoiding wheat flour. Its texture is close to flour and cornstarch.

1. Preheat oven to 350°F. Grease a 13" × 9" cake pan with unsalted butter and set aside. In small bowl, combine 1½ cups rice flour and chocolate milk; mix well and set aside. In another small bowl, combine tapioca flour, xanthan gum, salt, baking powder, baking soda, and ½ cup cocoa powder; mix well; set aside.

2. In large bowl, combine ½ cup brown sugar, sugar, eggs, mayonnaise, butter, and vanilla and beat until light and fluffy. Add rice flour mixture and beat well, then beat in tapioca flour mixture. Spread batter into prepared pan.

3. In small bowl, combine ½ cup rice flour, ¼ cup cocoa powder, and ½ cup brown sugar; mix well. Stir in ¼ cup melted butter until crumbly. Sprinkle over batter in prepared pan.

4. Bake 35–45 minutes, or until cake is set and begins to pull away from sides of pan. Let cool completely on wire rack. Cut into squares to serve.

Caramel Frosting

Cream cheese helps cut the richness of this excellent frosting.

Calories: 280.09
Fat: 10.13 grams
Saturated Fat: 6.40 grams
Carbohydrates: 48.76 grams
Sodium: 107.13 mg

1. In large saucepan, combine brown sugar, butter, honey, water, and salt. Bring to a boil over medium heat. Boil for 1 minute, stirring constantly.

2. Remove from heat and beat in cream cheese until blended. Add 2 cups powdered sugar and vanilla and beat well. Gradually add remaining powdered sugar until desired spreading consistency.

3. Use frosting, adding more water if necessary, as frosting will thicken fairly quickly.

1 cup brown sugar
½ cup butter, softened
¼ cup honey
¼ cup water
⅛ teaspoon salt
1 (3-ounce) package cream cheese, softened
2–3 cups gluten-free powdered sugar
1 teaspoon gluten-free vanilla
More water, if necessary

Make it Dairy Free!

This frosting can easily be made dairy free, too. Use gluten-free vegan margarine instead of the butter. Instead of the cream cheese, look for dairy-free vegan cheese, or soft vegan cheese made from rice milk. These products are usually available at health food stores, and can also be ordered online.

Calories: 131.39
Fat: 3.42 grams
Saturated Fat: 0.48 grams
Carbohydrates: 24.13 grams
Sodium: 111.67 mg

1½ cups all-purpose flour
½ cup whole-wheat flour
1½ teaspoons baking powder
½ teaspoon baking soda
½ teaspoon salt
¼ cup olive or vegetable oil
1 ripe banana, mashed
¾ cup rice milk
½ cup gluten-free orange juice
¼ cup honey
2 teaspoons gluten-free vanilla
2 teaspoons grated orange zest
1 cup gluten-free powdered sugar
2 tablespoons orange juice

milk eggs soy fish nuts

Banana-Orange Cupcakes

You can top these delicate cupcakes many ways. Use a traditional buttercream frosting flavored with orange, or use your favorite chocolate frosting.

1. Preheat oven to 350°F. In large bowl, combine flours, baking powder, baking soda, and salt and mix well with wire whisk.

2. In medium bowl, combine oil, banana, and rice milk and mash together using a potato masher. Stir in ½ cup orange juice, honey, vanilla, and orange zest and mix well.

3. Add banana mixture all at once to the dry ingredients and mix until combined. Stir 1 minute.

4. Fill prepared cups ¾ full. Bake 18–23 minutes, or until cupcakes are set and light golden brown. Let cool on wire rack 10 minutes.

5. In small bowl, combine powdered sugar and 2 tablespoons orange juice and mix well. Drizzle over warm cupcakes. Let cool completely.

Bananas in Baking

Make sure that the bananas you use in baking are very ripe. The skins should be yellow, with no green color at all, and dotted with black. Bananas are a good substitute for eggs in most baking recipes, since they add moisture and a bit of structure to the batter. If you have a lot of ripe bananas on hand, they freeze very well.

milk wheat eggs soy fish nuts

Cinnamon Crisps

The combination of flours and starch in these cookies makes them delicate and crisp at the same time.

1. Preheat oven to 375°F. In small bowl, combine rice flour, honey, vegetable oil, and vanilla and mix well.

2. In food processor, combine potato-starch flour, tapioca flour, xanthan gum, brown sugar, and rolled oats. Process until fine, then stir in salt and ½ teaspoon cinnamon. Stir in rice flour mixture until a dough forms, then add currants.

3. Roll dough into ¾" balls. On plate, combine sugar with remaining ½ teaspoon cinnamon and mix well. Roll dough balls in cinnamon mixture; place on ungreased cookie sheet.

4. Flatten cookies with the bottom of a glass. Bake 11–15 minutes, or until cookies are light golden brown; cool completely on wire rack. Store tightly covered at room temperature.

Yields 24 cookies

Calories: 85.94
Fat: 2.55 grams
Saturated Fat: 0.28 grams
Carbohydrates: 15.27 grams
Sodium: 26.36 mg

½ cup superfine rice flour
¼ cup honey
¼ cup vegetable oil
2 teaspoons gluten-free vanilla
2 tablespoons potato-starch flour
2 tablespoons tapioca flour
½ teaspoon xanthan gum
⅓ cup brown sugar
½ cup gluten-free rolled oats
¼ teaspoon salt
1 teaspoon cinnamon, divided
½ cup dried currants
2 tablespoons sugar

Calories: 159.77
Fat: 7.43 grams
Saturated Fat: 2.98 grams
Carbohydrates: 22.04 grams
Sodium: 42.70 mg

¾ cup solid shortening
2 tablespoons coconut oil
1 cup brown sugar
½ cup sugar
1 egg
1 egg yolk
3 tablespoons rice milk
2 teaspoons gluten-free vanilla
1 cup superfine rice flour
¾ cup white sorghum flour
½ cup potato-starch flour
1 teaspoon xanthan gum
½ cup gluten-free oatmeal, ground
1 teaspoon baking soda
½ teaspoon salt
¼ teaspoon cream of tartar
3 cups gluten-free semisweet chocolate chips

milk   wheat   soy   fish   nuts

Chocolate Chip Cookies

Ground oatmeal adds a subtle chewiness and crunch to these delicious cookies. If oatmeal is a no-no for you, just omit it, or substitute plain, not superfine, rice flour.

1. In large bowl, combine shortening, coconut oil, brown sugar, and sugar; beat until light and fluffy. Add egg, egg yolk, rice milk, and vanilla and beat well.

2. Stir in rice flour, sorghum flour, potato-starch flour, xanthan gum, ground oatmeal, baking soda, salt, and cream of tartar and mix until a dough forms. Stir-in chocolate chips. Cover dough and chill at least 2 hours.

3. Preheat oven to 325°F. Shape dough into 1" balls; place on parchment paper or Silpat-lined cookie sheets. Bake 13–17 minutes, or until cookies are golden brown around edges. Let cool on cookie sheets 2–3 minutes; remove to wire racks to cool. Store covered at room temperature.

Changing Cookies

If you're allergic to eggs, you can still make the recipe above and just about any recipe except those calling for beaten egg whites; just use a dairy-free vegan egg substitute. One egg is usually equal to about ¼ cup of the substitute. Be sure to read the label for substitution amounts and preparation directions.

wheat eggs soy fish nuts

Melting Tea Cakes

These tender cookies crumble when you bite into them, then they melt in your mouth. If you'd like a spicier cookie, add cinnamon.

1. Preheat oven to 400°F. In large bowl, beat butter until fluffy. Add powdered sugar and vanilla and beat until blended. Stir in remaining ingredients except additional powdered sugar.

2. Form dough into balls about ¾" in diameter. Place on ungreased cookie sheet. Bake 8–13 minutes, or until cookies are very light golden brown on the bottom.

3. Immediately drop hot cookies into powdered sugar and roll to coat. Place on wire rack until cool, then reroll in powdered sugar. Store covered at room temperature.

Yields 36 cookies

Calories: 91.53
Fat: 5.24 grams
Saturated Fat: 3.28 grams
Carbohydrates: 10.62 grams
Sodium: 52.58 mg

1 cup butter, softened
½ cup gluten-free powdered sugar
2 teaspoons gluten-free vanilla
1½ cups superfine rice flour
½ cup white sorghum flour
¼ cup cornstarch or tapioca flour
¼ teaspoon salt
¼ teaspoon ground cardamom
1 teaspoon xanthan gum
More gluten-free powdered sugar

Chocolate-Lemon Layer Bars

Chocolate and lemon is a wonderful combination that adds a nice twist to a classic lemon-bar cookie recipe.

Yields 16 cookies

Calories: 202.04
Fat: 6.61 grams
Saturated Fat: 1.33 grams
Carbohydrates: 34.71 grams
Sodium: 204.09 mg

1 cup Gluten-Free, Soy-Free Baking Mix (page 67)
¼ cup brown sugar
3 tablespoons gluten-free cocoa powder
6 tablespoons dairy-free, vegan margarine, melted
⅔ cup dairy-free, vegan egg substitute
¾ cup sugar
½ cup lemon juice
¼ cup cornstarch or tapioca flour
1 teaspoon baking soda
½ teaspoon cream of tartar
¼ teaspoon salt
1 cup gluten-free powdered sugar
2 tablespoons gluten-free cocoa powder
Pinch salt
2 tablespoons chocolate rice milk or almond milk
2 tablespoons dairy-free, vegan margarine, melted

1. Preheat oven to 350°F. In small bowl, combine Baking Mix, brown sugar, and 3 tablespoons cocoa powder; mix well. Add 6 tablespoons melted margarine and stir until crumbs form. Press into a 9" square pan. Bake 12–14 minutes, until set.

2. In medium bowl, combine egg substitute and sugar and beat well. Add lemon juice. In sifter, combine cornstarch or tapioca flour, baking soda, cream of tartar, and salt and sift into lemon mixture; stir with wire whisk to mix well. Pour over hot cookie base.

3. Bake 18–23 minutes longer, or until filling is set. Let cool completely.

4. In small bowl, combine powdered sugar, 2 tablespoons cocoa powder, pinch salt, chocolate milk, and 2 tablespoons melted margarine and mix with wire whisk. Pour evenly over cooled bars and spread to cover. Let stand until set. Cut into squares to serve. Store in refrigerator.

Cocoa Powder

For celiac patients and those allergic to gluten, you want to look for gluten-free cocoa powder. There are organic varieties available in health food stores and some grocery stores. Dutch-process cocoa powder has been processed with alkali to neutralize the acids, while natural cocoa is more acidic, with a stronger chocolate flavor.

wheat soy fish nuts

Truffle Brownies

*Truffles are thick and creamy, decadent
and full of chocolate, just like these brownies.*

Yields 16 brownies

Calories: 302.55
Fat: 17.10 grams
Saturated Fat: 10.78 grams
Carbohydrates: 37.46 grams
Sodium: 102.17 mg

1. Preheat oven to 325°F. Grease a 9" square baking pan with unsalted butter and dust with cocoa powder; set aside. In heavy saucepan, combine butter, coconut oil, and chopped chocolate; melt over low heat, stirring frequently, until smooth. Remove from heat; beat in sugars; let stand 5 minutes.

2. Beat in eggs, one at a time, then stir in vanilla. In sifter, combine rice flour, cornstarch, xanthan gum, cocoa, and salt and sift into batter. Stir just until combined. Fold in half of the semisweet chips and half of the milk chocolate chips.

3. Spread batter into prepared pan. Bake 40–50 minutes, or until brownies have a shiny crust and just begin to pull away from sides of the pan. Place on wire rack.

4. While brownies are still warm, in small saucepan combine remaining chocolate chips and heavy cream; cook and stir over low heat until mixture is smooth. Pour over brownies and spread to coat. Let stand until cool, then cut into small bars.

Unsalted butter
Gluten-free cocoa powder
½ cup butter
¼ cup extra-virgin coconut oil
3 (1-ounce) squares gluten-free semisweet chocolate, chopped
1 cup brown sugar
½ cup sugar
2 eggs
2 teaspoons gluten-free vanilla
½ cup superfine rice flour
3 tablespoons cornstarch
¼ teaspoon xanthan gum
3 tablespoons gluten-free cocoa powder
¼ teaspoon salt
1 (12-ounce) package gluten-free, semisweet chocolate chips, divided
1 cup gluten-free, milk chocolate chips, divided
¼ cup heavy cream

No-Gluten Peanut Butter Cookies

Yields 24 cookies

Calories: 193.17
Fat: 11.15 grams
Saturated Fat: 1.87 grams
Carbohydrates: 20.25 grams
Sodium: 113.92 mg

*2 cups crunchy natural
    peanut butter*
½ cup sugar
*½ cup gluten-free
    powdered sugar*
1 cup dark brown sugar
2 eggs
1 teaspoon baking soda
Granulated sugar

*Yes, this recipe really works! Just be sure to bake
the cookies on foil or Silpat silicone liners, because
they stick to even greased cookie sheets.*

1. In large bowl, combine all ingredients except the extra granulated sugar. Cover; chill in refrigerator until dough is firm.

2. Preheat oven to 350°F. Roll dough into 1" balls; roll in sugar. Place on parchment paper, foil, or Silpat-lined cookie sheets. Using a fork, flatten balls with a crosshatch pattern. Bake 8–9 minutes, or until cookies are set. Let cool on cookie sheet 5 minutes, then carefully remove to wire rack to cool completely.

Powdered Sugar

Most powdered sugar has cornstarch added to prevent lumps and help stabilize whipped cream and other soft mixtures. You can make your own powdered sugar. Combine regular granulated sugar with a pinch of arrowroot powder in a blender and blend until very fine. Use as a substitute for powdered sugar in any recipe.

milk · wheat · eggs · fish · nuts

Cranberry Cakes

These cupcakes can be sprinkled with powdered sugar or frosted with Creamy Vanilla Frosting (page 281).

1. In large microwave-safe bowl, combine brown sugar, ½ cup cranberry juice, water, dried cranberries, and margarine. Microwave on high power until mixture boils, about 3–4 minutes. Remove and stir, then return to microwave on high power and let boil another 2 minutes. Remove and let cool.

2. Preheat oven to 350°F. Spray 18 muffin tins with nonstick gluten-free cooking spray and set aside. Stir sparkling water into cranberry mixture, then add vanilla, Flour Mix, salt, cinnamon, and cardamom; mix well. Divide batter among prepared muffin tins.

3. Bake 15–20 minutes, or until cupcakes are light golden brown and tops spring back when lightly touched with finger. Remove from tins and let cool on wire rack.

4. In small bowl, combine 2 tablespoons cranberry juice and powdered sugar; drizzle over cooled cupcakes.

Yields 18 cupcakes

Calories: 223.33
Fat: 4.22 grams
Saturated Fat: 0.62 grams
Carbohydrates: 45.07 grams
Sodium: 119.92 mg

1 cup brown sugar
½ cup gluten-free cranberry juice
¼ cup water
1 cup gluten-free dried cranberries
⅓ cup dairy-free, vegan margarine
¼ cup sparkling water
1 teaspoon gluten-free vanilla
2 cups Flour Mix II (page 69)
½ teaspoon salt
1 teaspoon cinnamon
⅛ teaspoon cardamom
2 tablespoons cranberry juice
1 cup gluten-free powdered sugar

Gluten-Free Caramels

Make your own candies to make sure they are gluten free! These treats are good for the holidays, or melt some to make Oatmeal Caramel Bars (page 277).

Yields 48 candies

Calories: 105.96
Fat: 4.74 grams
Saturated Fat: 2.97 grams
Carbohydrates: 16.87 grams
Sodium: 38.00 mg

Unsalted butter
1 cup sugar
1 cup brown sugar
1 cup gluten-free light corn syrup
½ teaspoon salt
½ cup gluten-free dark corn syrup
2 cups heavy cream
¾ cup unsalted butter
2 teaspoons gluten-free vanilla

1. Grease a 13" × 9" baking pan with unsalted butter and set aside. In large heavy saucepan, combine sugar, brown sugar, light corn syrup, salt, and dark corn syrup; bring to a boil over medium heat, stirring frequently.

2. Reduce heat to low and gradually stir-in cream, whisking constantly. Then add butter; stir until melted. Attach a candy thermometer to side of pan, making sure it doesn't touch the bottom. Cook candy over low heat until temperature reaches 240°F.

3. To cook without a candy thermometer, when mixture thickens and boiling begins to slow down, start testing by dropping a bit of the hot candy into cold water. When it forms a firm ball that can still be shaped with your fingers, remove it from the heat.

4. Remove pan from heat and stir in vanilla (be careful, mixture will boil up and steam). Pour into prepared pan. Let stand until cool. Cut into squares and wrap individually in parchment paper.

Candy Thermometers

There are quite a few different types of candy thermometers; all work well as long as you follow a few rules. Make sure that the thermometer bulb is totally immersed in the boiling candy, but is not touching the bottom or sides of the pan. Rinse the thermometer with hot water to bring it up to temperature more quickly, and cool it slowly at room temperature.

milk · wheat · eggs · fish · nuts

Peppermint Patties

There's even mint in the chocolate coating in this easy candy recipe. Your kids will love it.

1. In large bowl, combine sugar and salt; mix well. Add margarine, corn syrup, both extracts, and rice milk and beat with electric mixer until thoroughly combined. You may need to add more sugar or rice milk to reach desired consistency.

2. Roll mixture into 1" balls and place on waxed-paper-lined cookie sheet. Flatten with bottom of drinking glass until ¼" thick. Cover; chill 1 hour.

3. Place 1½ cups of chocolate chips in microwave-safe glass measuring cup; melt on 50 percent power 2 minutes; remove and stir. Microwave on 50 percent power at 30 second intervals, stirring after each interval, until chocolate is melted and smooth. Add remaining ½ cup of chips and stir constantly until they are also melted.

4. Dip the peppermint centers into the chocolate mixture, shaking off excess. Place on cookie sheet and chill until chocolate is set. Store in airtight container at room temperature.

Yields 48 candies

Calories: 76.92
Fat: 3.02 grams
Saturated Fat: 1.47 grams
Carbohydrates: 13.50 grams
Sodium: 16.26 mg

4 cups gluten-free powdered sugar
⅛ teaspoon salt
3 tablespoons dairy-free, vegan margarine, softened
1 tablespoon gluten-free corn syrup
2 teaspoons gluten-free peppermint extract
½ teaspoon gluten-free mint extract
¼ cup rice milk
2 cups gluten-free, semisweet, mint-flavored chocolate chips

No-Bake Honey Balls

These sweet and chewy no-bake cookies
are a good choice for beginning cooks.

Yields 30 cookies

Calories: 65.32
Fat: 0.08 grams
Saturated Fat: 0.02 grams
Carbohydrates: 16.29 grams
Sodium: 7.10 mg

½ cup honey
½ cup gluten-free golden
    raisins
½ cup gluten-free dry milk
    powder
1 cup crushed crisp rice
    cereal
¼ cup gluten-free
    powdered sugar
1 cup finely chopped dates
1 cup crushed crisp rice
    cereal

1. In food processor, combine honey and raisins; process until smooth. Scrape into a small bowl and add milk powder, 1 cup crushed cereal, powdered sugar, and dates; mix well. You may need to add more powdered sugar or honey for desired consistency.

2. Form mixture into ¾" balls and roll in remaining crushed cereal. Store tightly covered at room temperature.

Dates

Do not buy the precut dates that have been coated in sugar for most recipes. They are too dry and too sweet and will upset the balance of most recipes. To chop dates, use scissors occasionally dipped into very hot water. If you can find them, Medjool dates, usually found in health food and gourmet stores, are richer than Deglet Noor dates.

wheat eggs soy fish nuts

Oatmeal Caramel Bars

This simple recipe is a variation on a classic. It's chewy, full of chocolate and oats, and really delicious.

1. Preheat oven to 350°F. Grease a 13" × 9" pan with unsalted butter and set aside. In large bowl, combine Baking Mix, oats, and brown sugar and mix well. Add melted butter and mix until crumbly.

2. Reserve half of the crumb mixture and press remainder into prepared pan. Sprinkle with chocolate chips and set aside.

3. In medium, microwave-safe bowl, combine caramels and light cream. Microwave on 50 percent power about 5 minutes, stirring after each minute, until caramels are melted and mixture is smooth. Drizzle evenly over chocolate chips.

4. Sprinkle reserved crumb mixture on top. Bake 20–25 minutes, or until caramel bubbles around the edges and the crumbs are toasted. Cool completely on wire rack then cut into squares to serve.

Yields 36 bars

Calories: 208.84
Fat: 7.55 grams
Saturated Fat: 4.08 grams
Carbohydrates: 33.22 grams
Sodium: 136.61 mg

Unsalted butter
2 cups Gluten-Free, Soy-Free Baking Mix (page 67)
2 cups quick-cooking, gluten-free rolled oats
1½ cups brown sugar
1 cup butter, melted
2 cups gluten-free, semisweet chocolate chips
1 (13-ounce) package gluten-free caramels, unwrapped
⅓ cup light cream

Calories: 456.48
Fat: 9.68 grams
Saturated Fat: 1.35 grams
Carbohydrates: 88.56
grams
Sodium: 140.21 mg

1 cup apple juice
1 cup oatmeal, divided
1¾ cups flour, divided
¼ cup whole-wheat flour
1 teaspoon baking powder
½ teaspoon baking soda
1 teaspoon cinnamon,
*   divided*
⅛ teaspoon cardamom
¼ teaspoon salt
1½ cups brown sugar,
*   divided*
½ cup sugar
2 tablespoons vegetable oil
¼ cup applesauce
1 ripe banana, mashed
2 teaspoons vanilla
1 tart apple, peeled and
*   chopped*
¼ cup vegan, dairy-free
*   margarine*

Apple Snack Cake

This is an excellent cake for lunchboxes, or you can serve
it as a breakfast bread to eat on the run.

1. Preheat oven to 350°F. Spray a 9" square pan with nonstick baking spray containing flour and set aside.

2. Place the apple juice in a microwave-safe glass measuring cup; micro-wave on high 2–3 minutes, or until boiling. Remove from microwave. Stir in ½ cup of the oats; mix well and set aside.

3. In large bowl, combine 1½ cups flour, whole-wheat flour, baking powder, baking soda, ¾ teaspoon cinnamon, cardamom, and salt and mix well. In medium bowl, combine 1 cup brown sugar, ½ cup sugar, vegetable oil, applesauce, banana, and vanilla and beat until creamy.

4. Stir applesauce mixture and oat mixture into flour mixture and stir just until combined. Fold in the apple and spoon into prepared pan.

5. For topping, combine ½ cup oats, ¼ cup flour, ½ cup brown sugar, and ¼ teaspoon cinnamon, and mix well. Add margarine and mix until crumbly. Sprinkle over batter in pan. Bake 30–35 minutes, or until cake tests done with toothpick.

Oatmeal for Nuts

Oatmeal can often give a similar texture to nuts in toppings and streusel. Use old-fashioned oats for more texture and quick-cooking oats for a lighter texture. For more flavor, try toasting the oats in a dry saucepan over medium heat for a few minutes. Shake the pan frequently until the oats turn slightly darker and are fragrant.

milk wheat nuts soy fish

Flourless Chocolate Cake

Use the best-quality gluten-free chocolate you can find for this rich cake. Callebaut is an excellent brand.

1. Preheat oven to 300°F. Grease a 10" springform pan with 1 tablespoon coconut oil and dust with 2 teaspoons cocoa powder; set aside.

2. In heavy saucepan, combine chopped chocolate, coconut oil, vegetable oil, sugar, salt, and brown sugar over low heat. Cook and stir until chocolate and coconut oil melt and sugar dissolves, stirring frequently. Pour into large bowl.

3. Add cocoa and vanilla and beat for 1 minute. Then add eggs, one at a time, beating well after each addition.

4. Pour batter into prepared pan. Bake 50–60 minutes, or until cake jiggles just slightly in the center when pushed. Let cool on wire rack; chill overnight in the refrigerator before removing pan.

5. Unmold cake and place on serving plate. In microwave-safe bowl, melt 5 ounces semisweet chocolate on 50 percent power 2–3 minutes; stir until smooth. Spoon over the cake and smooth with offset spatula. Let stand until firm. Cut into very small pieces to serve.

Melting Chocolate
There are a few rules to follow when melting chocolate. Make sure that you don't allow even a drop of water to come into contact with the chocolate; it will make the chocolate "seize" and turn grainy. Use low heat, and stir very frequently, if not constantly, so it doesn't burn.

Serves 16

Calories: 237.03
Fat: 16.38 grams
Saturated Fat: 6.76 grams
Carbohydrates: 28.37 grams
Sodium: 20.52 mg

1 tablespoon coconut oil
2 teaspoons gluten-free cocoa powder
6 (1-ounce) squares gluten-free bittersweet chocolate, chopped
2 (1-ounce) squares gluten-free semisweet chocolate, chopped
⅓ cup coconut oil
3 tablespoons vegetable oil
¾ cup sugar
¼ teaspoon salt
¼ cup brown sugar
¼ cup gluten-free cocoa powder
1 teaspoon gluten-free vanilla
4 eggs
5 (1-ounce) squares gluten-free semisweet chocolate, chopped

Chocolate-Cherry Meringue Cookies

These chewy and crunchy cookies taste like chocolate covered cherries, but they're better!

Yields 24 cookies

Calories: 46.56
Fat: 0.45 grams
Saturated Fat: 0.14 grams
Carbohydrates: 10.18 grams
Sodium: 19.72 mg

3 egg whites
⅛ teaspoon cream of tartar
⅛ teaspoon salt
½ cup sugar
¼ cup gluten-free powdered sugar
¼ teaspoon gluten-free cherry extract
¼ cup gluten-free cocoa powder
½ cup gluten-free hard cherry-flavored candies, finely crushed
½ cup gluten-free semisweet chocolate chunks

1. Preheat oven to 350°F. Line a cookie sheet with parchment paper and set aside.

2. In large bowl, beat egg whites, cream of tartar, and salt until soft peaks form. Gradually add sugar, beating until stiff. Beat-in powdered sugar, cherry extract, and cocoa powder until well blended.

3. Fold-in crushed candies and chocolate chunks. Drop by tablespoons onto prepared cookie sheet. Bake 25–30 minutes, or until cookies are dry to the touch. Let cool 5 minutes, then carefully peel off paper; cool completely on wire rack. Store covered at room temperature.

milk   wheat   eggs   soy   fish   nuts

Creamy Vanilla Frosting

This delicious and creamy frosting is good for frosting cakes or cookies, or sandwich it between graham crackers for a quick treat.

1. In medium bowl, combine shortening, coconut oil, hot water, and 1 cup powdered sugar; beat until creamy. Add salt, vanilla, and 1 more cup of powdered sugar; beat well.

2. Alternately add remaining powdered sugar with enough rice milk to form desired consistency. Beat on high speed for 1 minute, then use frosting.

Solid Shortening

Look for solid shortenings that are trans fat free. Crisco now makes shortening with zero grams per serving. Shortening is a good alternative to butter when baking; it can work better in some recipes instead of vegan margarines because it has no water. Or look for extra-virgin coconut oil. It's also a good substitute for butter in baking and cooking.

**Yields 2 cups;
Serving size ¼ cup**

Calories: 331.36
Fat: 15.52 grams
Saturated Fat: 8.38 grams
Carbohydrates: 50.10 grams
Sodium: 3.65 mg

⅓ cup solid shortening
¼ cup extra-virgin coconut oil
1 tablespoon hot water
4 cups gluten-free powdered sugar, divided
¼ teaspoon salt
1 teaspoon gluten-free vanilla
2–3 tablespoons vanilla rice milk

milk   wheat   nuts   soy   fish

Strawberry Meringues

Yields 24 cookies

Calories: 41.04
Fat: 0.20 grams
Saturated Fat: 0.04 grams
Carbohydrates: 9.47 grams
Sodium: 19.68 mg

3 egg whites
⅛ teaspoon cream of tartar
⅛ teaspoon salt
½ cup sugar
*¼ cup gluten-free
    powdered sugar*
*½ teaspoon gluten-free
    strawberry extract*
*1 tablespoon organic
    gluten-free strawberry
    syrup*
*½ cup hard gluten-free
    strawberry-flavored
    candies, finely crushed*

These pink, chewy, and crunchy cookies are a great snack, and you can also use them in Strawberry Meringue Pie (page 301).

1. Preheat oven to 350°F. Line a cookie sheet with parchment paper and set aside.

2. In large bowl, beat egg whites, cream of tartar, and salt until soft peaks form. Gradually add sugar, beating until stiff. Beat-in powdered sugar, strawberry extract, and strawberry syrup until well blended.

3. Fold in crushed candies. Drop by tablespoons onto prepared cookie sheet. Bake 25–30 minutes, or until cookies are dry to the touch. Let cool 5 minutes, then carefully peel off paper; cool completely on wire rack. Store covered at room temperature.

Strawberry Syrup

Many health food stores and online stores carry organic, kosher, gluten-free flavored syrups. These syrups will not only flavor cookies and cakes, but can be used to make flavored sparkling drinks, as well as to flavor other beverages. They are quite concentrated, so you only use a tablespoon per cup.

milk wheat nuts soy fish

White Cake

This fluffy cake has a wonderful texture. Frost it with Creamy Vanilla Frosting (page 281) or Fudge Frosting (page 260).

1. Preheat oven to 350°F. Spray a 13" × 9" pan with nonstick gluten-free cooking spray and set aside.

2. In large bowl, combine rice flour, millet flour, tapioca flour, xanthan gum, sugar, baking powder, baking soda, and salt and mix well with a wire whisk.

3. In food processor, combine coconut oil and solid shortening; process until blended. Add to flour mixture along with apple juice, water, and vanilla. Beat until blended, then beat on medium speed 2 minutes.

4. Add the unbeaten egg whites, all at once, and beat 2 minutes longer. Pour batter into prepared pan. Bake 35–40 minutes, or until cake is beginning to pull away from edges and is light golden brown. Cool completely on wire rack.

Serves 12

Calories: 292.55
Fat: 9.22 grams
Saturated Fat: 5.28 grams
Carbohydrates: 50.03 grams
Sodium: 198.85 mg

1½ cups superfine rice flour
½ cup millet flour
¼ cup tapioca flour
1 teaspoon xanthan gum
1½ cups sugar
2 teaspoons gluten-free baking powder
1 teaspoon baking soda
½ teaspoon salt
¼ cup coconut oil
¼ cup solid shortening
½ cup apple juice
¼ cup water
2 teaspoons gluten-free vanilla
4 egg whites

Calories: 64.41
Fat: 2.52 grams
Saturated Fat: 1.48 grams
Carbohydrates: 9.98 grams
Sodium: 35.39 mg

1¼ cups Flour Mix II (Page 69)
1 cup brown-rice flour
⅓ cup brown sugar
½ teaspoon baking soda
1 teaspoon gluten-free baking powder
½ teaspoon salt
½ teaspoon cinnamon
⅓ cup coconut oil
3 tablespoons dairy-free, vegan margarine
3 tablespoons honey
1 teaspoon gluten-free vanilla
¼ cup rice milk
2–4 tablespoons cold water

milk wheat eggs fish nuts

Graham Crackers

Making your own graham crackers is a fun family project. Even small children can help measure the sugar and Flour Mix.

1. In large bowl, combine Flour Mix, brown rice flour, brown sugar, baking soda, baking powder, salt, and cinnamon; mix well with wire whisk.

2. In small saucepan, combine coconut oil, margarine, and honey. Heat over low heat, stirring frequently, until mixture is melted and smooth.

3. Add to dry ingredients along with vanilla, rice milk, and 2 tablespoons cold water; mix until a dough forms. You may need to add more water or Flour Mix to make a firm dough. Cover and refrigerate dough 2–3 hours.

4. Preheat oven to 325°F. Roll-out dough between sheets of waxed paper until it is ⅛" thick. Cut into 2" squares and place 1" apart on Silpat-lined cookie sheets.

5. Prick crackers with a fork. Bake 20–30 minutes, or until crackers are deep golden brown, removing some of them if they start looking too dark. Cool completely on wire rack.

Baking Cookies
When you're baking cookies and crackers, your oven temperature must be accurate for best results. Use an oven thermometer, and watch the cookies carefully as they bake, especially toward the end of baking time. You may need to rotate the cookie sheet or remove some cookies that test done before others.

Chapter 15
Desserts

Strawberry Cream Parfaits

Serves 4

Calories: 487.80
Fat: 18.05 grams
Saturated Fat: 9.94 grams
Carbohydrates: 81.94 grams
Sodium: 55.24 mg

3 cups strawberries
1 (4-ounce) package soy-
    based gluten-free
    chocolate pudding mix
1 (12-ounce) package silken
    tofu
1 cup dairy-free, gluten-free
    whipped topping
1 cup miniature, gluten-free
    chocolate chips
6 Strawberry Meringues,
    crumbled (page 282)

These chocolaty, crunchy parfaits are perfect for a dinner party because you make them ahead of time. For an egg-free dessert, use 1 cup Spicy and Sweet Granola (page 24) instead of the Meringues.

1. Hull strawberries, slice, and set aside. In blender or food processor, combine pudding mix and silken tofu; blend or process until smooth and creamy.

2. Pour into medium bowl; fold in whipped topping.

3. In 6 parfait glasses, layer pudding mix, strawberries, chocolate chips, and crumbled Meringues. Cover and chill at least 2 hours before serving.

More Parfait Options

You can make parfaits using different fresh or frozen fruits. Just substitute your favorite fruit for the strawberries and top the parfait with Spicy and Sweet Granola (page 24) instead of the meringues. Parfaits are a fun way to serve your guests. You can even make them ahead of time and let your guests serve themselves.

milk   wheat   eggs   fish   nuts

Frozen Pops

Use any frozen fruit to make a rainbow of frozen popsicles.
These little treats are perfect for a hot summer day.

1. Make the Smoothies, but add chopped bananas and cinnamon when blending or processing the mixture.

2. Pour into 8 popsicle molds. You could also use paper drink cups and wooden popsicle sticks. Cover and freeze until firm.

Frozen Desserts

Frozen desserts are ideal for cooling down on a hot day. For best results, make sure that your freezer is set at 0°F, and use a freezer thermometer to check on the temperature. Do not thaw and refreeze desserts; this will cause large ice crystals to form and will ruin the texture of the dessert.

Yields 8 pops

Calories: 173.29
Fat: 3.41 grams
Saturated Fat: 0.36 grams
Carbohydrates: 34.43 grams
Sodium: 44.16 mg

2 recipes Blueberry
*   Smoothie (page 34)*
2 bananas, peeled
½ teaspoon cinnamon

Serves 6

Calories: 353.88
Fat: 20.72 grams
Saturated Fat: 16.83 grams
Carbohydrates: 42.34 grams
Sodium: 153.20 mg

½ cup medium-grain white rice
10 tablespoons sugar
2 cups rice milk
2 cups coconut milk
1 whole cardamom pod
¼ teaspoon salt
1 teaspoon gluten-free vanilla extract
⅓ cup gluten-free cocoa powder
1 tablespoon coconut oil

Cocoa Rice Pudding

*Coconut milk adds a smooth richness to this rice pudding.
Top it with raspberries and eat it for breakfast!*

1. In large saucepan, combine rice, sugar, milks, and cardamom pod; bring to a rolling boil. Reduce heat to very low, cover pan, and simmer 70–80 minutes, stirring frequently, or until rice is very tender.

2. Remove from heat and stir-in salt, vanilla, cocoa powder, and coconut oil; blend well. Remove cardamom pod and pour into bowl; let cool 30 minutes. Press plastic wrap directly onto pudding surface. Refrigerate until cold.

milk wheat eggs soy fish nuts

Cornmeal Pie Crust

**Yields 2 9" pie
crusts; Serves 16**

*Using waxed paper to roll out the dough will prevent sticking,
and makes the dough easier to handle.*

Calories: 132.13
Fat: 7.65 grams
Saturated Fat: 3.64 grams
Carbohydrates: 15.17
grams
Sodium: 73.58 mg

1. In food processor, combine cornmeal, masa, rice flour, millet flour, xanthan gum, sugar, and salt and process until mixed. Add shortening and coconut oil in small pieces. Pulse several times until mixture resembles small peas.

2. Add rice milk and half of the cold water; pulse several times. Add more water if necessary, pulsing a few times, until dough comes together.

3. Remove pastry from processor, wrap in plastic wrap, and chill 2–3 hours.

4. Preheat oven to 400°F. Divide dough in half and roll out between pieces of waxed paper to 11" circles. Fill and bake as recipe directs.

5. For baked pie crust, place one circle in 9" pie plate, fold edges under, flute edge, and prick with a fork. Bake 12–18 minutes, or until crust is light golden brown. Remove from oven and cool on wire rack.

½ cup yellow cornmeal
½ cup masa harina (corn
   flour)
½ cup superfine rice flour
½ cup millet flour
1 teaspoon xanthan gum
2 tablespoons sugar
½ teaspoon salt
6 tablespoons solid
   shortening
3 tablespoons coconut oil
1 tablespoon rice milk
3–4 tablespoons cold
   water

Solid Shortening

You can now find solid shortening that is trans fat free. It's a little more solid and stiff than the old formulation, but still bakes the same. If you prefer, the combination of solid shortening and coconut oil makes an excellent pastry, but you can use all solid shortening if there is an allergy to coconut in your family.

Serves 16

Calories: 430.70
Fat: 17.22 grams
Saturated Fat: 8.61 grams
Carbohydrates: 70.14 grams
Sodium: 214.24 mg

½ recipe Gluten-Free
    Caramels (page 274)
½ cup milk
6 Golden Delicious or
    Granny Smith apples,
    peeled
2 tablespoons lemon juice
⅓ cup sugar
1 tablespoon superfine rice
    flour
1 teaspoon cinnamon
¼ teaspoon salt
½ cup superfine rice flour
½ cup potato-starch flour
1⅓ cups gluten-free oats or
    rice grits
1¼ cups brown sugar
½ teaspoon cinnamon
¼ teaspoon salt
½ cup butter
¼ cup coconut oil

Apple Crumble

A caramel topping nestles on top of tangy and sweet apples sitting under a crumbly crust in this fabulous dessert.

1. Preheat oven to 350°F. Spray a 9" × 13" glass baking dish with nonstick gluten-free cooking spray and set aside. In small microwave-safe bowl, combine Caramels and milk. Microwave on 50 percent power 6–9 minutes, stirring after each minute, until mixture is melted and smooth.

2. Meanwhile, slice the apples ¼" thick and toss with lemon juice; place in prepared dish. In small bowl, combine sugar, 1 tablespoon rice flour, 1 teaspoon cinnamon, and ¼ teaspoon salt; mix well. Sprinkle over apples.

3. When caramels are melted, drizzle over apple mixture. In large bowl, combine ½ cup rice flour, potato-starch flour, oats or rice grits, brown sugar, ½ teaspoon cinnamon, and ¼ teaspoon salt; mix well.

4. In small saucepan, melt butter and coconut oil over low heat. Pour over oat mixture and mix until crumbly. Sprinkle over caramel layer. Bake 50–60 minutes, or until apples are tender and topping is deep golden brown. Serve warm.

milk wheat eggs fish nuts

Sorbet Parfaits

Parfaits are really easy to make and the perfect dessert for entertaining because they have to be made ahead of time.

1. In small bowl, combine Soy-Yogurt Cheese, powdered sugar, and cinnamon and mix well.

2. In each of 6 parfait glasses, layer the Soy-Yogurt Cheese mixture, sorbet, and Granola, ending with Granola. Cover and freeze at least 4 hours, until ready to serve.

About Sorbet

Most sorbets are dairy free and gluten free; again, read labels to make sure. They come in some fabulous flavors, including mango and chocolate. Try different flavor combinations in this super-easy dessert. You can also make your own sorbet if you have an ice-cream maker (see page 293).

Serves 6

Calories: 338.30
Fat: 6.18 grams
Saturated Fat: 0.96 grams
Carbohydrates: 65.97 grams
Sodium: 48.94 mg

1 cup Soy-Yogurt Cheese
    (page 70)
½ cup gluten-free
    powdered sugar
½ teaspoon cinnamon
2 cups gluten-free, dairy-
    free sorbet, any flavor
2 cups Spicy and Sweet
    Granola (page 24)

Gluten-Free Sweet Crepes

Crepes are very thin, unleavened pancakes. You can fill these with sorbet, sautéed apples, or the chocolate pudding from Strawberry Cream Parfaits (page 286).

Yields 12 crepes

Calories: 79.84
Fat: 1.92 grams
Saturated Fat: 0.23 grams
Carbohydrates: 12.78 grams
Sodium: 55.54 mg

½ cup superfine rice flour
¼ cup brown-rice flour
¼ cup tapioca flour
½ teaspoon xanthan gum
2 tablespoons sugar
⅛ teaspoon salt
¾ cup vegan egg replacer
1 tablespoon vegetable oil
1 teaspoon gluten-free vanilla
4–6 tablespoons rice or soy milk

1. In food processor or blender, combine all ingredients except rice milk; process or blend until smooth. Add enough rice milk to make a thin batter. Let stand 5 minutes.

2. Heat a nonstick 6" skillet over medium heat. Brush with a bit of oil. Using a ½-cup measure, pour about ⅓ cup of the batter into the hot pan. Immediately lift and tilt the pan so the batter coats the bottom. Cook 2–3 minutes, or until crepe is set and slightly crisp; turn and cook 30 seconds on second side.

3. As the crepes are finished, place on kitchen towels to cool. Do not stack crepes or they will stick together. You can freeze these, separated by parchment paper or waxed paper, up to 2 months. To thaw, let stand at room temperature for 20–30 minutes.

milk wheat eggs soy fish nuts

Strawberry Sorbet

Sorbets are basically sugar, water, and fruit; that's all!
The vodka, or other alcohol, gives it a softer texture
by keeping it from freezing rock hard.

Yields 4 cups;
Serving size ½ cup

Calories: 150.24
Fat: 0.41 grams
Saturated Fat: 0.02 grams
Carbohydrates: 35.40 grams
Sodium: 38.11 mg

1½ cups water
1 cup sugar, divided
6 cups strawberries
1 tablespoon lemon juice
⅛ teaspoon salt
2 tablespoons gluten-free
*   vodka, if desired*

1. In heavy saucepan, combine water and ¾ cup sugar and bring to a boil. Simmer over low heat 7–8 minutes, or until sugar dissolves completely. Remove from heat and let cool.

2. Hull strawberries and slice. Sprinkle with remaining ¼ cup sugar and stir. Let stand 30–40 minutes, or until sugar dissolves.

3. Combine strawberry mixture, lemon juice, salt, vodka, and ½ cup of the sugar syrup in a food processor; process until smooth. Strain, if desired, to remove seeds. Stir in remaining syrup. Cover and chill until very cold.

4. Freeze in an ice-cream maker according to manufacturer's directions.

Distilled Alcohols

Since vodka can be made from grain, celiacs and those allergic to wheat may shy away from it. But the American Dietetic Association has concluded that distilled alcoholic beverages, like vodka, whiskey, and rum, are safe to consume. But, as always, listen to what your doctor says and to what your body tells you. And if you're making this for kids, omit the alcohol.

milk   wheat   eggs   fish   nuts

Melba Crisp

Serves 8

Calories: 425.00
Fat: 13.12 grams
Saturated Fat: 7.00 grams
Carbohydrates: 74.32 grams
Sodium: 60.74 mg

5 peaches, peeled and sliced
1 cup frozen raspberries
½ cup sugar, divided
2 tablespoons cornstarch
1¼ cups Flour Mix II (page 69)
1 teaspoon gluten-free baking powder
½ cup certified gluten-free oatmeal or ¼ cup flaxseed
¼ cup brown sugar
1 teaspoon cinnamon
¼ cup coconut oil
3 tablespoons dairy-free, vegan margarine
2 tablespoons orange juice

Melba is a combination of peaches and raspberries. This delicious recipe is perfect served warm from the oven.

1. Preheat oven to 350°F. Spray a 2-quart, shallow baking dish with non-stick gluten-free cooking spray. In medium bowl, combine peaches, raspberries, ¼ cup sugar, and cornstarch; toss to coat. Place in prepared baking dish.

2. In large bowl, combine Flour Mix, baking powder, oatmeal or flaxseed, ¼ cup sugar, brown sugar, and cinnamon and mix well.

3. In small saucepan, combine coconut oil, margarine, and orange juice. Cook over low heat, stirring frequently, until melted and smooth. Drizzle over dry ingredients and stir until crumbly.

4. Sprinkle over fruit in baking dish. Bake 40–50 minutes, or until fruit is bubbling and tender and topping is crisp and browned. Let cool 30 minutes before serving.

milk   wheat   eggs   fish   nuts

Cherries Jubilee Crepes

This festive dessert can be made without the cream cheese for a dairy-free treat.

Serves 6

Calories: 226.33
Fat: 2.87 grams
Saturated Fat:0.45 grams
Carbohydrates: 44.69 grams
Sodium: 156.64 mg

1 (15-ounce) can gluten-free dark sweet cherries
2 tablespoons cornstarch or potato-starch flour
½ cup sugar
⅓ cup orange juice
1 teaspoon vanilla
8 Gluten-Free Sweet Crepes (page 292)
1 (3-ounce) package dairy-free, vegan cream cheese, softened

1. Preheat oven to 350°F. Make sure that all of the cherries have pits removed. Drain cherries, reserving juice; set aside.

2. In medium saucepan, combine ⅓ cup reserved cherry juice, cornstarch or potato-starch flour, sugar, and orange juice; mix well with wire whisk. Place over medium heat and cook, stirring constantly, until mixture thickens and becomes clear.

3. Remove from heat and stir-in cherries and vanilla. Let stand 10 minutes; remove the cherries from the sauce using a slotted spoon.

4. Arrange Crepes on work surface and carefully spread each with some cream cheese. Top with the cherries and roll up. Place in prepared baking dish, seam-side down. Bake 7–9 minutes, or until heated through.

5. While crepes are baking, reheat sauce over medium heat. When crepes are hot, remove from oven, place on serving platter, and pour hot sauce over all. Serve immediately.

Flaming Desserts!

If you'd like to flame this dessert, add ¼ cup brandy to the cherry sauce with the cherries and vanilla. When the sauce has been heated and poured over the hot crepes, ignite the sauce using a long lighter. Be careful, and stand back! The flame will burn itself out, then you can serve the crepes.

Creamy Raspberry Sorbet

Serves 6

Calories: 312.64
Fat: 8.45 grams
Saturated Fat: 7.14 grams
Carbohydrates: 61.60 grams
Sodium: 54.64 mg

1 cup sugar
1 cup water
1 cup coconut milk
2 cups fresh raspberries
2 cups frozen raspberries
⅛ teaspoon salt
2 tablespoons orange juice

For this recipe, you do need an ice-cream maker for best results. This creamy sorbet is rich and delicious.

1. In heavy saucepan, combine sugar and water and bring to a boil. Boil until sugar dissolves completely, about 1 minute. Remove from heat and let cool completely.

2. In food processor, combine sugar mixture, coconut milk, fresh and frozen raspberries, salt, and orange juice. Process until smooth. Cover and refrigerate until very cold, about 3–4 hours. Freeze according to your ice-cream maker's instructions.

Graham Cracker Pie Crust

Yields 1 pie crust; Serves 8

Calories: 224.99
Fat: 13.81 grams
Saturated Fat: 10.64 grams
Carbohydrates: 25.41 grams
Sodium: 69.04 mg

15 Gluten-Free Graham Crackers (page 284) or rice-bran graham crackers, crushed
½ teaspoon cinnamon
¼ cup brown sugar
⅓ cup coconut oil, melted

There are some gluten-free graham crackers on the market that are pretty good; rice bran is the closest to the real thing.

1. Preheat oven to 350°F. In medium bowl, combine Graham-Cracker crumbs, cinnamon, and brown sugar; mix well. Drizzle with melted coconut oil; mix with spoon until crumbs are coated.

2. Press into bottom and up sides of a 9" pie plate. Bake 7–9 minutes, or until set. Cool completely, then fill as desired or use in recipe.

milk wheat soy fish nuts

Banana-Split Parfait

*Now this is quite a dessert! If you love banana splits,
this is one recipe you'll make often.*

1. Peel bananas; slice ½" thick. In medium bowl, combine lemon juice, honey, and cinnamon and mix well. Toss bananas in mixture.

2. Crumble the Meringues. In each of six parfait glasses, layer bananas, crumbled Meringues, Strawberry Sorbet, and Chocolate Sauce. Serve immediately, or store in freezer up to 6 hours.

Parfaits

Parfaits are great last-minute desserts, and can be made with many ingredients. Layer fruit with vegan whipped topping and add some chocolate chips. Crumble some cookies and layer with frozen tofutti and toasted coconut. You can drizzle the layers with chocolate, caramel, or marshmallow sauce; you get the idea!

Serves 6

Calories: 375.32
Fat: 1.87 grams
Saturated Fat: 0.37 grams
Carbohydrates: 89.45 grams
Sodium: 88.84 mg

3 bananas
2 tablespoons lemon juice
1 tablespoon honey
½ teaspoon cinnamon
*12 Chocolate-Cherry
    Meringue Cookies
    (page 280)*
*2 cups Strawberry Sorbet
    (page 293)*
*½ cup Chocolate Sauce
    (page 304)*

milk   wheat   eggs   fish   nuts

Chocolate Sorbet Sandwiches

Yields 12

Calories: 263.71
Fat: 6.10 grams
Saturated Fat: 1.03 grams
Carbohydrates: 50.25 grams
Sodium: 84.82 mg

24 Cinnamon Crisps (page 267)
½ cup Chocolate Sauce (page 304)
2 cups dairy-free, vegan chocolate sorbet

You can make these little sandwiches with prepared chocolate sauce if you can find some that meets your dietary needs.

1. Prepare Cinnamon Crisps and let cool completely. Prepare Chocolate Sauce and let cool completely.

2. Spread some chocolate sauce on each cookie and make sandwiches using the chocolate sorbet. Wrap in waxed paper and freeze until firm.

wheat   eggs   soy   fish   nuts

Sorbet Pie

Serves 8

Calories: 318.51
Fat: 6.48 grams
Saturated Fat: 3.74 grams
Carbohydrates: 62.36 grams
Sodium: 104.16 mg

2 cups gluten-free chocolate sorbet
2 cups Strawberry Sorbet (page 293)
½ cup Chocolate Sauce (page 304)
1 Cornflake Pie Crust, baked and cooled (page 299)

Any flavor of commercial sorbet can be used in this easy pie. You could also use a Graham Cracker Pie Crust (page 296) if you'd prefer.

1. Layer chocolate sorbet, Strawberry Sorbet, and Chocolate Sauce in the cooled pie crust. Cover and freeze 4–6 hours, until firm.

2. To serve, let pie stand at room temperature 10–15 minutes before slicing. Serve with more Chocolate Sauce, if desired.

milk wheat eggs soy fish nuts

Grilled Peaches and Mangoes

Grilled fruit is a great treat, not only in summertime, but all year round. Serve the fruit over Strawberry Sorbet (page 293).

1. Prepare and preheat grill. Peel peaches and cut into slices. Peel mango and cut into slices. Place fruit in the center of a 12" × 18" piece of heavy-duty aluminum foil.

2. In small bowl, combine remaining ingredients. Drizzle over the fruit. Bring the short edges of the foil together and fold over twice, then fold up the other edges, leaving some room for heat expansion.

3. Grill fruit 10–12 minutes, turning foil packet once during grilling time. Open packet and serve with Cocoa Rice Pudding (page 288) or frozen sorbet.

wheat eggs soy fish nuts

Cornflake Pie Crust

Any kind of flaked cereal that you can eat can be used in this easy recipe. Be sure it's cooled before you add the filling.

1. Preheat oven to 350°F. Be sure the crumbs are finely crushed. Combine crumbs and sugar in medium bowl. In small saucepan, combine butter and cream cheese; cook over low heat, stirring frequently, until mixture is melted and smooth. Stir in corn syrup until blended. Drizzle over crumb mixture, tossing to coat.

2. Press into bottom and up sides of a 9" pie plate. Bake 8–11 minutes, or until light golden brown. Cool completely; fill as desired.

3. For tartlet shells, divide mixture among four 4" tartlet pans. Bake 4–6 minutes, until light golden brown.

Serves 4

Calories: 188.78
Fat: 0.34 grams
Saturated Fat: 0.05 grams
Carbohydrates: 47.32 grams
Sodium: 80.21 mg

2 ripe peaches
1 ripe mango
¼ cup honey
¼ cup brown sugar
1 teaspoon cinnamon
⅛ teaspoon salt
2 tablespoons gluten-free port wine, if desired

Yields 1 pie crust; Serves 8

Calories: 105.63
Fat: 4.9 grams
Saturated Fat: 3.01 grams
Carbohydrates: 15.09 grams
Sodium: 36.96 mg

1¾ cups cornflake crumbs or rice flake crumbs
3 tablespoons sugar
3 tablespoons butter
1 tablespoon cream cheese
1 tablespoon corn syrup

milk wheat eggs soy fish nuts

Apple Tart

Serves 6

Calories: 294.92
Fat: 7.34 grams
Saturated Fat: 3.99 grams
Carbohydrates: 58.97 grams
Sodium: 106.01 mg

½ recipe Cornmeal Pie
    Crust (page 289)
5 Granny Smith apples
2 tablespoons lemon juice
⅓ cup brown sugar
¼ cup gluten-free
    applesauce
1 teaspoon cinnamon
⅛ teaspoon cardamom
¼ teaspoon ginger
¼ teaspoon nutmeg

A rustic apple tart that doesn't need a pie pan! This is a good recipe for first-time pie bakers because the crust is so simple.

1. Preheat oven to 350°F. Roll out Pie Crust to a 12" circle; place on ungreased cookie sheet and set aside.

2. Peel and core apples; slice into ¼" slices, sprinkling with lemon juice as you work. Mound the apples in the center of the Pie Crust, leaving a 2" border.

3. In small bowl, combine remaining ingredients and mix well. Spoon over the apples. Gently fold the edges of the Crust up and over the apples, pleating as necessary. Crust will not meet in center.

4. Bake 40–50 minutes, until apples are tender and bubbling in center of pie, and crust is deep golden brown. Let cool 30 minutes before serving.

Apples for Baking
The best apples for baking keep their shape and are tart and sweet at the same time. Use Northern Spy, Pippin, Granny Smith, Rome, Braeburn, Winesap, Cortland, and Pippin. Because apples darken quickly when cut, sprinkle them with lemon juice as they are peeled and sliced.

wheat   soy   fish   nuts

Strawberry Meringue Pie

If you're allergic to eggs, just omit the meringue and serve this pie with either sweetened whipped cream or a vegan whipped topping.

1. Arrange whole strawberries, point-side up, in cooled Pie Crust; set aside. In medium, heavy saucepan, combine sliced strawberries and sugar; let stand 10 minutes. Using a potato masher, mash the strawberries. Bring to a boil over medium heat.

2. Meanwhile, in small bowl, combine cornstarch or potato-starch flour and orange juice; whisk until smooth. Add water and stir again. Add to the strawberry mixture and stir well. Cook, stirring frequently, until mixture thickens, about 8 minutes.

3. Stir in vanilla, then pour mixture over berries in the Crust and immediately place in refrigerator. Chill for 1 to 2 hours until set.

4. Preheat oven to 375°F. In medium bowl, combine egg whites and cream of tartar; beat until foamy. Gradually add ⅓ cup sugar, beating until stiff peaks form. Spoon onto pie, sealing edges of meringue to Crust.

5. Bake 10–14 minutes, or until meringue is lightly browned on peaks. Chill in refrigerator at least 3 hours before serving.

Serves 8

Calories: 245.01
Fat: 4.96 grams
Saturated Fat: 3.02 grams
Carbohydrates: 48.97 grams
Sodium: 58.27 mg

1½ cups whole
   strawberries, hulled
1 Cornflake Pie Crust,
   baked and cooled
   (page 299)
2 cups sliced strawberries
¾ cup sugar
3 tablespoons cornstarch
   or potato-starch flour
¼ cup orange juice
⅓ cup water
1 teaspoon vanilla
3 pasteurized egg whites
⅛ teaspoon cream of tartar
⅓ cup sugar

Caramel Sauce

Caramel sauce can be drizzled over sorbet or other frozen desserts, spice cake, or fresh fruit.

Yields 1 cup; Serving size 2 tablespoons

Calories: 183.76
Fat: 5.45 grams
Saturated Fat: 2.03 grams
Carbohydrates: 30.48 grams
Sodium: 98.92 mg

½ cup dark brown sugar
½ cup light brown sugar
½ cup dairy-free, vegan coffee creamer
¼ cup rice or soy milk
2 tablespoons dairy-free, vegan margarine
⅛ teaspoon salt

1. In heavy, medium saucepan, combine sugars, coffee creamer, and rice or soy milk; mix well with spoon.

2. Cook over medium heat until it comes to a boil. Then boil 3 minutes, stirring frequently. Remove from heat and add margarine and salt. Let cool at least 1 hour before serving. Store leftovers in refrigerator up to 1 week.

Coffee Creamer

Remember, "nondairy" does not mean that there is no milk protein in a product. The best way to ensure that your coffee (or recipes) are dairy free is to look for the words "vegan" or "contains no dairy." Vegan coffee creamers are a good substitute for milk or cream in many baking and cooking recipes.

milk wheat eggs fish nuts

Easy Cheesecake

This cheesecake is creamy and rich; you'll love it. Top it with some sliced, sweetened strawberries or peaches.

1. Preheat oven to 325°F. Prepare Pie Crust, but press crumbs into bottom and 1" up sides of a 9" springform pan; set aside.

2. In food processor, combine remaining ingredients. Process until smooth, scraping down work bowl several times. Spoon into springform pan.

3. Bake 65–75 minutes, or until filling is just set in center. Let cool 1 hour on wire rack; cover and chill 3–4 hours before serving.

Serves 8–10

Calories: 387.73
Fat: 15.01 grams
Saturated Fat: 8.85 grams
Carbohydrates: 52.23 grams
Sodium: 499.33 mg

1 Graham Cracker Pie
    Crust (page 296)
2 (8-ounce) packages
    dairy-free, vegan cream
    cheese
1 (8-ounce) package firm
    tofu
¼ cup coconut oil
½ cup Evaporated Rice
    Milk (page 66)
1 cup sugar
⅓ cup gluten-free
    powdered sugar
1 tablespoon cornstarch or
    potato–starch flour
2 teaspoons gluten-free
    vanilla
⅛ teaspoon salt

milk · wheat · eggs · soy · fish · nuts

Chocolate Sauce

Yields ¾ cup; Serving size 2 tablespoons

Calories: 164.82
Fat: 0.70 grams
Saturated Fat: 0.0 grams
Carbohydrates: 39.95 grams
Sodium: 34.68 mg

½ cup gluten-free cocoa
    powder
¾ cup sugar
½ cup water
¼ cup gluten-free corn
    syrup
Pinch salt
½ teaspoon gluten-free
    vanilla

Chocolate sauce that is rich and thick without any allergenic ingredients is a real treat. You can use it in hundreds of different ways.

1. In small saucepan, combine cocoa powder, sugar, water, corn syrup, and salt; mix well. Cook over medium heat, stirring frequently, until mixture comes to a boil; boil 3 minutes, stirring constantly.

2. Remove pan from heat and beat in vanilla. Let cool completely, stirring occasionally. Store covered in refrigerator.

Chocolate Sauce

You can make the chocolate sauce and serve it over sorbet or granita, or use it to make Banana-Split Parfaits (page 297). The sauce will keep, tightly covered in the refrigerator, for up to 2 weeks. You may need to heat it before serving so it thins enough for good pouring consistency. Or add more corn syrup, whisking well, until pourable.

milk   wheat   eggs   fish   nuts

Peaches and Cream Pie

Peaches and cream perfectly describes this easy pie. You can use fresh peaches if you'd like; just toss with some lemon juice before arranging on the filling.

Serves 8
_____

Calories: 331.84
Fat: 6.24 grams
Saturated Fat: 3.28 grams
Carbohydrates: 65.71 grams
Sodium: 110.50 mg

1. In blender or food processor, combine pudding mix, silken tofu, cream cheese substitute, and vanilla; blend or process until smooth and creamy. Pour into Pie Crust and set aside.

2. Drain peaches and arrange on top of filling. In small saucepan, combine jam, lemon juice, and cinnamon; heat until melted. Spoon over peaches. Refrigerate pie until firm, about 4–5 hours.

1 (4-ounce) package soy-based vanilla pudding mix
1 (12-ounce) package silken tofu
1 (3-ounce) package vegan cream cheese substitute
1 teaspoon gluten-free vanilla
1 Graham Cracker Pie Crust, baked and cooled (page 296)
2 cups frozen peach slices, thawed
½ cup gluten-free peach jam
1 tablespoon lemon juice
½ teaspoon cinnamon

Vegan Cream Cheese

If you need cream cheese that is dairy free, look for vegan cream cheeses. Tofutti makes a great one called "Better Than Cream Cheese." It comes in several flavors, too, so it can be used to make appetizer dips. Use it to make delicious frostings, too; just combine with an equal amount of vegan margarine, 4–5 cups powdered sugar, and vanilla.

Appendix A
Glossary

Abnormal
Outside the range of normal responses. A food allergy is an abnormal reaction to a common substance.

Allergen
Any substance that triggers an allergic reaction. Allergens from food are protein molecules.

Allergic Reaction
A reaction that is triggered by the immune system against an allergen. Symptoms include coughing, wheezing, edema, itching, hives, nausea, and vomiting.

Anaphylaxis
Also known as anaphylactic shock. A whole-body reaction to an allergy that can be severe enough to cause death. Symptoms include itching, swelling, difficulty breathing, low blood pressure, and loss of consciousness.

Antibody
Part of the immune system, antibodies are proteins with specifically shaped tips called epitopes that match up to antigens and start an allergic reaction.

Antigen
A molecule that stimulates the immune system into an allergic response.

Antihistamine
A drug that counters and neutralizes the effects of histamine released during an allergic reaction. The antihistamine replaces the histamine at receptor cells.

Biopsy
Surgical removal of tissue from the body to diagnose disease. Microscopic evaluation of the tissue is usually necessary.

Celiac Disease
Also known as celiac sprue, this autoimmune disease causes a reaction to gluten found in wheat, barley, and rye, which damages the lining of the small intestine.

Crohn's Disease
An irritable bowel disease (IBD) with symptoms similar to celiac disease. It causes inflammation in the small intestine, and is unrelated to food allergies.

Dermatitis
Noninfectious itching and inflammation of the skin, often caused by an allergic reaction.

Diagnosis
The naming of a disease or syndrome by identifying a collection of symptoms. Diagnosis can be obtained by observation, biopsy, and other medical tests.

Eczema
A condition of the skin characterized by itching, redness, swelling, and dryness. Can be a symptom of a food allergy.

Edema
Increase in fluid retention of any organ, from the skin to the muscles, which causes swelling.

Eggs
Eggs are produced by animals and plants alike. One of the eight major allergens, eggs from poultry contain a yolk and white surrounded by a membrane and shell. Egg substitutes are made from protein, cornstarch, and flour.

Enzyme
A protein molecule that speeds up or enhances chemical reactions in the body.

Epinephrine
A natural hormone released by the body during the "fight or flight" syndrome. Used to stem an allergic reaction, it increases blood pressure and heart rate.

Fever
A body temperature higher than 98.6°F. It is the body's response and defense against infection, that helps activate the immune system.

GI Tract
The Gastrointestinal tract starts at the mouth and ends at the anus, and is a collection of organs that processes the food you eat.

Gliadin
One of two proteins that make up gluten, the substance in wheat that causes celiac disease and wheat intolerance.

Gluten
The protein molecule in wheat that causes the set of reactions known as celiac disease. Gluten is made up of two proteins: glutenin and gliadin.

Histamine
A chemical compound made in the body that is released in response to an allergic reaction. Causes swelling, itch-

ing, low blood pressure, and dilation of blood vessels. Usually stored in mast cells and released when an allergen is present.

Hives
A skin condition, usually caused by an allergy, that presents as itching, red welts, and circular spots.

IgA
Antibodies that protect the mucous membranes of the body, including eyes, nose, mouth, and ears.

IgE
Antibodies produced in the skin, mucous membranes, and lungs that react against foreign substances like dander, pollen, and other substances that cause allergies.

IgG
The most common antibody found in bodily fluids. Fights intruders like bacteria and viruses.

Immune System
Organs, fluids, and cells in your body that help protect against foreign invaders. These can range from fungus to bacteria and viruses to food, when the system misidentifies an invader.

Intestines
The last part of the alimentary canal or GI tract, starting at the stomach. This is where most of the nutrients of the body are absorbed.

Intolerance
Food intolerance is a negative reaction to a food, usually in the intestinal tract, that causes symptoms like vomiting, diarrhea, and cramps. Intolerance is not an allergy.

Lactose
The sugar found in milk. Many people are lactose intolerant; that is, they lack the enzyme to process this compound. Lactose intolerance is not a food allergy.

Mast Cell
A cell found in tissues that contains histamines. It reacts with antigens in allergic reactions.

Milk
A liquid produced by mammary glands in mammals, milk is one of the eight major food allergens. It provides nutrition for newborns. Milk can come from cows, goats, sheep, or humans. A substitute can be made from rice or soy.

Nuts
The dried fruit of a legume (peanut) or tree (tree nuts). The seed is encased in a hard shell.

Placebo
A compound or chemical that is inert but is used in scientific tests to study the effect of chemicals on disease and therapy.

Prednisone
A corticosteroid drug used to treat allergy symptoms.

Protein
Large compounds comprised of amino acids arranged in a chain. The smaller compounds are attached to each other with peptide bonds. Proteins are almost always the allergen in allergic reactions.

RAST
Short for radioallergosorbent test, this is a test used to determine food allergies. It is performed by withdrawing blood and testing for the presence of IgE antibodies.

Respiratory System
The system in your body that transfers oxygen from your lungs to all of the tissues of the body. Includes lungs, bronchial tubes, arteries, and the nasal cavity.

Saliva
The clear liquid produced in your mouth. It's made in the salivary glands and used to start the food digestion process.

Shock
A potentially life-threatening situation where blood does not flow to the body's tissues. Medical shock is not the same as emotional shock.

Skin
The largest organ in the body, the skin reacts to allergens with hives, itching, and eczema. The skin can become involved in contact allergies if the person is very sensitive.

Soy
One of the eight major allergens, soy is a legume. The seeds, also called soybeans, are used to make tofu, soy sauce, and other foods.

Stomach
A hollow organ where food is digested. This is the second stage of digestion; the first occurs in the mouth with mastication and enzymes found in saliva.

Symptom
Literally meaning "change" or "mishap" in Greek, this is a change in body function experienced by human beings. It can be evidence of a disease or allergy.

Tolerance
The normal reaction to proteins found in food. The immune system should recognize proteins in food as harmless. When they do, you are tolerant of a food.

Wheat
Wheat is a grass plant. The seed is used to make flour and is a staple food around the world. One of the eight major allergens, it contains gluten, which can cause harm to the intestines in Celiac Disease.

Appendix B
Menus

Dinner for the Boss

Chicken Mushroom Tartlets / 122
Tomato Arranged Salad / 88
Honey Rolls / 59
Chicken Paillards with
Zucchini / 161
Stuffed Potatoes / 211
Flourless Chocolate Cake / 279

Holiday Dinner

Stuffed Bacon Mushrooms / 127
Greens and Fruit Salad / 89
Light Dinner Rolls / 62
Roasted Lemon Chicken / 170
Sparkly Carrots / 253
Truffle Brownies / 271

School-Morning Breakfast

Crisp Brown-Sugar Waffles / 26
Mango Spread / 34
Banana-Raspberry Smoothie / 37

Lunch for Friends

Light Fruit Dip / 128
Curried Salmon-Apple Salad / 96
Tomato Corn Soup / 133
Banana-Split Parfait / 297

Summer Cookout

Stuffed Cherry Tomatoes / 123
Spicy Chicken Burgers / 165
Southwest Potato Salad / 99
Tomato Beef Burgers / 178
Sorbet Pie / 298

Birthday Dinner

Spicy Sausage Tartlets / 125
Spinach Fruit Salad / 88
Creamy Fruit Salad / 103
Savory Grilled Steaks / 172
Mashed Potatoes / 272
Rich Chocolate Cara-
mel Cake / 263

Casual Lunch

Green Salad with Ranch
Salad Dressing / 108
Tortellini Soup / 140
Mustard Steak Wraps / 172
Apple Crumble / 290

Family Dinner

Crunchy Snack Mix / 110
Chicken Risotto / 159
Sourdough French Bread / 49
Spinach Fruit Salad / 88
Pea Sauté / 248
Oatmeal Caramel Bars / 277

Holiday Breakfast

Bacon Eggs Benedict / 23
Cherry Coffee Cake / 40
Blueberry Smoothie / 34

Breakfast on the Run

Cornmeal Cranberry Muffins / 45
Banana Bread / 52
Fruit Sparkle Salad / 106

Casual Get-Together

Dairy-Free Olive Cheese Ball / 113
Spaghetti Bolognese / 181
Seasoned Breadsticks / 48
Apricot Glazed Beans / 246
Apple Snack Cake / 278

After-Easter Brunch

Sautéed Yellow Squash
and Carrots / 247
Ham Manicotti / 190
Tomato Arranged Salad / 88
Decadent Cinnamon Choco-
late Bars / 262

Lunchbox Goodies

Citrus Raisin Broccoli Slaw / 90
Pizza Wraps / 224
Chocolate Chip Cookies / 268

Index

Note: Page numbers in **bold** type indicate recipe category lists.